the Practical Naturalist

Audubon

DK

the Practical Naturalist

Explore the wonders of the natural world

DK

LONDON, NEW YORK, MELBOURNE, MUNICH, AND DELHI

Senior Art Editor	**Project Editor**
Maxine Pedliham	Ruth O'Rourke-Jones
Designers	**Editors**
Rebecca Tennant, Silke Spingies,	Martha Evatt,
Simon Murrell, Stephen Knowlden,	Laura Palosuo,
Elaine Hewson	Cressida Tuson
Production Editor	**US Editor**
Tony Phipps	Jill Hamilton
Creative Technical Support	**Indexer**
Adam Brackenbury, John Goldsmid	Hilary Bird
Jacket Designer	**Production**
Duncan Turner	Mandy Inness
Illustrator	**Picture Researcher**
Dan Cole/The Art Agency	Laura Barwick
Managing Art Editor	**Managing Editor**
Michelle Baxter	Sarah Larter
Art Director	**Reference Publisher**
Phil Ormerod	Jonathan Metcalf

First American Edition, 2010

Published in the United States by
DK Publishing
375 Hudson Street
New York, New York 10014

10 11 12 13 14 10 9 8 7 6 5 4 3 2 1

A catalog record for this book is available from the Library of Congress.

ISBN 978-0-7566-5899-1

DK books are available at special discounts when purchased in bulk for sales promotions, premiums, fund-raising, or educational use. For details contact: DK Publishing Special Markets, 375 Hudson Street, New York, New York 10014 or SpecialSales@dk.com.

Color reproduction by Media Development Printing Ltd, UK.
Printed and bound by Tien Wah Press, Singapore.

Discover more at
www.dk.com

Consultant Editor

Chris Packham developed a fascination with wildlife from an early age and studied zoology at Southampton University, England. He has written several books on wildlife and has hosted many nature-based TV shows for the BBC including, *Springwatch* and *Autumnwatch*. Chris is involved with many wildlife conservation organizations including The Wildlife Trusts, The Wildfowl and Wetlands Trust, The Bat Conservation Trust, and is a Vice-President of the RSPB.

Contributors

Steve Backshall (Mountain and hillside) is a naturalist, author, and television presenter, who has traveled to more than a hundred countries, discovered new species, and climbed some of the world's highest mountains.

David Chandler (Web of life; Lake, river, and stream) is a freelance writer and environmental educator. David's books include the *RSPB Children's Guide to Bird Watching*, *All About Bugs*, and *100 Birds to See Before You Die*.

Chris Gibson (Coast) is a lifelong naturalist who writes, teaches, and broadcasts about the natural world. He is a senior specialist for Natural England.

Robert Henson (Weather) is a meteorologist and science journalist based in Colorado. He has worked as a tornado researcher and written extensively on climate change.

Rob Hume (What a naturalist needs; Forest; Consultant) worked for the RSPB for 30 years, editing *Birds* magazine for 15, and has written around 30 books.

James Parry (Tropical forest; Scrubland and heath; Grassland; Desert) is a writer and lecturer who has traveled widely to study wildlife and different habitats. He has written several books on natural history.

Dr. Katie Parsons (Close to home; Farm and field) has a PhD in animal behavior and ecology. She is currently a freelance conservation consultant and science writer.

Elizabeth White (Tundra and ice) is a documentary film-maker for the BBC Natural History Unit. She has a PhD in animal behavior and has filmed wildlife across the globe, including Antarctic and the high Arctic.

Steve Kress (Consultant) is a staff biologist for the National Audubon Society and a research fellow at Cornell University Laboratory of Ornithology. With Audubon, he started Project Puffin to restore seabirds such as Atlantic puffins and terns to the coast of Maine.

Contents

ABOUT THIS BOOK
This book is intended to be an inspirational guide to
exploring, understanding, and observing the natural world,
wherever you may be. The species included are examples of the
type of wildlife that exists in each habitat, wherever they
occur in the world. Not all examples shown for a given habitat
will be found together or in one specific geographical location.

Foreword

There is something comforting about knowing the name of an animal, plant, or rock—perhaps because names provide us with a sense of order. Naturalists of the 18th and 19th centuries focused on naming plants and animals previously unknown to them, seeking order in new lands, and then moving on to increasingly remote places in their quest to discover new species. Nearly all birds, fish, and mammals now have names—both scientific and common. Large, conspicuous creatures are especially well-described because taxonomists—a breed of naturalists with a special fondness for order—paid particular attention to the details that make them similar and different from each other. But as Benjamin Franklin once said, "What signifies knowing the names, if you know not the nature of things?" It is deceiving to think that naming things offers anything but the simplest understanding of life.

Our understanding of the natural world—and even the naming of animals and plants—is far from complete. We have only begun to describe the variety of life on Earth, and we know very little about the behavior, interactions, and habits of most animals.

The same observation skills that have helped us tag and categorize larger life forms are now necessary to discover the smaller creatures that live in seldom-explored habitats like rainforest canopies, ocean depths, caves, and soils. In these little-visited places lie vast numbers of life forms yet to be described. For example, there are about 350,000 beetles with scientific names, but probably several million more beetle species that haven't been named yet!

Not only are most plant and animal species yet to be described, but the lives of even the most familiar animals are little known. Only recently did biologists discover that elephants can communicate with family members many miles away, and that shorebirds only two months old have the ability to migrate nearly 7,000 miles from their hatching places to their winter homes—without stopping and without their parents. The race to discover more species and to understand their behavior has never been more important. Habitats rich in species are disappearing due to human actions before their precious life forms have even been discovered.

Today's naturalists have new tools for exploration, such as solar-powered computers, night-vision binoculars, remote-sensing cameras, geolocators, GPS loggers, and miniature high-definition video cameras. But the principal tools of today's naturalists are the same ones championed by Charles Darwin, John Muir, and others. Dedicated naturalists are careful, patient observers with an insatiable curiosity and a sense of wonder about the world. They know that nature is still far from being well-known and tame.

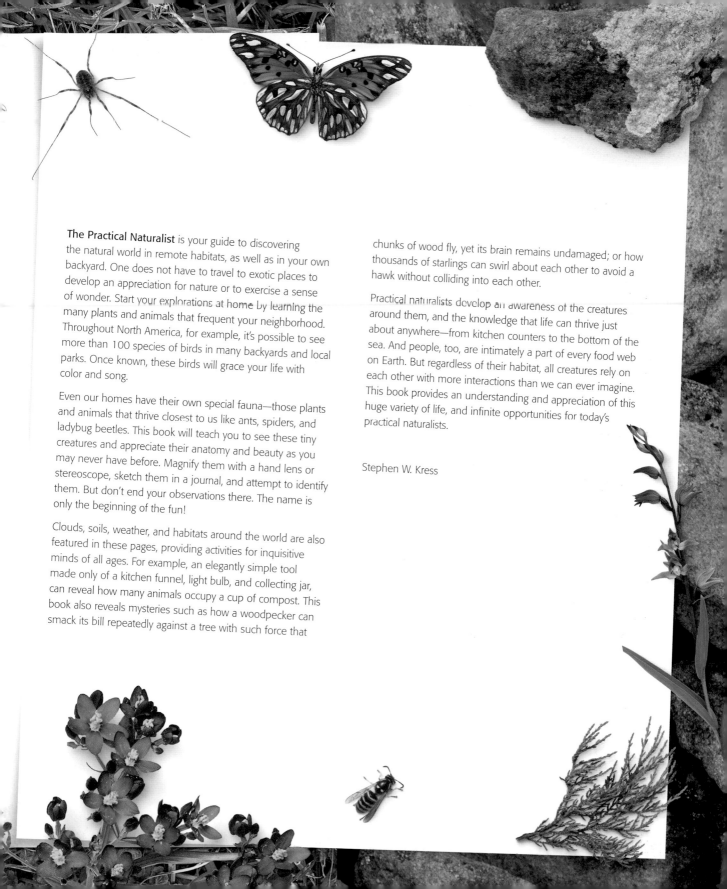

The Practical Naturalist is your guide to discovering the natural world in remote habitats, as well as in your own backyard. One does not have to travel to exotic places to develop an appreciation for nature or to exercise a sense of wonder. Start your explorations at home by learning the many plants and animals that frequent your neighborhood. Throughout North America, for example, it's possible to see more than 100 species of birds in many backyards and local parks. Once known, these birds will grace your life with color and song.

Even our homes have their own special fauna—those plants and animals that thrive closest to us like ants, spiders, and ladybug beetles. This book will teach you to see these tiny creatures and appreciate their anatomy and beauty as you may never have before. Magnify them with a hand lens or stereoscope, sketch them in a journal, and attempt to identify them. But don't end your observations there. The name is only the beginning of the fun!

Clouds, soils, weather, and habitats around the world are also featured in these pages, providing activities for inquisitive minds of all ages. For example, an elegantly simple tool made only of a kitchen funnel, light bulb, and collecting jar, can reveal how many animals occupy a cup of compost. This book also reveals mysteries such as how a woodpecker can smack its bill repeatedly against a tree with such force that chunks of wood fly, yet its brain remains undamaged; or how thousands of starlings can swirl about each other to avoid a hawk without colliding into each other.

Practical naturalists develop an awareness of the creatures around them, and the knowledge that life can thrive just about anywhere—from kitchen counters to the bottom of the sea. And people, too, are intimately a part of every food web on Earth. But regardless of their habitat, all creatures rely on each other with more interactions than we can ever imagine. This book provides an understanding and appreciation of this huge variety of life, and infinite opportunities for today's practical naturalists.

Stephen W. Kress

The web of life

The simple beauty of life can be relished on many levels.
A single bright-red ladybug on a fingertip is perfect.
The fresh scent of a rose is sublime. The tiny rainbows seen
flashing from the wings of aphids on the rose's stem are also
unexpected gems, and the marvel of a myriad of ants flying
up into the summer sky makes an urban spectacle. Each is
individually remarkable, but then, so are the relationships
that essentially and intrinsically link them all. There is
an undeniable and satisfying beauty to be found in an
understanding of these webs that knit life together.

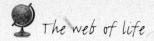

The nature of the planet

Much of the time, we are aware only of life immediately around us, yet this is only a small part of a much larger network. Life on Earth exists in many places—some very different to others, but all are connected.

The thin green line

Life in all its forms is found exclusively on the Earth's outermost layers, including the land, oceans, and the atmosphere surrounding the planet. This narrow strip is known as the biosphere—a word that literally means "life ball." Within it are millions of species, of which humans are one, with each dependent on others for their survival. The biosphere isn't uniform, however—it is a collection of different, yet interconnecting habitats, which have many ill-defined boundaries between them.

TUNDRA
Exposed, cold, and treeless, with many lichens and mosses, tundra is a habitat of the far north.

Key

- Grassland
- Desert
- Tropical forest
- Temperate forest
- Coniferous forest
- Mountains
- Polar regions and tundra
- Rivers and wetlands
- Coral reef
- The oceans

WORLD BIOMES DISTRIBUTION
The scientific word for a habitat is a biome. This map shows the variety of these biomes and their distribution, which is determined by climate and geology. Human impact on the environment isn't indicated—areas shown as temperate forest, for example, may now be farmland.

GRASSLAND
Grassland includes savannas, steppes, and prairies. It experiences more rainfall than deserts, but is drier than forests.

REED BEDS IN NORFOLK, UK
Many of these important habitats would be lost today if they were not periodically managed.

HABITAT-MAKER

Left to their own devices, some habitats are transient, changing from time to time. Reed beds are a good example. Often, dead vegetation builds up at the base of the reeds. This dries out the reed bed, allowing other species to gain a foothold. Scrub may take over, and ultimately woodland, which is a much more stable habitat.

AQUATIC
Aquatic habitats include lakes and streams to rivers and oceans. They may be saltwater or freshwater.

More than one home

Some animals have a very strong connection with a single habitat. Europe's bearded tits, for example, are small birds found mainly in reed beds. Other species make themselves at home in many habitats—the adaptable carrion crow can be seen in woods, uplands, and foraging on estuaries, among other places. Dragonflies make a big habitat change when they become adults.

adult winged dragonfly emerging from its larval "skin"

TRANSFORMER
The first part of a dragonfly's life is spent underwater as a larva, yet once it matures, it becomes an aerial predator.

LIFE ON EARTH

All life on Earth exists as part of an intricate web of interconnections. These images help to put some of these into context. They start with an individual of one species, and, step by step, move on to the biosphere. Individuals of any species don't generally live in isolation—others of their kind normally reside in the same area. Together, these make up a population. Add populations of other species in the same area and this builds into a community. The community lives in a specific habitat, with a certain climate, geology, and soil—together these living and non-living components make up an ecosystem. Put all the ecosystems together and you have the biosphere. In this way life on earth is interconnected, and we should take care to not tip the balance.

Find your own biome on the map. Perhaps it was once temperate forest.

FOREST
Forests are highly varied and species-rich habitats. Types of forest include northern boreal, tropical, and temperate forests.

DESERT
Deserts seem barren, experiencing almost no rain and possessing little or no vegetation. However, many species have adapted to desert life.

INDIVIDUAL
As a naturalist, you might encounter just one individual of a species. However, it is part of a larger group.

POPULATION
The individuals of a species in one area make up the population. Different species have different sized populations.

COMMUNITY
All the populations together form a community, where population fluctuations for one species have an impact on species.

ECOSYSTEM
Ecosystems may be large or small, and combine living components with an area's physical characteristics.

BIOSHPERE
This is the "ball of life." It is made up of all individuals in every population in every community and all habitats on the planet. The true worldwide web.

The diversity of life

The diversity of life on Earth is extraordinary. As a naturalist, there is always something new to understand, experience, and enjoy.

Scientists have identified about 1.8 million species, and it is estimated that as many as 6 to 12 million more are waiting to be discovered. Humans are just one animal species among many, but we have a unique role to play in understanding and conserving the rest.

Evolution

Just as human families exhibit variations in, for example, eye color, animals vary within a species. As differences are passed on to subsequent generations, they slowly change, or evolve, into creatures with varied appearances and capabilities. Suppose one bird has a larger bill than its neighbor and is better at feeding its young so that more of them survive. Some of its chicks also have larger bills, and, with time, more offspring acquire larger bills until they look quite different from their smaller-billed relatives. If there comes a time when the large bills can no longer breed successfully with the small bills, a second species has been created.

SLOW PROGRESSION
The elephants we recognize today are believed to have evolved from a prehistoric animal called *moeritherium*—an animal that more closely resembled modern tapirs.

MAMMALS
Mammals make up around 5,500 known species, including these raccoons, tiny bats, massive whales, camels, kangaroos, polar bears, cheetahs, giraffes—and humans.

BIRDS
The 10,000 known bird species are widely diverse, ranging from ostriches to penguins, albatrosses to eagles, ducks and starlings to owls, hummingbirds, and sparrows.

REPTILES
These are cold-blooded vertebrates and their bodies are usually covered in scales. There are close to 8,000 known species, including lizards, snakes, turtles, and crocodiles.

AMPHIBIANS
These animals have adapted to life both in water and on land. There are about 5,000 species of amphibians including caecilians, salamanders and newts, and frogs and toads.

FISH
Earth's brackish, fresh, and saltwaters are home to almost 31,000 known fish species, including salmon.

INSECTS
Around 950,000 insect species share the planet with us—over 500,000 of them are beetles. From dragonflies to bees, cockroaches to butterflies, the forms seem endless.

FLOWERING PLANTS
Around 260,000 flowering plant species have been recorded, on land and in water. These include grasses, trees, and more familiar blooms, such as these sunflowers.

TREES
The definition of what is considered a tree is not absolute, but there are an estimated 100,000 tree species in the world.

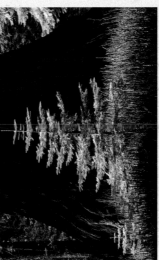

FUNGI
There are around 100,000 species of fungi. Toadstools and mushrooms belong to this group.

EVOLUTION IN ACTION
The five digits in this skeletal paw, and what looks like a thumb, belong to the giant panda, a member of the bear family. The "thumb" is actually a wrist bone, but it is much larger than that of, say, a brown bear. It can also move, is padded, and works with the true digits to make it easier for the panda to handle bamboo, its preferred food. This appendage may have evolved over thousands of years as a trait that was beneficial to the panda's survival.

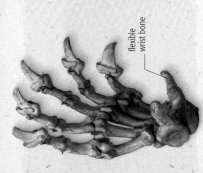

flexible wrist bone

Amazing adaptations
Evolution is about change, and if an inherited characteristic increases the chance of survival by making an animal better at finding food or avoiding predation, for example, then those attributes are more likely to be passed on to the next generation. Within the animal kingdom, some species have—over many generations—evolved an array of adaptations to meet the challenges of life, including capabilities such as camouflage or super-sharp senses, a bill that functions as a specialized feeding tool, antifreeze in the blood, or even feathers that hold water.

MIMICRY
Predators may keep their distance from some nonvenomous species of milk snake, which have evolved to resemble highly venomous coral snakes.

CORAL SNAKE

red touches black bands, not yellow

MILK SNAKE

PERFECTLY ADAPTED
Sword-billed hummingbirds use ultra-long bills to reach nectar in flowers, pollinating them in the process.

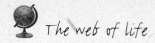
Animal life

Animals occupy particular niches within the complex web of life, and have evolved various strategies and behaviors to ensure survival.

Herbivores, carnivores, and scavengers

Simply put, green plants use the Sun's energy to grow, herbivores eat the plants, and carnivores eat herbivores. But feeding relationships are often more complex. Carnivorous foxes prey on herbivorous rabbits, but also eat fruit. Crows may scavenge from the dead bodies of both animals, but also eat seeds, fruit, insects, and small animals. They are taking advantage of evolutionary niches by developing different eating habits.

SCAVENGER

HERBIVORE

CARNIVORE

Early bird or night owl?

Not all animals are active at the same time, which can reduce competition between species; for example, butterflies take nectar from flowers during the day, while most moths do so at night. Animals that are active during the day, such as most lizards, are "diurnal" and those that are active at night, such as hedgehogs, are "nocturnal" (see pp.54–55). Some animals are "crepuscular," which means you are most likely to see them at dusk and dawn.

FLEXTIME

The snowy owl is a crepuscular hunter that raises its young on the Arctic tundra, where, in the very far north, there is no darkness for months during the summer. At this time of year, while the female is brooding the young, the male can have sole responsibility for feeding up to 11 youngsters, the female, and himself. To do this, he adapts his usual habits, hunting in the day.

NIGHT AND DAY
Hedgehogs are nocturnal mammals found in Europe, Africa, and Asia. Lizards can be diurnal or nocturnal—this viviparous lizard is diurnal.

DIURNAL

NOCTURNAL

Getting away from it all

Mammals need to eat to stay warm, but in winter food can be hard to find. Some survive by hibernating. During this time their metabolisms are turned down to a minimum, and they use the fat deposits they laid down while food was plentiful to fuel this low-energy winter existence. There are also invertebrates, reptiles, and amphibians that hibernate. Migration is a strategy that is employed most visibly by some birds, but also by fish, butterflies, moths, and land and sea mammals. These creatures travel huge distances, often along well defined routes, in search of food and breeding grounds.

LAND MIGRATION
Migrating caribou can travel over 3,100 miles (5,000 km) a year, crossing water if necessary. No other land mammal covers such a distance.

Migrating humpbacks can be seen from locations on the Pacific coast.

EPIC JOURNEY
Humpback whales migrate farther than any other mammal. Their journey, between the Central American Pacific and the Antarctic, is over 5,000 miles (8,000 km).

HOW MIGRATING BIRDS NAVIGATE

A bird's ability to navigate between breeding grounds and wintering areas, which can be thousands of miles apart, is staggering. Visual clues assist them, for example a river may keep them on track, and the Sun acts as a compass, with birds using their "internal clock" to compensate for its apparent movement. At night they use the stars as a guide. Birds can also detect the Earth's magnetic fields and use these to navigate. As they get closer to their destination smell may help: petrels, for example, find their burrows by smell.

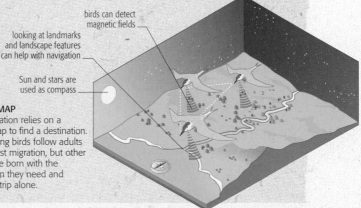

birds can detect magnetic fields

looking at landmarks and landscape features can help with navigation

Sun and stars are used as compass

MENTAL MAP
True navigation relies on a mental map to find a destination. Some young birds follow adults on their first migration, but other species are born with the information they need and make the trip alone.

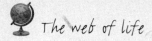
Back from the brink

Human intervention in the natural world can have a dramatic impact on the lives of animals and plants.

Humans can have a detrimental effect on animal and plant populations through a variety of means. However, we also have the capacity to turn things around, and in some cases this has happened. The sea otter is one such example. Once hunted to near extinction for their fur, now, thanks to successful conservation initiatives, they can again be seen in waters off North America's Pacific coast. Conservation projects have also helped the American bison, after hunting had decimated herds that once totalled many millions, and the osprey, which, by 1916, had been persecuted to oblivion in the UK by egg collectors and hunters. Similarly, the large blue butterfly had disappeared from the UK by 1979, but has been successfully reintroduced. Although successes like these can be achieved, many species of plants and animals remain threatened.

OSPREY
Ospreys returned to Scotland in 1954. Around-the-clock protection and recent reintroduction to England has helped UK numbers rise to around 150 pairs.

AMERICAN BISON
The American bison has been brought back from the brink of extinction. Over 150,000 now live on ranches and reserves.

LARGE BLUE BUTTERFLY
Reintroduction and appropriate land management has helped save the UK's large blue population from extinction.

Weather and sky

Perhaps no greater factor has a more important or powerful influence on all life than the weather—from the very short to the very long term. Hourly, daily, or seasonal variations exert profound effects on species and their populations, and individual events can provoke catastrophe or celebration. A cloudburst in the desert, for example, is the source of an explosion of life, but the same event could extinguish it elsewhere. The impact upon our species seems set to become ever more critical as we pitch our predictive abilities against increasingly turbulent fluctuations in the world's atmospheric conditions. Thus, understanding weather is fundamental to understanding all life on Earth.

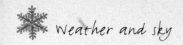

Climate and seasons

You can see variations of weather in daily and seasonal cycles and regional patterns. Together, these produce a climate: the norms and extremes that occur at a given place.

The Sun

Without solar energy there would be no climates on Earth. Daily cycles of sunshine and darkness result from the planet's rotation, and seasons are caused by the tilt of Earth's axis as it orbits the Sun. Because this orbit is not absolutely circular, Earth is closer to the Sun in January than in July. In about 13,000 years, however, the opposite will be true, which should warm northern summers.

POLAR CLIMATE
Some bird and whale species migrate to the polar regions, as regional sea ice expands and retreats seasonally.

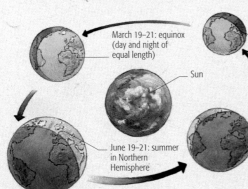

March 19–21: equinox (day and night of equal length)

Sun

December 19–21: summer in Southern Hemisphere

September 19–21: equinox (day and night of equal length)

June 19–21: summer in Northern Hemisphere

SOLSTICES
Solstices are the twice-yearly times when the Sun reaches its highest or lowest point in the sky. Due to Earth's tilt, what is summer in the north will be winter in the south.

Currents

Continents, sunlight, and Earth's rotation all influence the movement of seawater. Trade winds help drive surface water west across the tropics. The main ocean currents then move toward the poles in the western Pacific and Atlantic oceans, and toward the equator in the eastern Pacific and Atlantic. Far more heat lies in Earth's vast, dense oceans than in its relatively thin atmosphere. It is this marine influence that helps keep northerly London fairly mild, and equatorial Lima, Peru, surprisingly cool. Meanwhile, a broad "conveyor belt" threads through the global oceans (see map, above).

JET STREAMS
These fast-moving air currents help regulate the climate by connecting areas of contrasting temperatures and air pressure.

OCEAN WARMTH
Despite being near Antarctica, southern Chile is insulated from extreme cold by the surrounding ocean, making it habitable for temperate-zone species.

KEY

	Polar
	Tundra
	Subarctic
	Continental
	Temperate
	Warm, oceanic
	Mediterranean
	Semiarid
	Arid
	Subtropical
	Equatorial
	Mountain

Global zones

All habitats and biomes (see pp.10–11) are affected by climatic factors such as sunlight and moisture. The Earth is grouped into a system of climate zones (see below), with latitude, the distance from the equator, by far the strongest influence. Ocean currents and surface types are also important. Coastal deserts get little or no rain, thanks to cool offshore waters and stable air, yet thunderstorms rage across temperate zones, where heat builds more easily and air masses often clash.

RICH DIVERSITY
Huge tree canopies in tropical rainforests serve as sunscreens, keeping the air constantly warm and moist, which is ideal for animals such butterflies and frogs.

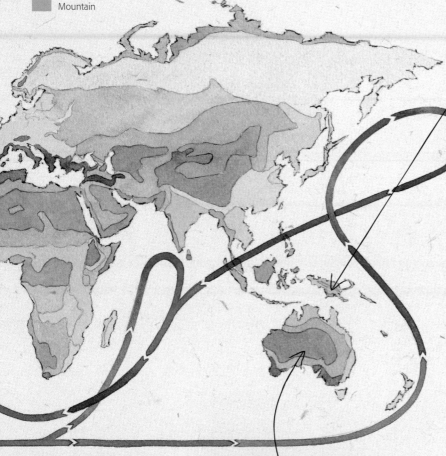

CORIOLIS EFFECT

As the planet revolves, it turns more quickly west to east in the tropics (its widest part) than in polar regions. When air currents flow from the tropics to the poles, the speed forces them to bend right over the planet's surface—a phenomenon known as the Coriolis effect. Air moving toward the equator also turns right, creating trade winds (see opposite). This effect helps explain the direction of prevailing winds and the presence of gyres.

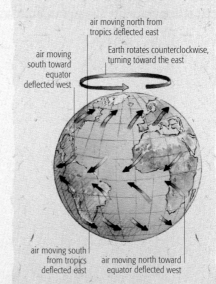

air moving north from tropics deflected east

Earth rotates counterclockwise, turning toward the east

air moving south toward equator deflected west

air moving south from tropics deflected east

air moving north toward equator deflected west

KEY

WARM SURFACE CURRENT

COLD, SALTY, DEEPWATER CURRENT

CONVEYOR BELT
Warm surface water flows from the tropical Pacific and Indian oceans around Africa, then north across the Atlantic. The water gradually sinks, forms cold bottom water, then completes the loop.

ARID CLIMATE
Despite dry conditions and large daily swings in temperature, many creatures and plants, such as lizards and spinifex grass, are well adapted to deserts.

21

Cloud spotting

Learning to read the sky's dazzling variety of clouds is useful for understanding air currents and can help you forecast upcoming weather.

How a cloud is formed

Water vapor is at the heart of every cloud. As warm air is forced upward, it cools, and the relative humidity increases. The rising air becomes saturated, and the water vapor collects around dust, salt, or other airborne particles to form a cloud. The type of cloud is dictated by its temperature, moisture content, and the air flow surrounding it.

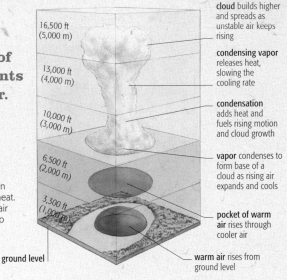

CLOUD FORMATION
As water condenses in rising air, it releases heat. The heat warms the air mass, and causes it to rise farther until it reaches the same temperature as the air surrounding it.

- 16,500 ft (5,000 m)
- 13,000 ft (4,000 m)
- 10,000 ft (3,000 m)
- 6,500 ft (2,000 m)
- 3,300 ft (1,000 m)
- ground level

cloud builds higher and spreads as unstable air keeps rising

condensing vapor releases heat, slowing the cooling rate

condensation adds heat and fuels rising motion and cloud growth

vapor condenses to form base of a cloud as rising air expands and cools

pocket of warm air rises through cooler air

warm air rises from ground level

Identifying clouds

The higher the cloud, the lower its temperature. Some are made of ice crystals, others of water droplets, and the composition gives each a different form. Our classification of clouds is based on one created by English pharmacist Luke Howard. In 1783, intrigued by the vivid sunsets created by volcanic eruptions, he developed a cloud-naming system, presenting it to scientists in 1802. Howard divided clouds into four types: stratus (meaning "layer"), cumulus ("heap"), nimbus ("rain"), and cirrus ("curly").

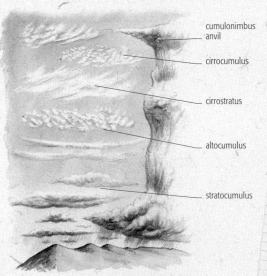

- cumulonimbus anvil
- cirrocumulus
- cirrostratus
- altocumulus
- stratocumulus

Each cloud has a two-letter code: useful to note when out making observations

Cloud codes

- cirrus (Ci)
- cirrocumulus (Cc)
- cirrostratus (Cs)
- altocumulus (Ac)
- altostratus (As)
- nimbostratus (Ns)
- stratocumulus (Sc)
- stratus (St)
- cumulus (Cu)
- cumulonimbus (Cb)

CLOUD LEVELS
Many clouds are combinations of the main categories, so that nimbostratus, for example, is a layer of rain cloud.

SPOTTING SPECIAL CLOUDS

Some types of clouds appear rarely and only in certain areas. Noctilucent (night-shining) clouds form at heights of around 50 miles (80 km). Once observed only at high latitudes (in the north or south), noctilucent clouds are now reported closer to the equator. Sometimes resembling a stack of dinner plates, lenticular clouds develop when a particular arrangement of wind layers passes over a mountain peak or range.

NOCTILUCENT CLOUD
Earth's highest cloud is most likely to be seen just after sunset or before sunrise in summer.

LENTICULAR CLOUD
With such an otherworldly appearance, lenticular clouds may be mistaken for unidentified flying objects.

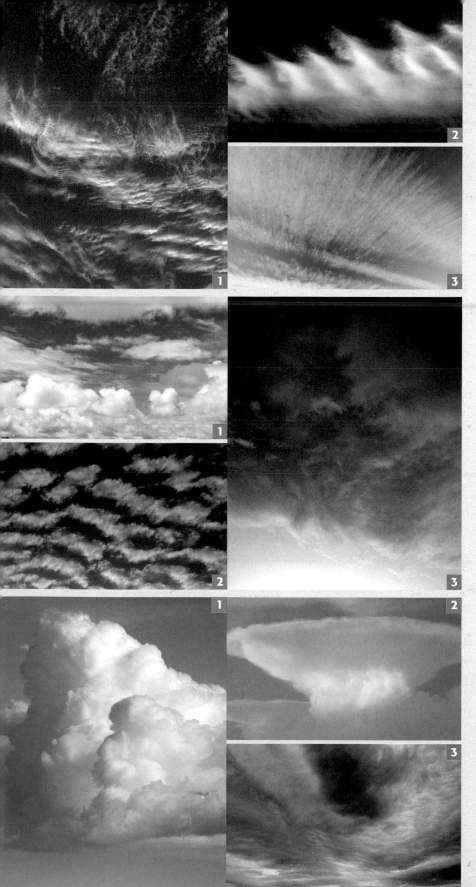

High-level clouds

Forming 3–9 miles (5–15 km) above sea level, high-level clouds consist mainly of sheets, patches, or streaks associated with cirrus formations. These clouds are often the first sign of an upcoming weather event, from a passing thunderstorm to a longer-lasting storm system. As sunshine or moonlight plays on cirrus clouds, ice crystals produce a range of optical effects.

1 Highly variable wind and moisture patterns can lead to a patchwork of cirrus clouds.

2 Recurring wave patterns, caused when wind blows faster above the clouds than below them, are a hallmark of Kelvin–Helmholtz cirrus clouds.

3 Contrails—narrow clouds produced by aircraft exhausts—can interact with existing cirrus clouds or spread out to form new cirrus clouds.

Medium-level clouds

The medium-level zone, ranging from around 1–3 miles (2–5 km) above sea level, represents a transition region. Here, clouds take on a wide variety of shapes and sizes, affected by movements above and below the layer as well as within it. Most clouds in this region are preceded by the prefix *alto*, a Latin term meaning "high."

1 Cumulus clouds often push upward into the medium-level cloud zone. In this image, cumulus (bottom) clouds are joined by altocumulus (top).

2 Altocumulus often appear as vast sheets of broken cloud, especially over the ocean. Small eddies (where wind doubles back on itself) help shape these clouds into lines or arrays of cloud parcels.

3 If more moisture is present at medium levels than below, a mid-level cloud may form rain or snow that quickly evaporates as it falls, producing streaks that hang from dark clouds. These streaks are called *virga* (from the Latin for "branch" or "twig").

Low-level clouds

Warmth and moisture near Earth's surface help make low-level clouds the most dynamic and fastest-growing. Low clouds may form when conditions are calm, which can lead to fog (see p.25). In highly unstable conditions they can set the stage for cumulonimbus clouds (thunderstorms).

1 Towering cumulus clouds extend from a smooth base upward to heights of 6 miles (10 km) or more.

2 A vigorously developing cumulus cloud that extends to heights where the temperature is below freezing becomes a cumulonimbus, with an anvil-shaped top made up of a sheet of cirrus ice crystals.

3 Stratocumulus in the wake of a storm may appear ragged, as turbulence and wind shear—changes in wind speed or direction—eat into parts of the cloud formation.

Wet weather

After evaporating, water vapor stays airborne for a week or so. Vapor molecules condense to form clouds, before returning to Earth.

Rain

Some parts of the planet experience virtually no rain; others are deluged almost daily. How much rain falls plays a large part in the species of plants and animals that inhabit an area. Cloudy, cool areas feel more damp than their sunny, warm counterparts, which can be deceptive—on average, sunny Dallas, Texas, gets nearly twice as much rain as cloudy London, England.

1 Frontal rain occurs as weather fronts push their way across the landscape and water condenses in the air that rises above them. Intense, frontal rain ends quickly once the front clears.

2 Orographic rain results when an air mass is forced over high terrain, such as a mountain, causing moisture to rise and condense.

3 Warm, moist air topped by cooler, drier air can lead to showers and thunderstorms that may be scattered across a summer landscape or focused along a strong front. This is called convective rain.

4 Cyclonic rain is caused by a low-pressure system. Moist air spirals toward the area of lowest pressure, producing extensive clouds and precipitation.

How raindrops form

Raindrops often start as snowflakes that grow around a nucleus of dust within high, cold clouds. Once large enough, they fall into warmer air and melt, turning to rain before hitting the ground. In warm climates, raindrops form without any ice being present: tiny water droplets collide, scooping up even more droplets and growing as they fall.

AIR CURRENTS
When warm air rises and cools, water vapor condenses to form clouds. When rain or hail form and start to fall, a downdraft is created by the falling precipitation.

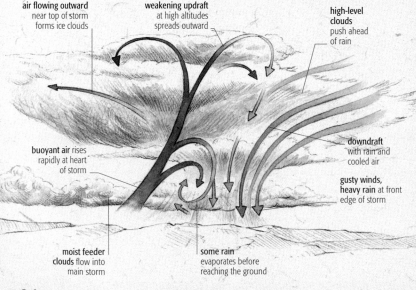

air flowing outward
near top of storm
forms ice clouds

weakening updraft
at high altitudes
spreads outward

high-level
clouds
push ahead
of rain

buoyant air rises
rapidly at heart
of storm

downdraft
with rain and
cooled air

gusty winds,
heavy rain at front
edge of storm

moist feeder
clouds flow into
main storm

some rain
evaporates before
reaching the ground

Snow and hail

Many parts of the world get precipitation in frozen form. While snow develops only in clouds with temperatures that are below freezing, it may accumulate at ground level even when temperatures are slightly above freezing. Once in place, a heavy snowpack reflects sunlight, helping cold surface air to remain. Hail forms when moisture-packed updrafts in a thunderstorm bring water to high, cold altitudes; it freezes, accumulates, and falls as ice.

SNOWFALL
On average, 1/16 in (1 mm) of water yields about 3/8 in (1 cm) of snow. The yield is usually higher in the dry, fluffy snow of cold climates.

HAILSTONES
Sometimes as big as a grapefruit, hailstones are a spectacular and sometimes dangerous form of precipitation, causing enormous damage to crops and vehicles.

SNOWFLAKES

The entrancing variety of snowflakes is due to ice crystals' tendency to grow in six-sided structures (hexagons). Different kinds usually form at different temperatures. Near-freezing conditions often lead to clusters of needles or plates. Colder air favors columns, plates, or dendrites.

SECTOR PLATE

DENDRITE

THIN PLATE

Frost and dew

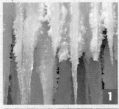

At night, especially when it is clear and calm, air near the ground can cool enough to bring relative humidity to 100 percent. More cooling leads to condensation on grass and other surfaces; this is either frost or dew, depending on temperature. The deposit normally disappears as temperatures rise the next morning.

1 Rime frost, often very beautiful, is the result of water droplets that hover in below-freezing air and turn to ice when they encounter a surface.

2 Hoar frost is created when ice forms on surfaces as air close to the ground drops below freezing.

3 Dewdrops are a common sight on clear, calm summer mornings. They evaporate soon after sunrise as air warms and the relative humidity drops.

4 As surface air cools overnight, it flows into valleys and "frost hollows," where dew and frost may be especially thick.

Mist and fog

Literally a cloud on the ground, fog forms when a layer of air just above the Earth's surface cools enough so that water condenses to form cloud droplets. Even "pea soup" fog may extend only a few yards above ground level. Mist is a less dense form of fog. When visibility is more than 0.6 mile (1 km) the moisture is called mist, below that it is called fog.

SEA OF FOG
Cold Pacific water near San Francisco, California, leads to frequent fogs, as moist, salt-laden air flows up the city's steep hills and engulfs the Golden Gate Bridge.

Stormy weather

Whether gentle, gusty, or gale-force, wind is the atmosphere in motion as it rushes toward and around low-pressure regions.

Breezes

You can feel the most reliable winds in the form of land and sea breezes found near coasts—the result of temperature differences. Asia's monsoons are caused by a season-long pattern: summer heat warms the continent, which pulls tropical moisture inland. Localized breezes affect local habitats—and people—in very specific ways, not least by creating unique microclimates.

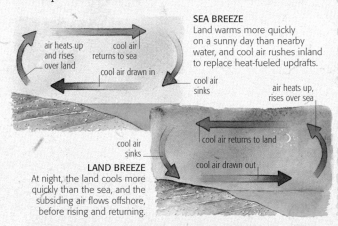

SEA BREEZE
Land warms more quickly on a sunny day than nearby water, and cool air rushes inland to replace heat-fueled updrafts.

air heats up and rises over land

cool air returns to sea

cool air drawn in

cool air sinks

air heats up, rises over sea

cool air returns to land

cool air sinks

cool air drawn out

LAND BREEZE
At night, the land cools more quickly than the sea, and the subsiding air flows offshore, before rising and returning.

LOCAL WINDS

There are many localized winds that blow in regions around the world. The mistral, for example, is a cold northern wind that blows through southern France toward the Mediterranean Sea. In addition to relentless winds, its low pressure also causes headaches in many people, and makes children and animals restless and irritable. The harmattan brings a thick haze of Saharan dust to North Africa.

HURRICANE
Winds pull energy and moisture from warm seas. Each year 40 to 50 of these tropical storms grow strong enough to be called hurricanes, typhoons, or cyclones—all names for the same type of storm. Many cause little or no damage, but some bring extreme winds inland, causing devastation.

Cyclones

Any area of low atmospheric pressure is, technically, considered a cyclone, although the term is usually associated with a spiraling storm. In the USA, for example, "cyclone" was once another name for a tornado, and both hurricane and typhoon are alternative names for a tropical cyclone. What we usually think of as cyclones are huge storms that generate rain, snow, and wind, and these begin as deep areas of low pressure. Winds rush in to "fill the gaps" and, due to the Coriolis effect (see p.21), begin to spiral upward—counterclockwise in the Northern Hemisphere and clockwise in the Southern Hemisphere.

Tornadoes

The world's strongest ground-level winds occur in tornadoes—reaching speeds of 300 mph (485 kmph) or more. These spinning columns—small, brief, but often violent—extend from thunderstorms. Tornadoes are most frequent and destructive in Bangladesh and the USA, where temperature contrasts and moisture abound, but they occur in most midlatitude areas. Beware—if a tornado appears to be stationary but growing, it may be moving toward you.

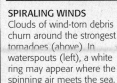

SPIRALING WINDS
Clouds of wind-torn debris churn around the strongest tornadoes (above). In waterspouts (left), a white ring may appear where the spinning air meets the sea.

TRACKING TWISTERS

Because "twisters"—another name for tornadoes—grow and die quickly, scientists must "chase" them to gather the data for research. Truck-mounted radar, introduced in the 1990s, has allowed scientists to profile dozens of tornadoes. Storm-chasing may look glamorous in movies and on TV, but it is mostly long, hard work. An entire season may yield only a few minutes of tornadoes.

STORM CHASERS IN TEXAS

Thunder and lightning

Thunderstorms generate lightning through intense electrical fields that are produced when ice crystals and water droplets collide. Cloud-to-ground strikes are the ones that threaten people and property, but most lightning actually occurs within and between clouds. A single thunderstorm can produce many thousands of bolts in just a few hours' time. The intense heat generated by a lightning strike causes a rapid expansion of air in the lightning channel. This explosion of air produces thunder.

FORKED LIGHTNING
Cloud-to-ground lightning strikes are stunning to behold, but can be very dangerous to people and animals.

CLOUD-TO-CLOUD LIGHTNING
Sheets of cirrus cloud, or anvils, may extend dozens of miles beyond the top of a thunderstorm updraft. These highly electrified regions can generate spectacular lightning displays that you can see long before a storm arrives and after it departs.

Making predictions

Weather forecasting has developed from superstition into science. Yet with a sharp eye, you can spot the basics that drive weather—and make predictions of your own.

FORECASTING
Meteorologists draw on data collected daily at weather stations around the globe.

The professionals

Forecasters predict upcoming weather by feeding observations from across the globe into computers. Highly complex software packages interpret the data, based on our physical understanding of the atmosphere. While still not perfect, one- to three-day forecasts have become far more accurate in recent decades; extended models hint at what weather might arrive as far as ten days in advance.

WEATHER MAP
Synoptic maps show warm and cold fronts and isobars (lines of equal air pressure).

Home weather station

If you're interested in setting up your own weather station, you can choose from a wide range of digital equipment to collect and display daily readings and store them on a home computer. Displays are linked to instruments that measure temperature, humidity, barometric pressure, wind, and precipitation. You can even upload data to public or private networks that collect observations from people all over the world.

ANEMOMETER
The rotor (left) measures wind speed; the tail of the weathervane (right) keeps it pointed into the wind, indicating wind direction.

DIGITAL WEATHER STATION
By using modern equipment, you can view a detailed portrait of weather conditions, such as temperature and humidity, at a particular location at any time.

air pressure in inches of mercury

FORECASTING A WARM FRONT

In areas such as North America and Europe, you can predict a warm front by observing a distinctive sequence of clouds. As a front approaches, warm, moist air sweeps overhead, eroding cold air below. This results in thick, low cloud, and causes an overcast sky for a few hours. Steady rain or snow may eventually develop, ending with a surge of warm air.

1 Thin cirrus clouds (see p.22) are often the first sign of an approaching warm front.

3 The Sun may appear fainter as existing clouds lower and thicken, forming a deck of altostratus clouds (see p.22).

2 A halo or ring may be seen around the Sun or Moon as cirrus clouds thicken into a layer of cirrostratus clouds.

4 Heavy bursts of rain often occur before a warm front passes, but may end abruptly.

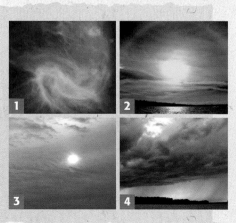

PREDICTING A SHOWER

You can spot an approaching storm by observing cumulus clouds—formed by unstable, rising air (see p.22). When warm, moist cumulus clouds rise into much colder air, they may trigger thunderstorms. Weaker showers grow and die in an hour or two; stronger storms can be set off by a cold front or embedded within a cyclone (see p.26).

1 Fair-weather cumulus often develop into small, puffy clouds that do little more than block the Sun as they pass by.

2 Moderate cumulus stretch higher into the sky, indicating the risk of a shower or storm in the next few hours.

3 Towering cumulus reach toward frigid atmospheric layers. If they keep growing, a thunderstorm may develop.

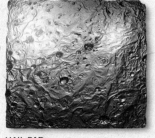

HAIL PAD
Sheets of aluminum foil spread on top of polystyrene pads make a simple way of measuring the size of any hailstones that fall in your garden.

RAIN GAUGE
This simple, centuries-old technology remains a standard, reliable method of measuring rainfall.

THERMOMETER
"Max–min" types store the day's high and low readings.

air pressure in millibars

static pointer set to indicate current pressure at last reading

moving pointer indicating pressure

BAROMETER
An indoor weather instrument, a barometer tracks the rise and fall of atmospheric pressure, which is closely related to approaching storms.

Hang seaweed indoors. If it feels moist, it might rain soon.

SEAWEED

Weather folklore

Many cultures have developed unique ways of interpreting Earth's atmospheric behavior. Common observation surrounding weather threads emerge in folklore. In many different countries, poetic sayings link the look of the sky, or the state of animals or plants, to some future weather event. And while modern forecasting has generally replaced folklore, some of these old weather sayings and practices do, in fact, work.

An open cone indicates warm, dry weather. PINE CONE

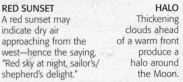

RED SUNSET
A red sunset may indicate dry air approaching from the west—hence the saying, "Red sky at night, sailor's/shepherd's delight."

HALO
Thickening clouds ahead of a warm front produce a halo around the Moon.

SUPERSTITIONS

Unlike sayings based on atmospheric conclusions, superstitions assign supernatural meanings and explanations to what are really ordinary weather events. In some North American and European traditions, if the sun shines on February 2 (often called "Groundhog Day"), it supposedly means a prolonged period of wintry weather. Rainbows, which are caused when sunlight refracts through moisture in the air, are especially prone to mystical interpretations.

RAINBOW
Various cultures have seen rainbows as spiritual bridges or portents of fortune or disaster.

Climate change

A global climate has evolved since Earth formed, but human activity now appears to be forcing the atmosphere to change in new and complex ways.

Causes of climate change

Although both natural and human activity have an impact on the evolution of Earth's climate, human causes far outpace the gradual changes produced by various natural causes. Homes, vehicles, factories, and power plants burn vast amounts of coal, oil, and gas, releasing carbon into the air, where it then combines with oxygen to form carbon dioxide (CO_2). This invisible, odorless gas traps heat from Earth in the atmosphere, pushing up the planet's temperature. Airborne CO_2 has increased 30 percent since the 1950s and global temperatures keep rising—with potentially dramatic results for habitats and wildlife.

NATURAL CAUSES
Major volcanic eruptions actually cool Earth's climate by releasing sulfur dioxide, which reflects sunlight, but they also add carbon dioxide to the atmosphere.

A big eruption throws dust and gases into the atmosphere.

HUMAN CAUSES
Burning coal for power is one of the most significant human-produced causes of carbon dioxide in the atmosphere.

PLANTS AND CLIMATE CHANGE

In warm regions, trees help cool the climate by shading the soil and trapping moisture. Planting trees in these areas may help offset global warming. Plants also absorb carbon, but the carbon eventually returns to the air whenever a plant dies and decays. Conversely, trees have a warming effect in subpolar regions, where dark evergreens absorb more sunlight than snow-covered ground. Plants and oceans absorb about half the carbon dioxide emitted from human activity, and plant-stressing droughts can have the effect of cutting that absorption in half for up to a year.

EARLY SIGNS OF SPRING
In Japan, where the timing of cherry blossoms has been tracked for centuries, the blooms now arrive almost a week earlier than they did in 1950.

Signs of change

Many natural indicators point to a warming climate. Most glaciers around the world have retreated in the last century and the Arctic Ocean is losing more sea-ice in summer. As air warms, more water evaporates into it, so drought-stricken ground tends to dry further while heavy rains become heavier. Sea levels are rising as glaciers melt and oceans warm and expand. Climate change threatens the habitats of many plant and animal species, which could lead to their extinction.

RISING SEAS
The average sea level has risen nearly 8in (20cm) in the last century. Coral atolls and low-lying deltas are most threatened by further rises.

GLACIAL THAW
Polar bears and other creatures rely on the Arctic Ocean's sea-ice. The average extent of late-summer ice has dropped more than 30 percent since 1980.

Tracking changes

Amateur naturalists around the world help scientists keep track of changes in plants, animals, and insects as the climate warms. Through programs such as Project BudBurst (see panel, right), and the National Phenology Network in the USA, UK's Nature's Calendar, and other similar projects worldwide, volunteers record changes they see and report their observations on the internet. These efforts will become more and more valuable over time as climate change unfolds and the amount of data grows.

PROJECT BUDBURST

Thousands of Americans take note of spring's progress each year through Project BudBurst, a program sponsored by a museum, a university, and a research center. The volunteers record such events as buds opening and fruit ripening. Hundreds of plant species are now being tracked through the project, and thousands of observations are submitted each year.

CYCLES OF CHANGE
Once endangered in the UK, the comma butterfly is now more frequently observed. Its adaptable life cycle has allowed it to expand its range as far north as Scotland, responding to favorable weather conditions.

Use binoculars to see even more stars.

Night watch

Nothing stretches the imagination and prompts us to question our place in the universe like stars. The sky on a crystal-clear night is an incredible sight, and it is surprising how much you can see.

The Moon

The Moon is a wonderful, even magical, sight. It is our nearest neighbor in space and revolves in time with its orbits around Earth, which means we only ever see one side of it. It is best studied when the low, raking light of the Sun picks out its mountains and crater walls in sharp definition. A full Moon reflects brilliant, intense light and minimizes contrast so, although you can see the entire Moon, it is the least rewarding Moon phase for observation. The brilliance of a new Moon also tends to overwhelm nearby stars.

MOON LIGHT
Moon phases are caused by the Sun lighting up the Moon. A new Moon is dark because the Sun is lighting up the side farthest from the Earth. As the Moon orbits the Earth, more can be seen until it is all visible at a full Moon.

Seeing stars

Stars are grouped into areas of the night sky called constellations, with names such as the Southern Cross and Orion. The stars in a constellation have no connection to each other—the "patterns" are created by chance and early civilizations named them partly to help with navigation and orientation. Knowing where to find constellations will help you understand the night sky better. Binoculars or a small telescope will help you see more stars than the naked eye, and enjoy the constellations and star clusters to the full.

STAR MAP
A star map is essential for navigating the night sky. Pick out the Big Dipper (part of the constellation Ursa Major), shown on this map.

MEASUREMENTS

The size of celestial objects and the distance between them are described in degrees and parts of a degree. Calculating degrees can be done by simply using your hand as a ruler. Hold it up to the sky, at arm's length, and use these standard measurements to help make your calculations.

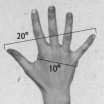

FINGERTIP DEGREE
A finger width, held at arm's length, measures about 1° across.

JOINT MULTIPLES
Finger joints are roughly 3°, 4°, and 6° across.

HAND AND PALM SPAN
An average adult handspan covers 20°; the palm is 10° across.

PREDICTED SIGHTINGS

Stars are fixed objects, but planets and other bodies move around the sky. Astronomers can predict where most will be on a given night, and many resources can tell you what to look for each month, such as which planets can be seen, or whether meteor showers or a bright comet are due.

COMETS

METEORITE

Planets

You can see Venus, Jupiter, Saturn, Mars, and Mercury with the naked eye or with binoculars. Venus and Mercury are evening or morning objects. Venus is usually the brightest of the planets, and all of them, except Mercury, are brighter than any star. Uranus and Neptune are faint compared to Venus, and you need binoculars, a precise location, and a star chart to spot them. Unlike stars, which are very far away and appear as points of twinkling light, planets are solid, much nearer to Earth, and do not twinkle.

MORNING LIGHTS
Venus and the Moon at dawn make a spectacular sight. At its brightest, Venus is more striking than any star. It is so bright that it has even been mistaken for an alien airship or UFO.

THROUGH BINOCULARS
Jupiter is so large that binoculars show its defined shape. Watch it on different days to see its brightest moons move around it.

Using telescopes

You can get great results from a telescope without spending a fortune. Choose a model with a wide lens or mirror—high magnification is far less important—which will gather maximum light and help you see objects such as faint stars, clusters, nebulae, and galaxies. A "go-to" system automatically points some telescopes to your chosen target and is often affordable. Balance cost with practicality, and always visit a good dealer for advice.

lens

eyepiece

counterweight

equatorial mount

leg and tripod

EQUATORIAL MOUNT

ALTAZIMUTH MOUNT

FOLLOW THE STARS
Mounts help telescopes follow the stars. An equatorial mount needs to be carefully aligned, while an altazimuth—such as the Dobsonian altazimuth mount shown here—moves freely from side to side and up and down.

What a naturalist needs

In these gadget-obsessed days, the excitement of preparing a "tool kit" that contains all the essentials for properly exploring the natural world is no longer the sole preserve of the geek. Whether young or old, being technically prepared is part of our lives, and there are plenty of new toys available for the modern naturalist. Field guides for cell phones, tiny cameras to reveal the private lives of nestlings, and chemical lures for specific moths join affordable night-vision binoculars and bat detectors that transfer recordings to your PC can be bought right off the shelf. But remember, the most critical part of the kit cannot be bought. It's a lifetime of curiosity!

A naturalist's kit

Curiosity, enthusiasm, and common sense are some of a naturalists's most important tools. Add a field guide and some way of taking notes, and you are well on your way.

Observing and recording

Becoming a naturalist is about becoming a systematic observer of nature. To do this, you need to have some way of recording what you have seen. It is only when you begin to log your discoveries that patterns and trends begin to emerge—which in turn make you a more focused observer. Some field guides (whether in printed form or digital) for identifying species and a notebook and pencil for jotting it all down are all you need to get started, but don't forget all the time-saving devices offered by modern technology.

DIGITAL NOTES
Modern cell phones provide numerous ways of taking on-the-spot notes in the wild. You can take quick photos or save observations as text messages or voice recordings.

QUICK RECORD
Use a digital camera to create a high-resolution record of your observations during the day. You can later add information like date and location to the files.

FIELD GUIDES
Either carry field guides with you, or take detailed notes of species you are not familiar with to identify later.

NOTEPADS, PEN, AND PENCIL

ADHESIVE TAPE

KEEPING A RECORD
Writing your observations in a notebook is an easy and economical way to keep a lasting record. Sketch your impressions and describe species in detail. Use tape to attach findings such as feathers and leaves to the pages.

ACCURATE NOTES
When making notes, either digitally or on paper, try to be as precise as you can to make comparisons easier later on. Always remember to record the location and date of your sightings. You may want to carry a ruler or tape measure to accurately record details such as size.

TAPE MEASURE

RULER

A host of high-tech extras can help identify and record what you see. CDs, mp3 players, and other devices allow you to you listen to and compare bird sounds on the spot. Digital field guides and mobile web browsers provide fast access to information, although often flicking through a book is more convenient and offers bigger images. Take time to decide what you need and what you like best—and how much you want to spend. There are no rules, so have fun exploring the possibilities at a local wildlife fair or nature reserve shop.

BIRD VOICE PEN
Point to a patch on a printed list to hear the bird song or call you want.

RECORDING DEVICE
Dictate notes as you go—but you'll need to transcribe them later, and you can't make sketches.

wide lens catches light

SCOPE
For steady closeups use a scope on a tripod. An angled eyepiece makes it more comfortable.

focusing ring

VIDEO CAMERA
Create an accurate record by taking a video. Later, you can use it to make written notes.

USING BINOCULARS

Binoculars allow you to get close to wildlife while causing the minimum amount of disruption. To balance any difference between the two eyes, first cover the right side; use the central wheel to focus a sharp object—like a TV aerial—with your left eye. Now cover the left side; use the right eyepiece adjustment to get the same object sharp with your right eye. Look straight at what you want to see, then bring the binoculars up to your eyes. Use only the central wheel to focus on different distances.

right eyepiece adjustment

central focusing wheel

objective lens gathers light

A STEADY GAZE
Use both your thumbs and fingers to help keep binoculars steady.

COMPACT BINOCULARS
Lightweight binoculars are great, but make sure they are comfortable to use.

NAKED EYE VIEW   8x MAGNIFICATION   20x MAGNIFICATION

MAGNIFICATION
A steady view magnified 7 or 10 times shows more than a wobbly one twice as large. Choose binoculars with a magnification between 7x and 10x at most.

A closer look

In order to learn more about certain plant and animal species, it is useful to take a closer look. For some difficult groups, a magnifying lens is essential for accurate identification. Try to observe the specimen as you find it and never collect wild plants or animals. If you catch an insect for closer study, always handle it with great care, and release it afterward.

EASIER VIEWING
Clear perspex boxes are best for observing insects and other small animals more closely, allowing you to view the specimen from all sides with minimal disruption. Some containers have a built-in magnifying lens for easier viewing.

LOOKING AT DETAIL
Use either a loupe lens or a larger magnifying glass to record details such as whether a flower stem is smooth or hairy, the shape of a beetle's jaw, or the wing structure of a dragonfly. Tweezers are useful for holding up small specimen you may find; live animals should only be observed in boxes.

TAKING SAMPLES
Never uproot a wild plant—if in doubt, leave well alone. Use a knife to take a leaf sample for identification later on.

COLLECTING CONTAINERS

CLOTH

LOUPE LENS

TWEEZERS

MAGNIFYING GLASS

CATCHING INSECTS
In order to catch insects for closer observation, make sure you have the right equipmen, such as a net or pooter. Take great care not to damage the animal in any way and always release it afterward.

NET   POOTER

BUTTERFLY NET

Being prepared

Life outdoors is unpredictable, but a changeable forecast is no excuse to stay in. You can take simple steps to be comfortable in most weather conditions.

Evaluating conditions

For the most part, the time of year, the weather forecast, a good map, and an idea of exactly what you are trying to achieve prepares you for most eventualities outdoors. Dress and pack accordingly, bearing in mind that you may be carrying everything with you all day. If buying new equipment or clothing, choose comfortable, lightweight options that allow maximum ease of movement. Your aim is to avoid being too cold, hot, wet, or getting sunburn.

HEAD LAMP

HEADGEAR

Always remember to protect your head outdoors. A warm hat is invaluable on a cold day, while a cap and sunglasses provide shade from the Sun.

HAT

CAP

POLARIZED SUNGLASSES

LAYERING

Wearing several thin layers allows you to easily add or remove clothing as conditions change. Layering is also the best way to keep warm—the air trapped between the layers is an efficient insulator.

fingerless gloves keep hands warm while writing or using equipment

FINGERLESS GLOVES

fleece jacket combines comfort with warmth

lightweight jacket is easy to wear and breathable, yet keeps you dry

base layer wicks perspiration away from body

waterproof zippers ensure that gear stays dry in all conditions

external pockets provide quick access to gear

SPEED LITE

20
500

TROUSERS
Choose trousers that are both robust enough to protect you from scratches and lightweight enough to be comfortable. Trousers with zip-off legs are ideal for changeable weather or an impromptu paddle.

zip-off legs
adjust for warm weather

RUBBER BOOTS

HIKING BOOTS

SANDALS

FOOTWEAR
Choose footwear according to the terrain. Sturdy sandals can be worn on flat ground, while hiking boots are ideal for rough terrain. Rubber boots can be useful when the ground is wet or marshy.

THE DAY PACK
The best knapsacks sit high on the back for comfort, have an abundance of zippered pockets, and are waterproof to keep out the rain. Like all outdoor gear, try it on before you buy. A belt bag is the ideal choice for short treks.

waist strap
helps distribute weight evenly, sparing shoulders

BELT BAG

WET GEAR
What you need depends on what you're doing, when, and where. A swimsuit, mask, and snorkel are all you need to explore aquatic wildlife when the weather is warm. A wetsuit is a good investment for snorkeling in cooler climes, or if you plan to spend long periods in the water.

MASK AND SNORKEL

FLIPPERS

BATHING SUIT

Getting around and staying safe

If you're heading further afield than your local area, make sure you've planned your excursion and have the right equipment to hand.

Finding your way

Exploring a new area requires a bit of preparation and research, but need not be difficult. A map or trail guide is an essential piece of equipment—simple ones are often available online. Plan your route in advance, and carry a map even when following marked trails to ensure you make it back before nightfall.

MAPS
A wide variety of maps is available for navigating in wilderness areas. Choose a large-scale contour map for maximum detail about the various features of the landscape.

FLASHLIGHT
With no other lights around, darkness can fall very quickly. Make sure you always carry a working flashlight.

WATCH
Keep track of the time to check your progress and assess when you need to turn back.

GPS DEVICE
GPS uses numerous satellites to calculate your position. They are especially useful when visibility is low.

USING A COMPASS

A compass is useful whenever you are using a map, but essential if walking on land outside marked trails. A compass, at its simplest, is an instrument that always points to the magnetic north. Use it to ensure that your map is oriented correctly, and to check your course of travel as you walk from point to point.

FINDING NORTH
Align your compass with map gridlines and rotate both until the needle points to "N."

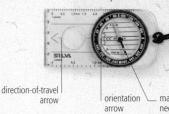

direction-of-travel arrow

orientation arrow

magnetic needle

PUBLIC RIGHTS OF ACCESS

Rights of access refer to the rights of the general public to use public and privately owned land for recreation. Access rights can vary considerably from country to country so always obtain up-to-date information from local authorities when visiting a new area. Access rights can be limited to rights of way, meaning that access to land is only permitted via a certain path or trail.

RIGHTS AND RESPONSIBILITIES
Rights of way are there to be used, but remember to close gates, avoid leaving litter, leave plants alone, and clean up after your dog if you have one.

Countryside Code
1. Plan ahead, be safe, and follow any signs.
2. Leave gates and property exactly as you found them.
3. Protect plants and animals and take your litter home.
4. Keep dogs on a leash.
5. Consider other people.

NAVIGATING IN THE WILD
It takes some time to learn to use a map and compass confidently, but it is a skill that will pay off time and again.

Staying safe outdoors

There are a few things to bear in mind to ensure your comfort and safety outdoors. Watch weather forecasts and be prepared—good conditions can turn bad quickly, especially on exposed ground and mountains. Be careful near the sea, especially on beaches and salt marshes with a large tidal range; you can find yourself a long way from safety when tides turn. Use a tide table (p.198) and watch out for strong winds. Though livestock rarely pose problems, it is wiser to avoid them if you can. Take precautions in unfamiliar places, especially if you are on your own, or as it gets dark. And always tell people where you're going and when you expect to return.

BITES AND STINGS
Spiders and insects rarely cause problems, but find out about any dangerous ones in the area.

INEDIBLE PLANTS AND FUNGI
The golden rule is, simply, don't eat anything unless you are absolutely sure of what it is.

SEVERE WEATHER
Don't venture far afield in difficult terrain if the weather looks bad—and always take suitable clothing.

SAFETY ESSENTIALS

A mobile phone is a safety essential, but you may not have coverage everywhere. Remember to program it with emergency numbers. Always pack a whistle—it can help rescue teams find you if you're unable to move. Be sure to also pack water, high-energy snacks, and basic first-aid supplies, especially if you're planning a long hike in unknown terrain.

tweezers to remove splinters

bandages to treat bleeding and breaks

information on emergency procedures

WHISTLE

FIRST-AID KIT

Photography

Taking photographs is a great way to record the natural world. Using the correct equipment and techniques can help you get some amazing shots.

Choosing your camera

It is the opportunistic and unpredictable nature of wildlife photography that makes capturing a great image so rewarding. Expensive gear is all very well, but being in the right place at the right time, and being alert, patient, and respectful are key. Regardless of what you want to do, you should be familiar with your camera, and it should be comfortable to use and kept with you at all times.

Get as close as you can to your subject without disturbing it.

shutter — flash — viewfinder

automatic zoom lens

navigation buttons

BACK OF DIGITAL CAMERA

DIGITAL CAMERA
Compact digital cameras make photography easy, allowing you to review your pictures instantly and create high-quality images without the cost of traditional film, or the weight and expense of professional gear.

shutter dial — flash mount

shutter

manual zoom lens

LCD screen

BACK OF AN SLR

SINGLE LENS REFLEX (SLR) CAMERA
The camera of choice for serious photographers is the SLR. They have a range of features that can be adjusted manually and also offer greater flexibility with interchangeable lenses.

USEFUL EQUIPMENT

A tripod is useful when your camera needs to be stable, whether for close-ups of tiny plants or insects, or to steady your hand when using a zoom lens. Your kit should also include a lens-cleaning cloth, blower brushes, spare batteries, and digital cards.

tripod attaches to bag

camera is protected by padding

CAMERA BAG
Expensive equipment needs protection when on the move. Carrying bags offer sturdiness, waterproofing, and balance with weight and comfort.

ZOOM LENS   WIDE ANGLE LENS

EXTRA LENSES
Zoom lenses are most suitable for close-ups, while wide angle lenses are ideal for landscape photography.

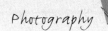

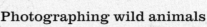

Photographing wild animals

Animals in the wild are fickle subjects due to their unpredictable natures you must take care not to approach or disturb potentially dangerous animals. Studying the techniques used by professional wildlife photographers can improve your chances of getting great shots at a safe distance. "Digiscoping," for example, where you fix a camera to a telescope via an adapter, allows you to shoot close-ups without disturbing your subjects or their environment.

BLINDS

A hide, or blind, is a shelter that offers protection for you and your equipment, and gets you close to your subject without being seen. Fixed shelters, such as a car, can be effective, but a hide built over a period of days to avoid alarming the subject, is often better. Tents can be adjusted for this purpose.

Light and exposure

To capture wildlife in action, and get a good depth of focus, you usually need as much light as possible for quick exposures. But don't look just for bright sun "spotlighting" the subject; think about different types of light, the moods they create, and the effect you want. Go out both early and late in the day and observe the play of light and shadow. Try taking shots with low, raking sunshine, or with light reflected by mist or snow. And don't forget the flash—it is essential for images in lowlight conditions.

Use a waterproof camera, to photograph underwater life.

1 A pheasant captured at full speed. Bright light allows a fast shutter speed to catch the action. A slow shutter speed would create a blur.

2 Bright, autumn sunlight has enriched this pheasant's colors. Dull light flattens color, but it can create a more subtle, atmospheric result.

3 An owl at night taken with a flash, probably triggered by an electronic motion sensor.

4 A subject, like a bird, can be emphasized by isolating it from its background using a shallow depth of field. Create this effect by using a large aperture.

Keeping a record

Recording your observations not only helps you learn more about what you have seen, but lets you to contribute to the data-collecting efforts of the naturalist community.

Field notes

Whether digital or hand-written, the notes you take in the field form an important part of being a naturalist. Note-taking helps focus your attention on the details of what you see—instead of a brown bird, you will learn to see a smallish brown and cream bird, with dark brown markings. Take photos or make sketches to form a more comprehensive picture, and use your notes to look up and learn the names of new species later on. A log of repeated observations allows you to link your discoveries to wider natural phenomena.

TAKING NOTES
Make notes while you are nature watching, or right after—it may be hard to recall details of what you saw.

KEEPING TRACK
A hand-counter is a useful tool for counting flocks of birds with ease.

CELL PHONE
A cell phone is a great tool for a naturalist. Use it to make notes, take photos, or even as a voice recorder.

remember to note date and location of sightings

always include name and any interesting information

note colors of plants and animals

make sketches and add details for later identification

include details of environment in which each species was seen

10/12/2010
Location Ham Lands
Nature Reserve, Richmond

– Rowan berries just changing color from orange to red—earlier than last year!

– Berries seem especially plentiful this year, due to wet summer?

– Gray-brown caps and light-brown stems – Grows in clumps of 2–3

Growing in the shade of trees, almost hidden by fallen leaves

stems 4–5 inches in length, caps up to 2 inches across

pale underside

Collared dove feather—under tall trees

SKETCHING

If you look at something superficially you will soon forget most of the details. If you take time to observe it and draw sketches, however, it will stick in your mind for years. You don't need to be a great artist to sketch the basic shape of an animal such as a bird. Record the overall shape first, then add the details such as tail shape and markings.

1 Use basic ovals to create a bird shape. Get the rough shapes and proportions down, then add a basic bill, tail, and legs.

2 Fill in the general shape and revise the bird's proportions. Is it upright, horizontal, slim, chubby, or long- or short-legged?

3 Add essential details: shapes, relative proportions —do the wings reach halfway along the tail or fall short?—and feather patterns.

4 Look closely at the head and note down the colors and pattern of the plumage and the shape and relative length of the bill.

5 Make sketches from different angles, if possible. Have you labeled everything? If not, take another look. Making notes around a sketch forces you to notice specific characteristics.

Data collection

note any items collected along the way

If taking notes on a regular basis, it is a good idea to transfer the data you collect in the field into a more systematic form for easier access later on. This could be note cards, a comprehensive diary, or a computerized observation log. Use field guides and online databases to identify species and compare your observations to other people's. Don't forget to add or scan in your photos and sketches. Regular, detailed records of the same subjects can help build up a set of valuable data not just for yourself but for the wider naturalist community. A single count of birds on a lake is interesting, but a series of weekly counts taken over a month or year can have real scientific value. Look for local or national surveys to which you can submit your findings.

ORGANIZED SYSTEM
Uploading your records onto your computer allows you to easily retrieve data collected over time. Use online databases for added detail and identification.

BIRDWATCHING
Your data can form part of a regional or national bird survey. Programmes all over the world, such as www.ebird.org in the USA, pool together data from naturalists.

Close to home

Tropical rain forests and Antarctic seas are home to many celebrity species, but it is in and around our own homes that we meet most of our wildlife. These encounters are formative at first, then ultimately much more rewarding than fantasies of exotic creatures fueled by television. To watch in "real time," to identify species that share our community, to relate to their lives and perhaps provide for them—even touch, feel, and smell them—this is the essential source of a real affinity with nature. And despite our worst efforts, so many animals and plants have managed to adapt to sharing the "manscape" that meeting them can be an everyday event.

Home

We all have a number of visitors in our houses. Wasps, birds, and bats may nest in your loft or roof space, while beetles and termites might burrow into wood. Peer into cracks in walls and you may find mice or cockroaches. Look around to see what's sharing your space, but don't view anything as a "pest"— these animals don't exist to aggravate us, but as part of the compex system of nature.

COMMON WASP

HORSESHOE BATS

Local habitats

You don't have to venture far to explore the natural world. Our homes, gardens, parks, streets, and railroads are teeming with wildlife—if you know how to look for it. Many animals and plants live well alongside humans.

Garden

Gardens are great for watching wildlife, especially if sensitively managed with nature in mind. Even the smallest outdoor space—a window box, terrace, or patio—can be stocked with plants to attract insects and the animals that feed on them. In larger gardens, ponds, compost heaps, brush piles, and nature reserves provide more opportunities for animals and plants to thrive. Bird baths, feeding stations, and nest boxes attract wildlife, too.

MOURNING DOVE

COMMON DAISY

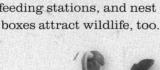

GARDEN SNAIL

Town park

Urban parks are oases of green that provide a much-needed "breathing space," both for people and wildlife. Established parks have mature trees and may include a pond, lake, and wildlife area. Look for small mammals such as squirrels, including groundhogs in North America, songbirds, and waterfowl.

CHESTNUT

GROUNDHOG
(WOODCHUCK)

Street

You may think there is little space for wildlife in the concrete jungle. However, look closely and you will see wildflowers growing through cracks in the pavement, and insects burrowing into the mortar of a wall. You might even catch sight of a rat or a fox scavenging in trashcans, and don't forget to look up to see birds roosting on buildings and street lamps.

BROWN
RAT

ZINNIA

Railroad

Next time you take a ride on the train, look out of the window for wildlife. Some plants, including ragwort (a type of daisy), flourish in the well-drained, gravelly conditions along tracks, and you may see mammals, such as wild rabbits. Disused tracks are often converted into footpaths, while old tunnels can be adapted for hibernating bats—but visit such areas with caution.

OXFORD
RAGWORT

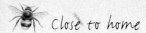
In the home

Our homes provide shelter for animals other than ourselves. We share our living space with an array of successful opportunists.

House guests

The most successful species in nature are those that can quickly adapt to change and capitalize on opportunities as they arise. As humans alter the landscape, wildlife must adapt to survive. Some animals have evolved to find their niche in our homes, which meet two basic needs—shelter and food. For example, a dry attic is a perfect place for a wasp to build her nest, while discarded food waste is a feast for a house mouse. Each species has its place in the world and many, such as spiders, provide a valuable service by keeping the levels of other house guests, such as flies, in check.

LIQUID DIET
Houseflies can contaminate food by passing bacteria from their feet and mouthparts. They suck in liquid food through a fleshy proboscis.

AN ITCHY VISITOR
Adult fleas need blood in order to reproduce. If you notice small, irritating bites, usually on legs and ankles, there may be fleas in your house. Their eggs often drop into bedding or carpets, where the larvae feed and pupate. New adults then jump on to a passing host.

TAKING A BATH
Some spiders can bite if threatened, but they come inside to feed on insects, so don't harm them.

GECKOS
Geckos make good house guests. They keep insects, such as mosquitoes, in check.

LOFTY AMBITIONS
Bats often roost in loft and roof spaces. They will not gnaw on wood and do no structural damage—their dry droppings are also rarely a nuisance.

Fleas have long back legs and can jump up to 350 times their body length.

CAT FLEA

Signs of life

Some visitors are unseen until you notice their tell-tale signs. If you live in the USA, Africa, or Australia, you may not be aware of a termite invasion until you see a nearby swarm, but they could have already been at work in your home. Other visitors are more obvious, and you'll see droppings or nests. You may also hear scratching or chattering in a ceiling or wall, or smell a distinctive odor.

LITTLE NICHES
Small holes in your furniture can be a sign of "woodworm": the common name for the beetle larvae that bore into wood.

BLISTERING PAINT
Buckling paint may mean termites are around. They can cause damage to structures by eating through wooden supports.

TINY DROPPINGS
Small, black pellets in cabinets or on floors are often a sign that mice are inhabiting your home.

HOLES IN CLOTHES
If you see small, light brown moths in your home, check your clothes and carpets. Adult moths do not eat, but their larvae feed on natural fibers, such as wool.

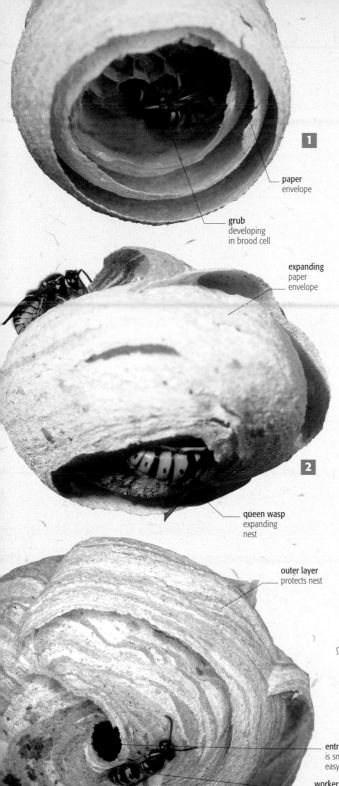

paper
envelope

1

grub
developing
in brood cell

expanding
paper
envelope

2

queen wasp
expanding
nest

outer layer
protects nest

entrance hole
is small and
easy to defend

worker wasp
continues to
enlarge nest

3

Homes from homes

A nest is usually an indication that an animal has set up home in your house. Wasps' nests are common in attics, garages, and lofts—try to look at them from a distance, or with binoculars. Basements, garages, and roof spaces are good places to hunt for the nests of small mammals, such as mice, while evidence of nests around your house may indicate that birds are living in your roof. Swallows and martins build their nests outside under roof overhangs, so you can watch them as they work to feed their young. Never disturb a nest unless it is unavoidable.

LONE QUEEN
A queen wasp uses her antennae to check the size of her nest.

Wasps' nest

1 Social wasps live in colonies in nests. A solitary queen begins the nest, laying a single egg in each brood cell as she completes it. The nest is a sequence of paper layers, made out of chewed wood fibers.

2 The queen tends and feeds her growing grubs with the caterpillars she has caught until they hatch into worker wasps. The workers then help the queen expand the nest, allowing her to spend more time producing eggs.

3 The nest has a small entrance hole that is easy to defend and also helps control the interior temperature and humidity. Workers continue constructing new outer envelopes to accommodate the growing colony.

HOUSE MICE
Mice build nests out of materials they find in and around homes, such as dry grass and soft fabric fibers.

swallows feed their young on insects caught in flight.

MOUTHS TO FEED
Look up, you may see birds such as swallows and martins building their nests beneath the eaves of houses or outbuildings.

51

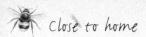

Spiders

Spiders are common in homes and gardens. The best way to find them is to look for their silken webs.

HOUSE SPIDER

Around 40,000 species of spider have been recorded worldwide. They build their webs out of lines of silk, expelled through silk-spinning organs (spinnerets) from glands in their abdomens. Some spiders maintain and repair the same web for some time, while others eat their webs in the evening and construct a new one the next day. The intricate webs of garden spiders are a spectacular sight on a dewy morning. Search carefully among bushes and shrubs, but be careful not to touch any part of the web or the spider will hide. Plain, brown house spiders do not construct such beautiful webs; look for flat, tangled webs in parts of the house that are not used very often. Other spiders you might see around your garden or home include wolf spiders, the females of which often carry a white egg sac under their abdomens; jumping spiders, such as zebra spiders that stalk their insect prey; and tiny money spiders, some of which construct fine, sheetlike webs in grass and hedgerows.

BANDED GARDEN SPIDER

TYPES OF WEBS

Different spiders spin different types of webs. Some spiders create a radial web with strands of silk extending around it that act as tripwires to alert the spider when an insect touches them. House spiders weave a tangled sheet of silk to catch insects that crawl or fly into it, and garden spiders spin orb webs across gaps to catch flying insects.

RADIAL WEB

SHEET WEB

ORB WEB

CLEVER CONSTRUCTION
Most orb web spiders, like this black and yellow garden spider, take only half an hour to spin a web. They move along the nonsticky rays (spokes) of the web so they do not get caught.

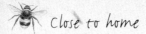
Round the clock

Garden visitors change over a 24-hour period. Diurnal animals are active in daylight hours, while those awake at night are nocturnal.

Daytime

Go out into the garden at dawn, as the first rays of sun peek above the horizon, and you will hear songbirds begin their dawn chorus (see p.98). As the Sun gathers strength, butterflies, dragonflies, and reptiles come out to bask in its warmth. Garden birds start to appear as the day wears on, you may notice them busily feeding themselves and looking for food for their young.

FIND A FOX
Foxes can be seen both during the day and at night, a pattern also followed by rabbits.

FOLLOWING THE SUN

Plants that turn to follow the Sun as it moves across the sky during the day are heliotropic, and the motion is known as heliotropism. They track the Sun with their leaves to maximize the amount of light they absorb for use in photosynthesis. Sunflower blooms also follow the Sun to attract insects that favour its warmth.

NIGHT OR DAY?

Animal behavior is influenced by a biological process called circadian rhythm, a daily cycle that provides cues as to when to sleep, wake, and feed. Many animals (including humans) are diurnal, and remain active during the day, but others are crepuscular (active during twilight hours), or nocturnal (active at night) (see p.14). Nocturnal animals may have adapted this behavior to avoid competition for food with similar diurnal species, to avoid dehydration in hot habitats, or to avoid predation.

DAYLIGHT HUNTER
Kestrels are diurnal birds of prey. They can hover for extended periods, so they can survive in a variety of habitats, including urban centers. Look for them hunting by roads.

SPOT A SQUIRREL
Squirrels are busy during the daytime, feeding and storing food for later. They are agile and very good at stealing food from garden birdfeeders.

SEE A SNAKE
Reptiles, such as snakes, bask in the morning sun to warm their bodies and speed up their metabolism.

LET FRUIT LIE
Leave fallen fruit on the ground in your garden to attract daytime feeders, such as birds and insects.

Night-time

If you sit quietly in your garden at dusk, you might see bats. They fly and hunt insects in the dark by using sound waves to create a mental image of their surroundings. This process is called echolocation. Other nocturnal creatures often have a heightened sense of sight, smell, or hearing. Light reflected in the eyes of a fox or cat is due to a special layer in the retina, called the tapetum, which takes in the maximum amount of light and gives them excellent night vision.

GARBAGE RAIDERS
Some mammals, such as raccoons and foxes, will scavenge in garbage cans during the night.

MAKE A SAND TRAP

A sand trap can tell you which animals visit your garden after dark. Spread a thin layer of sand in an area you think they may use regularly, perhaps a run under a garden hedge or around a feeding station, where you can leave some pet food to attract them. In the morning, see what prints have been made by visiting creatures and try to identify them.

raccoon paw print

SANDY PRINTS
Various animals might be tempted to cross the sand. These prints belong to a hungry raccoon.

LISTEN FOR OWLS
Tawny owls are night hunters. Like most owls, their *to-whit, to-whoo* cries are a male and female, calling to each other.

TEMPT A MOTH
Plant scented, night-blooming flowers to attract moths. The scent helps them find the flowers in the dark.

GO FOR GLOW
Tiny lights in rough grass at night indicate the presence of glow worms, a type of wingless female beetle or larvae.

FEED A BADGER
If badgers are in the vicinity, you might attract them into your garden with peanuts, raisins, fruit, and bread.

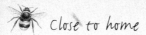
Garden birds

Watching birds in the garden can be truly rewarding. You can encourage your avian visitors by providing food, shelter, and water.

Attracting birds to your garden

The more habitats your garden provides, the better it is for birds and the more species you will attract. Provide shrub and tree cover for shelter and nesting places. Choose native plants that produce seeds and berries as well as those that attract insects, and avoid highly invasive species such as buckthorn. Offer a range of food on bird tables and in feeders and clean water for drinking and bathing, and put up nesting boxes (see p.61).

AUTUMN BERRIES
Hawthorn fruits in autumn are a favorite of berry-eating birds such as this mistle thrush, as are the berries of related species like cotoneaster.

SUNFLOWER
You can buy sunflower seeds for your birdfeeders, but why not plant the flowers? They not only attract insects, but once they have bloomed you can keep the dried heads for birds to feast on the oil-rich seeds.

BLACKTHORN

SAFE NESTING
Holly bushes provide safe nesting and hiding places for small birds, such as sparrows. The bright-red berries are eaten by larger birds, including towhees, thrashers, and blackbirds.

Bird studies

Enhance your observations by attracting birds to a feeding station or bird bath. Watch quietly from a window and don't make sudden movements that might startle your visitors. Depending on your location, you may spot birds from these common groups.

Thrush family

Thrushes are small to medium birds renowned for their beautiful song. Most species are brown or gray, with speckled underparts—apart from the brightly colored bluebirds from the Americas. Thrushes eat insects, but many also eat snails. Watch them using a stone to break the shells.

Starling family

Starlings usually have dark plumage with a metallic sheen. European starlings have white speckles, especially in winter, and can form huge flocks to feed and roost (see pp.72–73). They have been introduced to the Americas, Australia, and New Zealand. Other species of starlings include Asian myna birds and African starlings.

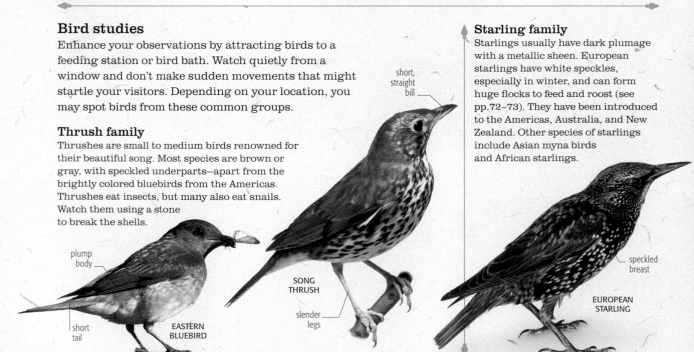

short, straight bill

plump body

short tail

EASTERN BLUEBIRD

SONG THRUSH

slender legs

speckled breast

EUROPEAN STARLING

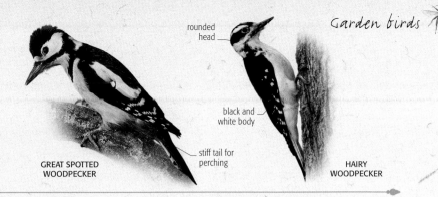

Woodpecker family

Woodpeckers are boldly patterned birds ranging in size from small, at about 6–7 in (15–18 cm) long, to the largest species being about the size of a crow. They have sharp, chisel-shaped bills for pecking or hammering holes in trees to find grubs and make their nests. Two of their toes face forward and two backward to help them grip.

rounded head

black and white body

stiff tail for perching

GREAT SPOTTED WOODPECKER

HAIRY WOODPECKER

white wing bar

tuft or crest

white cheek

white underparts

long tail

GREAT TIT

TUFTED TITMOUSE

BLACK-CAPPED CHICKADEE

Tit family

Birds of the tit family have small, round bodies and short, triangular bills. Some have crests, and some have very long tails. Many are brightly colored. North American members of the family are called chickadees or titmice.

Finch family

The finches are small birds with many plumage colors, including browns, greens, blacks, and some striking reds and yellows. Their bills vary widely in size and shape according to their diet. In addition to goldfinches, bullfinches, and greenfinches, the family includes grosbeaks, linnets, and siskins.

EUROPEAN GREENFINCH

forked tail

Crow family

Corvids are medium to large birds with strong, scaly feet and stout, robust bills. Many species are black or gray, but some are pied—for example, the magpie is white and black. Others, including American jays and the European jay, are brightly colored. The family also includes crows, jackdaws, ravens, and rooks.

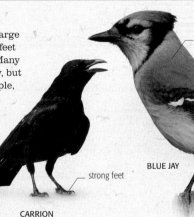

bright blue plumage

strong feet

CARRION CROW

BLUE JAY

BIRDS IN FLIGHT

Identifying flying birds is often challenging. However, a few clues may help you work out the family at least. Besides the rhythm of the flight, things to note include the size of the bird (often difficult to gauge at a distance), its wing shape, tail shape, color, and how it holds its neck and legs. For example, herons fly with their necks bent, whereas cranes fly with their necks outstretched.

FAST WING FLAPPING
Fast, direct flight in a straight line with rapid wing beats is typical of pigeons, ducks, and seabirds with short wings, such as auks.

SLOW WING FLAPPING
Herons, gulls, and barn owls fly with a slow, steady, almost lazy-looking wing beat, allowing them to scan for food as they fly.

wing beats

INTERMITTENT WING FLAPPING
Woodpeckers and finches show an undulating flight of flapping interspersed with pauses in which they seem to bound up and glide down.

RANDOM WING FLAPPING
Aerial insect-eaters such as swifts and swallows usually have a random flight pattern, dipping and diving after insects as they hunt.

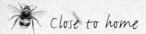

Feed the birds

Birds eat a range of foods, according to their species and the time of year. Some feed mostly on insects, especially in spring and summer when rearing their young, while others are mainly seed-eaters. Many birds gorge on berries and fallen orchard fruit in autumn and winter. You can enhance birds' survival by supplementing their natural diet with additional food.

GREAT BACKYARD BIRD COUNT

Why not get involved with the Audubon's Great Backyard Bird Count? This annual four-day event takes place in February. To take part you simply note birds anywhere for as little or as long as you wish during the allotted period. You then report your findings back online. For more information visit http://www.birdcount.org. You can also report your birdwatching activities through www.ebird.org.

FEEDER PLACEMENT
Offer a variety of feeders in different locations around the garden. Place feeders within 6½–9¾ ft (2–3 m) of shrubs so that the birds can dash away if they see a predator such as a cat or hawk approaching.

caged feeder allows birds to feed on the ground without predators or scavengers getting in

windows kill birds that fly into them, locate feeders either within 3⅓ ft (1 m) or more than 33 ft (10 m) away

elevated bird table fairly close to the house gives a good view of feeding birds

bird tables can be suspended from trees by chains

low bird tables may be used by timid species but ensure they are close to cover

tube feeders can be hung from tree branches or from brackets on walls

feeders on poles can be moved around the garden to find the birds' favorite feeding places

BIRD TABLES
Blackbirds are common visitors to bird tables. Offer a mix of flaked corn, black sunflower seeds, and peanut granules on your table.

USING CAMERAS

The key to successful bird photography is to be as unobtrusive as possible. Use a telephoto lens from the house, or turn the garden shed into a blind. Alternatively, place remotely operated cameras beside feeders or outside nest boxes to observe avian comings and goings. Some cameras are small enough to fit inside nest boxes so you can observe the growing family within.

NEST-BOX CAMERA
A small video camera mounted in a removable drawer in the roof of this box gives an excellent view of the nest inside.

MOTION SENSITIVE
Birds moving in front of the infrared sensor on this camera cause it to whirr into action, taking digital photos, videos, or a combination of the two.

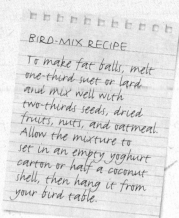

BIRD-MIX RECIPE

To make fat balls, melt one-third suet or lard and mix well with two-thirds seeds, dried fruits, nuts, and oatmeal. Allow the mixture to set in an empty yoghurt carton or half a coconut shell, then hang it from your bird table.

Different bird feeders

Variety, both of feeder design and food types, is essential to attract the most birds. Some birds like to hang from feeders; some perch; others feed on the ground. Suitable foods include black sunflower seeds, niger seeds, flaked corn, peanuts, mealworms, and dried insects.

1 Small birds such as these American goldfinches enjoy feeders with many perches specialized for holding small seeds. Niger seeds are small and black with a high oil content: a favorite of finches and siskins.

2 Nuthatches usually perch on tree trunks head-downward, so a wire-mesh feeder is ideal for them.

3 Birds, such as this North American tufted titmouse, particulary need our help in cold weather. Ensure your feeders are replenished regularly and keep them clear of snow.

4 In addition to visiting feeders containing a suet mixture, woodpeckers will feed on the ground or from logs drilled with holes and filled with a suet mixture, seeds, or nuts.

Do's and don'ts
1. Use good-quality bird food from specialist suppliers.
2. Clear away stale or moldy food.
3. Don't give leftover cooking fat, margarines, vegetable oils, or milk.
4. Never put out salted food or add salt to a birdbath.
5. Keep stored food dry.

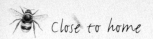

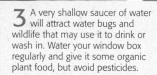

LADYBUG

Lavender in flower attracts butterflies and bees.

Wildlife garden

However big your garden, there are many things you can do to encourage wildlife. You will make a difference, and enjoy doing it.

Why have a wildlife garden?

Many suitable habitats for wildlife have been lost or degraded over the years, through changing land use and development, but with a little effort you can provide your own safe places for wildlife to breed, shelter, and find food. There are plenty of activities that don't cost much, but give wildlife a helping hand whether you have your own large garden or a small balcony or window ledge.

Making a window box

If you don't have much outside space, create a mini nature reserve in a window box. Give interest and a year-round food supply by choosing plants that bloom at different times. For example, spring bulbs attract early-flying bumblebees, while summer flowers provide nectar for sun-loving butterflies. Many herbs, such as lavender and catnip, are favorites with honeybees and they also smell pleasant. Evergreens, such as rosemary and ivy, provide shelter for insects such as ladybugs throughout the winter.

1 Start by filling your window box with soil, then plant a variety of plants far enough apart to give them room to grow.

3 A very shallow saucer of water will attract water bugs and wildlife that may use it to drink or wash in. Water your window box regularly and give it some organic plant food, but avoid pesticides.

2 Cover the surface with gravel or bark to help the soil retain moisture during the summer, and to insulate the window box during the winter.

Bucket of life

A bucket of water left outside the back door will soon be teeming with larval insect life. Mosquitoes lay their eggs in still water. Once they hatch, the larvae mostly stay at the surface to breathe, but tap the bucket and they will wiggle underwater. You may also see small red organisms called bloodworms, which are the larvae of nonbiting midges.

head end of the larva

TEEMING WITH LIFE
Mosquito larvae have mouth brushes on their heads for feeding on algae and bacteria in the water.

Bird bath

Birds require water to drink and wash in all year round. Place a bird bath close to bushes, but where the birds have good visibility. Clean and refill the bath regularly with fresh water, and break any ice. Water between 1 and 4 inches (2.5–10 cm) deep will suit a variety of species.

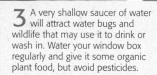

BATH IN THE AIR
Commercially produced bird baths include those that can be suspended from a tree.

SPLASHING AROUND
An up-turned trash can lid, supported by discarded bricks, makes an effective and affordable bird bath.

Helping the bees

Bees are vital for the pollination of many plants and food crops. They are in decline and need our help. Solitary bees nest in holes in the ground or in hollow plant stems. They seal an egg in a cell within the nest with some food for the larva to eat once it hatches. Give somewhere for the young to grow with a bought or homemade bee house. Place it in a sunny position and ensure rain can't get in.

BEE HOTEL

Make your own bee house from a bamboo cane, modeling clay, and a clay pot. Cut the cane into 20 equal lengths, according to the size of your pot. Bind the canes with tape and press the end of the bundle into the modeling clay. Wedge it into the pot with the open ends facing out.

Brush pile

Replicate the valuable habitat of fallen trees with a pile of logs and branches in a shady part of your garden. This creates a damp, dark refuge and source of food for numerous animals, including beetles, centipedes, toads, frogs, and newts. Leave the wood to decay and you may see some intriguing fungi as it rots, especially if the logs are from different tree species. Add new logs periodically.

ROTTEN MEAL

Stag beetle larvae feed on rotting wood for up to five years before pupating over winter, emerging as an adult in spring.

Leaf piles and nesting boxes

Provide nesting materials for small mammals by raking dead leaves into a pile and putting out pieces of animal wool and hair, which they can use for lining their nest. You can also build or buy nesting boxes suited to hedgehogs or dormice for example. It is best to let a leaf pile rot into nutrient-rich leaf mold that you can later spread on the garden.

Look for invertebrates, such as snails, in leaf piles.

HELP A HEDGEHOG

A hedgehog might hibernate in a nesting box in a quite corner of your garden. Hedgehogs eat slugs, so don't put down slug pellets, which can harm them.

COSY NEST

In addition to small mammals, hibernating toads may also use your leaf pile.

Bird and bat boxes

There are numerous types of bird and bat boxes designed for nesting and roosting. You should consider the species you are hoping to attract when choosing which one to buy or build. Attach the box to a tree, post, or wall in a sheltered, quiet part of your garden. Clean it out in the late winter or early spring to remove abandoned nests and make room for new ones.

1 Position several bat boxes around the tree so they offer different temperatures during the day. Bats enter through a narrow slit in the base.

2 A more natural looking bird or bat box can be fashioned out of a section of a hollow tree branch, slotted into a hollow tree trunk.

3 Small birds, such as blue tits, require a box with a small entrance hole. Site the box well out of the reach of predators such as cats.

Compost dwellers

ANT
Ants often nest inside compost heaps. They also feed on some composting materials.

CENTIPEDE
Centipedes patrol the top layers of compost heaps, feeding on other insects and spiders.

EARWIG
Earwigs eat plant matter in compost. They use the pincers at their back ends to deter predators.

OPOSSUM
Opossums and other small mammals might scavenge food from your compost heap.

Composting

Compost is a mixture of decaying organic substances. Making a compost heap is a fantastic way of recycling your garden refuse and some of your household waste. You will also reduce the amount of garbage going into landfill and produce an organic soil enhancer for your garden. The warm, moist environment attracts various animals to live and feed there. Add some old compost or soil to a new heap to introduce beneficial soil microbes and earthworms. Turn the pile regularly to add oxygen to it, but take care not to injure any animals.

RAW MATERIALS
Add fresh leaves, clippings, or food waste to the top of the pile. This provides a home for numerous insects, and will attract creatures that prey on them. You may even see birds picking over the top of your heap.

MATURING COMPOST
Bacteria cause most of the decay in a good heap. The heat they produce through digestion warms the heap and speeds up the composting process. Fungi, earthworms, and other invertebrates help, too.

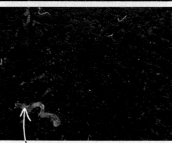

FINISHED COMPOST
The compost should be ready after four to eight months, depending on the heap's temperature. Add finished compost to flower beds and vegetable patches to improve the structure of the soil and help your plants grow.

RECYCLING NUTRIENTS
Add your kitchen and garden waste to your home composting bin, and it will turn into valuable nutrients to put back into your garden.

Ingredients of good compost

To make good compost, you will need a mix of nitrogen-rich "green" ingredients such as fruit and vegetable peelings and grass clippings, and dry, carbon-rich "brown" matter such as leaves, straw, and wood shavings. Keep the heap moist and well aerated, and be careful not to add meat or fat to the compost to avoid attracting rodents.

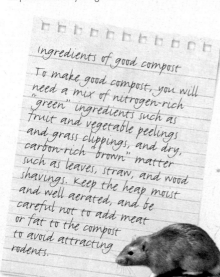

BROWN RAT

Worms can burrow as deep as 6 ft (1.6 m), but they surface after rain.

The different layers allow you to see how worms tunnel and process soil.

WORMERY

Earthworms add oxygen and nutrients to the soil. You can build a wormery in a clear container to watch them at work. Make drainage holes in the bottom, then add alternating layers of sand, soil, compost, and leaf litter. Finally, put in some earthworms. Keep the wormery in a dark place and watch the tunneling begin.

Making a pond in your garden

A pond is probably the most valuable asset to any wildlife garden. You should attract aquatic and semiaquatic insects, including pond skaters, water beetles, water snails, dragonflies and damselflies, and amphibians such as frogs and newts. It will also provide somewhere for birds and mammals to stop for a drink. Stock your pond with native plants; be careful not to introduce alien species that could cause damage. Avoid goldfish, too, because they eat water snails and tadpoles. Position your pond in a semishaded, sheltered location away from trees, and wait for the wildlife to arrive.

1 Dig a shallow hole with a sloping edge and shelved sections for access and gradients. Line the hole with a pond liner and temporarily weigh it down.

2 Cover the liner with sand, soil, and gravel. Ideally, fill the pond with rainwater from water butts, or allow it to fill naturally with rain.

3 Add plants, using bricks or stones if necessary to raise them to the required level in the water. A variety of submerged, floating, and emergent plants is recommended in order to attract as much wildlife as possible to your pond.

POND IN A BARREL
Even if you have no garden, you can turn a container into a small pond. Steep sides cause problems for small creatures, however, so be sure to make access points.

pond plants provide cover

BATHTUB POND
Old bathtubs make great ponds, especially if you sink them into the ground. Be sure to clear out any leaves that have fallen in.

Water plants

OXYGENATING
Hornwort helps keep the pond water clear, and also adds oxygen during photosynthesis.

DEEP WATER
Water hawthorn leaves float on the surface of ponds, but its bulbs can be planted up to 24 in (60 cm) deep.

MARGINALS
Water forget-me-nots grow at the pond margin, giving resting places for insects and protection for wildlife.

FLOATING
Frog's-bit plants float without putting down roots. They provide valuable cover on the pond's surface.

Butterflies and moths

You can make your garden more attractive to butterflies and moths, which can also be found in many other habitats worldwide.

Butterfly or moth?

Butterflies and moths both belong to the insect order Lepidoptera, meaning "scale wings," which has over 170,000 species. Most butterflies are diurnal, while many, though not all, moths are nocturnal. Many moths appear drab in comparison to more brightly-colored butterflies—their colors camouflage them while they are resting. Moths usually rest with their wings outstretched, while butterflies fold their wings vertically over their backs, unless they are basking in the Sun.

antenna is feathery and sensitive

dull color for camouflage

eyespot to deter predators

POLYPHEMUS MOTH (SATURNIID)
These North American moths live for only one week as adults—just long enough to breed.

forewing

METAMORPHOSIS

Butterflies and moths undergo a spectacular transformation, or metamorphosis, from leaf-munching caterpillars to winged adults. During a process called pupation, the juvenile cells in the caterpillar's body are destroyed, while the undifferentiated cells, known as imaginal disks, divide, elongate, and become specialized. The nervous system is restructured too. Butterfly pupae are encased in a hardened shell, called a chrysalis, while some moths spin a protective silk cocoon.

1 Butterflies and moths usually lay their eggs on plants. Look for clusters of tiny, hard-shelled eggs that are "glued" to the upper or lower surface of a leaf.

2 The eggs hatch into caterpillars that devour the plant. This is the growth stage. If you see a plant with ragged, eaten leaves, look for the caterpillar responsible.

pupa has a protective, hard case

3 When the caterpillar is fully grown, it looks for a safe place to pupate. Its skin splits to reveal the pupa, inside which it transforms into an adult.

wings expand as they fill with blood

4 When metamorphosis is complete, the adult breaks out of its chrysalis. It hangs upside-down while its moist wings unfold and gradually harden. It is now ready to disperse, mate, and breed.

hind wing

SWALLOWTAIL BUTTERFLY
There are over 600 species of the swallowtail butterfly family (Papilionidae) worldwide. Particularly prevalent in tropical regions, their name is derived from the pointed tips of the hind wings, which resemble the forked tail of a swallow.

tail on hind wing

MOTH AND BUTTERFLY BEAUTIES

Butterflies and moths come in an astonishing variety of sizes, colors, shapes, and patterns. Keep a record of those that you spot, noting any distinctive markings.

PEACOCK BUTTERFLY (NYMPHALID)

CINNABAR MOTH (ARCTIID)

SMALL WHITE BUTTERFLY (PIERID)

jointed antenna acts as a sensory organ

thorax

small head

eye is large and compound

Individuals within a species have generally the same wing pattern because the pigments are genetically predetermined.

distinctive, dark wing vein

scalloped wing marking

abdomen contains the digestive system and reproductive organs

tiny, coloured scales cover the wing

ATTRACTING BUTTERFLIES

Gardens can easily be made more butterfly-friendly. Plant flowering plants, such as butterflyweed or buddleia (below), in dense clusters in sunny positions, and grow the right food for their caterpillars. Avoid using pesticides and provide sunny resting spots and patches of wet soil, where they can get essential minerals.

SWALLOWTAIL WING DETAIL

Butterfly and moth wings are covered with rows of minute, overlapping scales that give the creature its distinctive color and pattern. The color comes from pigments or from reflected light.

Farm and field

Farmland may be a modified aspect of our landscape, but it is often the most accessible type of countryside for people to explore. And while it's true that some modern farmland and forestry support very few native species, in many places less intensive agriculture has actually created new habitats that are far richer than some natural environments, sometimes allowing small groups of species to prosper artificially. In the US, for example, meadowlarks and bobolinks are now largely limited to the hayfields so typical of man-made farmland, and who would not be excited by a walk across a flower-filled "unimproved" meadow? Indeed, these are all national—and natural—treasures.

ORCHID

Pasture

Grazing helps maintain grassland habitats for wildlife. Without livestock to crop vegetation, strong grasses and shrubs would take over, and many wildflowers such as orchids would be lost. Grasslands are vital to butterflies and birds such as the stone curlew, woodlark, and nightjar. Flooded water meadows provide a seasonal refuge for water birds, and many insects depend on livestock dung for reproduction and food.

SNOWY WAX-CAPPED MUSHROOMS

EUROPEAN MOLE

Farm and field

Farmland is an artificially created landscape in which wildlife has to adapt to constant changes. It is a mosaic of many habitats: pasture, crop fields, and meadows interspersed with hedges, woodland, ditches, and settlements.

Arable land

Arable fields, where crops are grown, are home to birds that prefer to nest on open ground. You might also see small rodents such as harvest mice and voles. The value of arable land for wildlife can be improved by leaving crop remnants in the fields during the winter after harvesting, rotating the crops, reinstating lost hedgerows, and leaving wide field margins.

CORNFLOWER

POPPY

SKYLARK

Field boundary

Much of the value of farmland to wildlife is found at field edges, where machines and chemicals are kept at bay. Hedgerows, ditches, and stone walls are all types of field boundary. They can provide wildlife, such as songbirds and reptiles, with food, shelter, and corridors through which they can safely travel.

COMMON SHREW

SONG THRUSH

Hay meadow

Wildflower-rich hay meadows aren't just beautiful—they support a myriad of insects that feed on nectar, including bumblebees, honeybees, and butterflies. Sadly, traditional hay meadows are now few and far between because of changes to cutting regimes and the use of herbicides. This has resulted in a reduction in insect numbers.

BUTTERCUP

Barns and outbuildings

Farm buildings provide homes for barn owls, swallows, bats, and rodents such as mice. When a little rundown and seldom disturbed, barns and outbuildings are excellent places to watch wildlife. An open window or gap in a door allows animals to enter and find shelter. Old farm buildings can be appropriately restored to ensure they continue to welcome wildlife in the future.

BARN OWL

HARVEST MOUSE

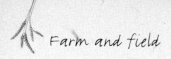
Nature's highways

Despite being cultivated, farmland can play host to an abundance of wildlife. Field boundaries provide animals with safe passage.

Field boundaries

Different farming systems have used different ways of defining fields according to their requirements, available materials, and the climate. Traditional methods include hedges, ditches, and stone walls, all of which provide opportunities for wildlife to inhabit and travel through the agricultural landscape. The loss of field boundaries from the environment, whether by removing hedgerows to create larger fields, or replacing stone walls with fences, is detrimental to the wildlife that depends on them.

VIEW FROM ABOVE
Look down from an airplane and you can see how fields are separated by hedges, tree lines, ditches, or walls. A mixture of boundary types creates the most wildlife-rich farmland.

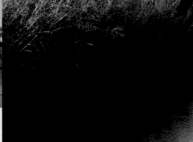

Hedges

Hedges are rows of shrubby plants grown to demarcate fields, the edges of lanes, or settlements. You can estimate a hedge's age by counting its plant species—some hedges can be hundreds of years old. Many different types of animals and plants thrive in the shelter created by hedgerows, including birds, insects, mammals, wildflowers, mosses, and fungi.

ADDER
Various reptiles find food and shelter in hedges, including snakes such as the adder (common viper). Adders are venomous, so don't get too close.

Ditches

Ditches drain low-lying land for agriculture, but they may also be home to insects, such as water beetles and dragonflies; water birds; newts and other amphibians; and mammals, including otters and water voles. Ditches must be managed to prevent silt blockage or clogging with vegetation. They may also be adversely affected by fertilizer and pesticide run-off from adjacent agricultural land.

AMERICAN MINK
The American mink is native to North America but has been introduced to Europe. You may see it using agricultural ditches for hunting and hiding.

FIELD VOLE
Field voles are tiny rodents native to Northern Europe that require grassy habitats. They may hide in hedges to escape being noticed by passing birds of prey—or run to them for protection.

WOOD DUCK
Wood ducks are just one species of waterfowl you might find in farmland ditches.

GERMINATION IN ACTION

Germination is the process by which a plant seed begins to grow into a plant. It can be monitored at home by placing some seeds on moist paper towels in a clear sealed plastic bag, and then leaving it for a week or so at room temperature. Seeds are contained within a fruit—or, in the case of beans, a pod, which splits open. Each bean is a seed that will become a new plant, provided that conditions such as temperature, water availability, and light intensity are suitable. Cactus hedges may be ideal for black-bean germination.

1 The black bean seed contains the plant embryo and a store of protein surrounded by a seed coat.

hilum scar where seed was attached to parent plant

radicle simple first root of plant

2 Germination begins, and an embryonic root called the radicle emerges from the seed and grows downward.

cotyledons first plant leaves, which begin process of photosynthesis

3 The seed leaves, or cotyledons, are pushed toward the surface by growth in the embryonic shoot, or hypocotyl.

secondary roots begin to anchor plant, and take in water and nutrients

Cactus hedges

Cactus hedgerows are found in arid areas where it is too dry for other hedging plants to survive. They are found in Central and South America, where people used cacti such as prickly pear to mark out their agricultural plots. Just as in European hedgerows, birds and other animals nest and find food in them, and the base of the hedge makes a good environment for wild plant seeds to germinate.

CACTUS POLLINATOR
Bats can pollinate cacti by drinking nectar from their flowers, and some disperse cacti seeds by eating the fruit and depositing the seeds.

JAVELINA
The javelina or peccary feeds on the prickly pear cactus. It can be found in South, Central, and parts of North America.

Stone walls

Stone walls have long been used to enclose fields or to terrace sloping agricultural land—for example, in Mediterranean olive groves. If built without mortar or cement, they provide plenty of nooks and crannies for plants and animals. Look for insects, reptiles, and amphibians that make their homes in stone walls, and study the surface of the stone closely to see lichens growing.

SUN LOUNGER
Reptiles, such as this wall lizard, bask on and hide between the warm rocks of stone walls.

MOUNTAIN MADWORT
This plant thrives in dry, rocky soil in Europe and Asia. Wildflowers like this may seed in wall crevices.

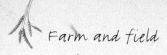

Shape shifters

The sight of starlings flocking is a thrilling spectacle. Moving as one, the birds morph gracefully over open land.

Watching flocking birds is one of nature's great displays. If you are fortunate you might see a flock of blackbirds or European starlings—gregarious birds that feed and roost together in the hundreds or thousands. Flocks are at their largest in autumn and winter. Look for them over farmland, especially grazing marshes, in the afternoon and early evening. After a busy day feeding, the birds fly together for up to half an hour on their way to nearby roosts in woodland, reedbeds, or urban areas. Flocking helps the birds avoid predation by making it difficult for birds of prey to pick out individuals. Groups of European starlings also exhibit an interesting behavior when feeding. As the lead birds move forward over the ground searching for insects, birds from the rear fly up and over to land in front. This behavior is called "roller feeding." During spring and summer, the starlings feed in open farmland, probing insects and larvae from the ground. In this way they aid farmers by controlling a number of crop pests. In the autumn and winter they turn to grain and fruit.

FLOCKING TECHNIQUES

It was previously thought that European starling flocks maintained their cohesion because each bird kept a set distance from its nearest neighbor. However, new research has shown that each starling tracks the location of an average of six or seven other birds within the flock, allowing it to make the necessary adjustments to its flight to keep the flock together. In this way the flock can expand and contract while maintaining cohesion and avoiding the risk of a lone bird breaking away.

AVOIDING A PREDATOR
The flock weaves about, splits, and reforms in the air in an effort to outwit predators such as peregrine falcons.

DRAMATIC DISPLAY
As the sun sets, thousands of European starlings appear to dance in synchrony as the flock prepares to settle in and roost for the night.

Beetles

Beetles can be found in almost all habitats, from deserts and ponds to the tops of mountains. They are thought to represent one third of all insects.

Beetle diversity and distribution

Beetles (Coleoptera) are arthropods, a major group of invertebrates that also includes arachnids and crustaceans. They have jointed legs and front wing cases (elytra) that cover and protect the more delicate hind wings. There are believed to be well over 350,000 species of beetle worldwide, with many more species yet to be discovered. Beetles play an important role in the natural world—they recycle nutrients by helping to break down animal and plant waste. Most species are herbivorous.

POTATO-EATER
Native to North America, the Colorado beetle (family Chrysomelidae) has been introduced widely. It can cause damage to potato crops.

Beetle varieties

There are currently around 188 different families of beetles, but their classification is constantly being reviewed. They range in size from tiny species smaller than a millimetre to giants, such as the titan beetle of the Amazon rainforest, that are nearly 8 in (20 cm) long. Here are some common families.

LADYBUG (COCCINELLIDAE)
Ladybugs are small, domed beetles. The most familiar pattern is red with black spots, but other colorways also exist.

ROVE BEETLE (STAPHYLINIDAE)
Rove beetles have long, flexible abdomens visible beneath short wing cases (elytra).

WEEVIL (CURCULIONIDAE)
Weevils, or snout beetles, are small plant-eaters with bent, clubbed antennae. Over 60,000 species are known.

SCARAB BEETLE (SCARABAEIDAE)
Scarab beetles vary enormously in color, shape, and size. All have a distinctive club at the ends of their antennae.

LONGHORN BEETLE (CERAMBYCIDAE)
These beetles are so-called because they possess antennae that may be as long as, or longer than, their bodies.

MAKING A BERLESE FUNNEL

light bulb
as heat and light source

soil or leaf litter sample on mesh

collecting jar with kitchen paper at the bottom

A Berlese funnel lets you see the variety of insects that hide in soil and leaf litter. Put some soil on a piece of mesh in a funnel, paper cone, or half an empty plastic bottle and suspend it over a jar with some kitchen paper in the bottom. Shine a lamp onto the sample from at least 4 in (10 cm) above. The heat and light coax any insects to move through the mesh into the jar. Ensure you let them go.

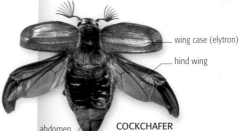

wing case (elytron)

hind wing

abdomen

COCKCHAFER (SCARABAEIDAE)
This common cockchafer's wings are outstretched for flying. Their antennae fan out to sense air currents.

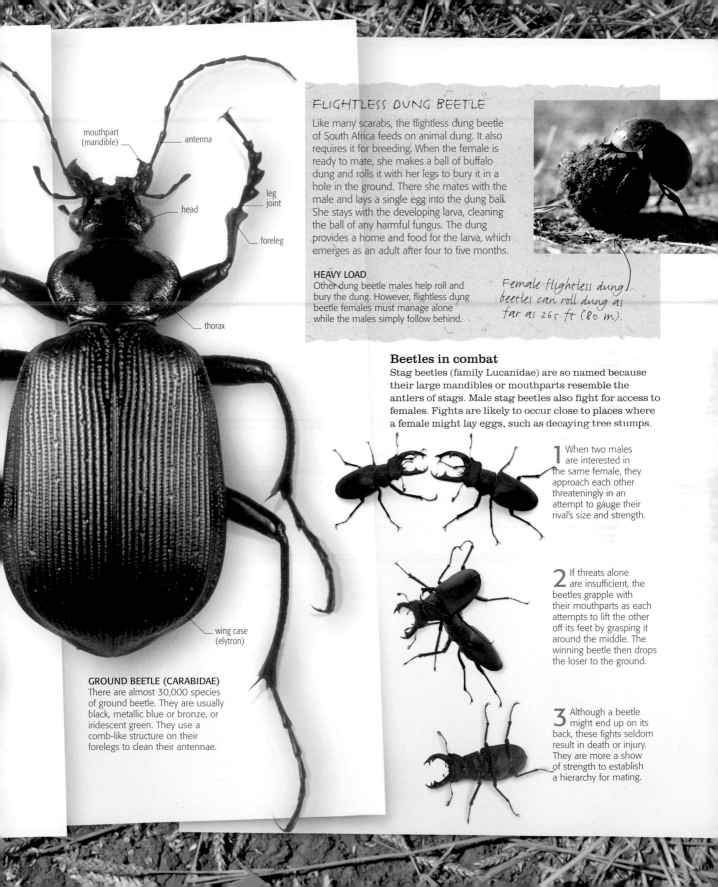

mouthpart
(mandible)

antenna

head

leg
joint

foreleg

thorax

wing case
(elytron)

GROUND BEETLE (CARABIDAE)
There are almost 30,000 species
of ground beetle. They are usually
black, metallic blue or bronze, or
iridescent green. They use a
comb-like structure on their
forelegs to clean their antennae.

FLIGHTLESS DUNG BEETLE

Like many scarabs, the flightless dung beetle
of South Africa feeds on animal dung. It also
requires it for breeding. When the female is
ready to mate, she makes a ball of buffalo
dung and rolls it with her legs to bury it in a
hole in the ground. There she mates with the
male and lays a single egg into the dung ball.
She stays with the developing larva, cleaning
the ball of any harmful fungus. The dung
provides a home and food for the larva, which
emerges as an adult after four to five months.

HEAVY LOAD
Other dung beetle males help roll and
bury the dung. However, flightless dung
beetle females must manage alone
while the males simply follow behind.

*Female flightless dung
beetles can roll dung as
far as 265 ft (80 m).*

Beetles in combat
Stag beetles (family Lucanidae) are so named because
their large mandibles or mouthparts resemble the
antlers of stags. Male stag beetles also fight for access to
females. Fights are likely to occur close to places where
a female might lay eggs, such as decaying tree stumps.

1 When two males
are interested in
the same female, they
approach each other
threateningly in an
attempt to gauge their
rival's size and strength.

2 If threats alone
are insufficient, the
beetles grapple with
their mouthparts as each
attempts to lift the other
off its feet by grasping it
around the middle. The
winning beetle then drops
the loser to the ground.

3 Although a beetle
might end up on its
back, these fights seldom
result in death or injury.
They are more a show
of strength to establish
a hierarchy for mating.

Open farmland

Farms cover huge tracts of land. If farmland is sensitively managed, wildflowers and animals can thrive at its edges, or within the fields themselves.

Exploring farmland

Farmland can be a great place for wildlife-watching, but take care before exploring it. If there are no public paths or roads (see p.40), you must get permission from the landowner before going on private land. Always keep on footpaths, bridleways, or field edges to avoid damaging crops. Don't startle livestock, always leave gates as you find them, and avoid any fields that have been recently sprayed with herbicide or fertilizer.

HARVEST TIME
The mechanization of farming during the last century has meant more arable land—but loss of wildlife habitat.

MOLE HILLS
Little heaps of earth in pastures are a sure sign that moles are tunneling beneath, looking for earthworms.

Wildlife

Farmland is home to insects such as honeybees and butterflies, and numerous birds and mammals, including deer, rabbits, foxes, and bats. A good way to observe farmland wildlife is to choose a position downwind on a footpath where you can watch from behind a tree or hedge without giving away your presence or disturbing any animals. Use binoculars to help you see and identify species. Look for wildflowers, such as poppies, cornflowers, and field pansies, which will be found mainly at the field edges due to the use of herbicides on crops.

MEADOW VOLE
These tiny rodents feed on grasses in open North American farmland. They are prey for larger animals, including birds and mammals.

ACTIVE ADAPTATION

Try looking for banded snails in fields and hedges. You may notice more dark-shelled snails on brown leaves and yellowish snails in grass, where they blend in and predators like thrushes find it hard to see them. Darker snails also thrive in cooler areas as their shells warm up faster.

BROWN-LIPPED

WHITE-LIPPED

SPARRING PARTNERS
Keep an eye out for boxing brown hares on open farmland—an exhilarating sight. It occurs in spring when females try to ward off the unwanted attentions of males.

Farmland birds

Many birds that inhabit farmland nest on the ground, including the skylark, lapwing, corn bunting, and gray partridge. They are difficult to see on their nests, but you may catch sight of them in flight or when feeding. Also look for birds of prey, such as kestrels or barn owls, hunting for small rodents. In Europe, farmland birds are declining in numbers, as are grassland birds in North America. This is thought to be largely due to changing agricultural practices. However, a number of major conservation efforts are under way to help reverse the decline, such as providing uncultivated areas within fields where birds can nest and forage, and growing flower-rich margins at field edges to attract insects.

LAPWING
Birds such as lapwings breed in arable fields and meadows. They eat insects and worms.

GRAY PARTRIDGE
Adult partridges feed on grain in grain fields. Their young eat insects in the field margins.

RING-NECKED PHEASANT
Ring-necked pheasants are native to Asia but were introduced to Europe and North America as game birds.

Cowpatties

Cattle dung has been shown to support over 200 different species, mainly because cowpatties are a great source of food for small insects such as flies, beetles, springtails, and worms. In return, these tiny creatures do a fantastic job of removing cowpatties from the fields and recycling the nutrients they contain back into the soil. Dung beetles also help keep numbers of flies, such as horn flies and face flies, low in farmland by outcompeting them in cowpatties.

SPRINGTAIL

DUNG FLY

DUNG BEETLE

COWPATTIE SOCIETY
You can see male common yellow dung flies establish territories on freshly deposited dung and wait for females to arrive. After mating, the females lay their eggs on the dung's surface.

A healthy dung insect community will remove a cowpattie from the soil's surface within 24 hours.

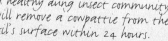

77

Farmland close-up

Farmland varies widely around the world and the wildlife inhabiting it depends upon the type and method of agriculture being practiced. Wherever you are, look along field margins for signs of life.

SWEET CHESTNUT

NUTS

THISTLE

TRAVELER'S JOY

WOOD BETONY

Autumn brings a rich harvest of fruits, nuts, and grains.

Look for blossoms adding color to fields in spring and seedheads in late summer.

CORN

HEDGE PARSLEY

WHEAT EARS

CRAB APPLE BLOSSOM

MAP BUTTERFLY

Look for butterflies in meadows and hedgerows.

PEACOCK BUTTERFLY

SOLDIER BEETLES

TWO-SPOT LADYBUG

Beetles may be found feeding on flower heads.

BIRD FEATHERS

Collect feathers of gamebirds and birds of prey but never disturb nests.

ABANDONED BIRD'S NEST

BLACKBERRIES

DRIED DUNG

Animal remains give valuable clues to the lives, and deaths, of farmland wildlife.

OWL PELLETS

OLIVES

MOLE SKELETON

DISCARDED SNAKE SKIN

Forest

You walk over grassland or heath, but you walk _in_ a forest. It envelops you, and this points to a significant difference: there are many more opportunities here for life to exploit distinct niches. Thus, forests support our richest biodiversities, especially those seasonally stable and ancient swathes that ring the Equator. These are complex places, where the connections between the species that form communities are still revealing surprises. Yet forests can also be difficult habitats to explore—you can't see the life for the trees. You will need a lifetime of patience to uncover their secrets.

Ancient woodland

A few forests have remained almost unchanged by human influence. In an area that has been consistently wooded for hundreds of years you may find rare plants, such as orchids growing on chalk in beech groves. Birds, such as owls, and mammals adapt well to modern woods, but older forests often attract a wider array of animals than younger woodlands, including more specialized insects and plants.

TAWNY OWL

OAK BEAUTY MOTH

Deciduous woodlands

From the tropics to temperate zones, broadleaved woods are beautiful habitats. Deciduous forests that are leafless in winter are found mainly in moist, relatively cool habitats, and at higher elevations closer to the tropics.

WILD GARLIC

Beech forest

Beech forests glow a brilliant green in spring and burn bright with glorious autumn colour. The dense canopy keeps the forest floor in deep shade so few shrubs grow here, but you can find plants such as wild garlic and abundant fungi springing up on the forest floor. Birds sing in the trees, insects flourish in the leaf litter, and you can find squirrels, foxes, and—if you're quiet—badgers among mammalian residents.

BEECH LEAF

Parkland

Parkland is largely artificial in North America and Europe, often associated with estates around large houses. The shrub layer is often weak or absent, so you won't see as many butterflies and forest flowers as on a heath or grassland area; however old, rotting trees still attract birds such as nuthatches and woodpeckers, as well as insects, and you may encounter mammals such as deer or squirrels.

FOXGLOVE

HORSE FLY

Temperate rain forest

Temperate rain forest along coasts as far apart as New Zealand and Chile, or North America and western Scotland, is even more threatened and fragmented than most tropical rain forests. Yet they have a great wilderness value—mature forest is often ancient, with a covering of spring flowers or ferns, while open glades encourage a dense growth of thick, tangled shrubs at their edges—all home to a host of wildlife.

JEWEL BEETLE

SWORD FERN

OAK LEAVES AND ACORNS

BLACKBERRIES

PURPLE EMPEROR

Remember to look up for birds and squirrels in the trees.

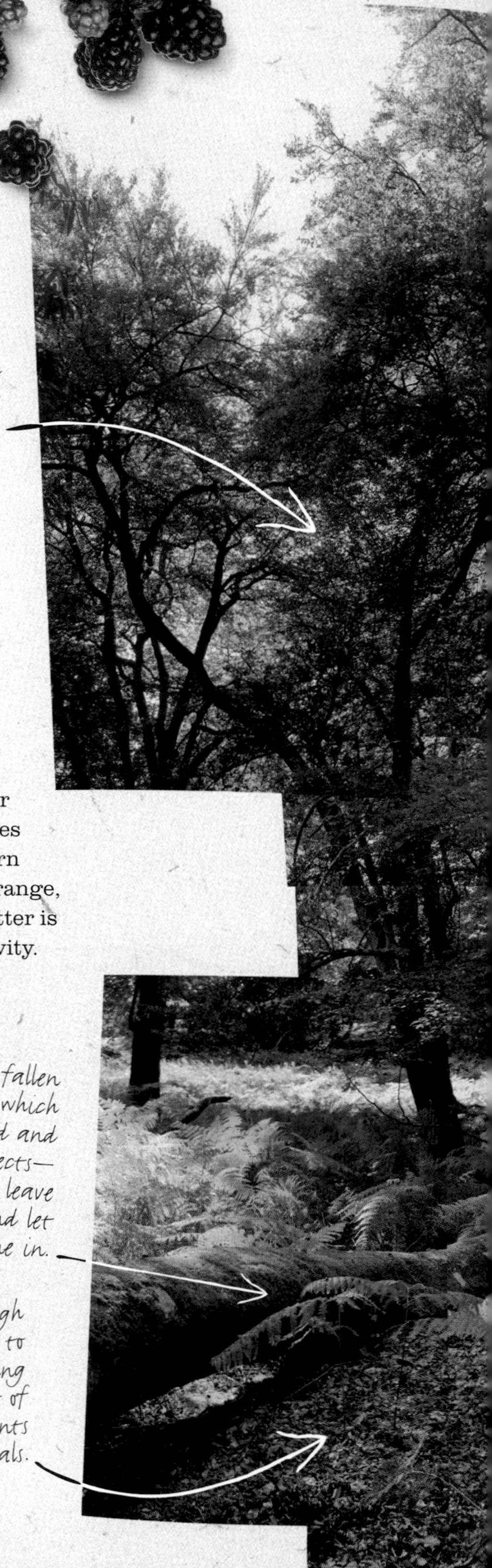

A walk in the woods

A deciduous wood is packed with a myriad of sights, smells, and sounds. Tall trees envelop you, shielding you from the interference of the man-made world.

The character of the wood changes dramatically with each season, so visit throughout the year to see how the forest develops. In spring, the wood comes alive with colorful flowers, insects, and birds. Trees are in full leaf during summer, providing food and shelter for insects in the canopy and covering the forest floor in shade. Look for fungi in autumn and for leaves of deciduous trees, which turn beautiful shades of yellow, orange, and red. In winter, the leaf litter is still a place of abundant activity.

BEECH NUT

Look at fallen branches, which create food and homes for insects—the gaps they leave behind let sunlight shine in.

Sift through rotting leaves to find a thriving habitat of tiny plants and animals.

SOLOMON'S SEAL

HAWKWEED

MAPLE
LEAF IN
AUTUMN

Look for holes
in trees—
many birds
nest in them.

NURSERY WEB
SPIDER

summer leaves
hide squirrels
and birds—listen
for their calls.

TULIP TREE
BLOSSOM

see how bracken thrives where
sunlight reaches through to
the ground.

FLOWERING
MOSS

HAIRSTREAK BUTTERFLY

5 CANOPY

Treetops create a canopy, letting through different levels of light according to the type of tree. Some animals, such as birds, butterflies, monkeys, and sloths, are canopy specialists, each choosing different "stories" for different needs. Birds such as thrushes feed and sing in the canopy, but nest at lower levels. Butterfly caterpillars may feed in the canopy, while adults feed from flowers far below.

WOOD THRUSH

GRAY SQUIRREL

5

Living space

From the roots to the canopy, trees provide living space for a wide variety of wildlife, thus increasing the habitable area of a forest.

Forest builders

Just a moment spent looking at a tree reveals that they abound with life. They provide food and shelter for animals both large and small, from the microscopic organisms in rotting leaves to the birds in the highest branches. Each tree creates a host of niches at every level—the larger the forest, the more diversity. Because the forest is so interdependent, it functions in much the same ways as a single living entity, with each species being reliant on another species for its survival. At the bottom of this chain is the soil.

FOREST WEB

Plant growth in the forest produces enough food to support three levels of consumers, from small herbivores to carnivores and large omnivores.

bear

fox jay owl skunk

beetle worm finch mouse vole deer

MEASURING UP

Trees are the Earth's largest living organisms. Measuring a tree and counting its annual growth rings can provide more than dimensions and age—it can also reveal how environmental conditions have affected it over the years. The growth rings on this tree are off-center, suggesting that one side of the tree may have been exposed to harsh, windy conditions.

rapid growth on sheltered side

CROSS-SECTION FROM FELLED TREE

GIRTH GROWTH

The girth (circumference) of a tree increases each year. Measure it with a tape measure at least 5 ft (1.5 m) above the ground. Keep a record of your measurements and compare your readings over a number of years to see how the tree is growing.

Tree shapes

Individual trees can develop unusual shapes, especially if they are growing in harsh conditions. Look for short, gnarled, and stunted trees at high altitudes, cold and windy areas, or poor soils. In dense forests you might find very tall and straight trees, while coastal trees tend to bend away from prevailing winds because twigs and branches on the exposed side die or fail to develop. Trees with bark, leaves, and branches stripped to a specific level may be showing damage from browsing animals, such as deer.

SPECIES SHAPES

The outline of a mature tree can help you identify it. With or without leaves, each species has its own characteristic shape based on the number and thickness of the smaller twigs and the angle at which they grow from the main branches.

BROAD
(BEECH)

BROAD COLUMNAR
(SWEET CHESTNUT)

SLENDER AND GNARLED
(SESSILE OAK)

COLUMNAR
(HOLLY)

NARROW AND WEEPING
(SILVER BIRCH)

CONICAL
(ALDER)

SPREADING
(HORNBEAM)

COLUMNAR TO SPREADING
(WILD CHERRY)

4 SHRUB
Shrubs and saplings grow beneath some trees, for example holly grows under oak to create a shrub layer.

VIBURNUM

3 FIELD
Herbs and low-growing flowers, ferns, and mosses create a field layer close to the ground.

COLUMBINE

2 LEAF LITTER
Rotting leaves from past seasons create leaf litter, which has a thriving wildlife system of its own. Oak and sycamore leaf litter is especially rich.

1 SOIL
Humus from rotting foliage and dead wood mixes with underlying minerals to create the soil on which all life depends.

EARTHWORM

Leaves

Leaves are the crowning glory of most plants, they convert energy from the Sun—the basis of all life on Earth.

How leaves work

Plants collect nutrients by photosynthesis. Chlorophyll in leaves uses sunlight to convert carbon dioxide from the air into starches and sugars. As leaf cells (stomata) take in carbon dioxide, water is lost, or transpired. Nutrient-rich sap rises, pulling water in from the soil via the roots in a process called osmosis.

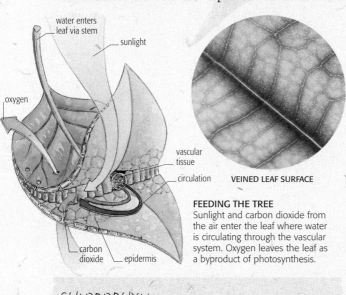

water enters leaf via stem

sunlight

oxygen

vascular tissue

circulation

VEINED LEAF SURFACE

carbon dioxide

epidermis

FEEDING THE TREE
Sunlight and carbon dioxide from the air enter the leaf where water is circulating through the vascular system. Oxygen leaves the leaf as a byproduct of photosynthesis.

CHLOROPHYLL

Chlorophyll is an essential pigment contained in plants. It is responsible for the great variety of greens you can see in different kinds of plants and achieves this by mostly absorbing blue and red light and reflecting green light. Known as a "photoreceptor," chlorophyll is essential for photosynthesis. In winter, when days are shorter, photosynthesis is not possible and chlorophyll is withdrawn from the leaf cells, leaving them an orange-brown. Trees shut down and survive on stored starches until spring.

young leaf

old leaf

LEAF SURFACE
A waxy cuticle reduces water loss and tiny hairs control evaporation. When old leaves pit and mottle they lose this function.

Leaf structure

You will notice most conifers have needlelike leaves, but broadleaved deciduous tree leaves have a stiff midrib and a broader blade with supporting side ribs. A stalk provides mobility, reducing wind damage.

Leaf shape

Leaves come in a great variety of shapes and sizes. They may be simple or compound, with a number of leaflets such as "palmate" (hand-shaped) and "pinnate" (several leaflets in a row). Teeth, notches, points, and lobes encourage water to gather and drip away.

OVAL (ELLIPTIC)

TEARDROP (ARISTATE)

ROUND (ORBICULAR)

COMPOUND (PEDATE)

HEART-SHAPED (CORDATE)

ELONGATED (LINEAR)

Arrangement

Look for leaves with different arrangements. Some are solitary, while others are clustered. Where they have stalks they can be opposite each other or they can be alternate.

branch from same point

OPPOSITE

branch alternately on each side

CLUSTERED

branch from central point

ALTERNATE

Color varieties

Leaves come in a variety of colors. Some have a red pigment overlying the chlorophyll, creating "copper" varieties. Others have yellow pigments or appear almost white. Dying leaves in the autumn make sugar, which is trapped as a red pigment.

green upper side

silver underside

CONTRAST (SILVER MAPLE)

AUTUMN RED (RED MAPLE)

newer leaf

older leaf

NEW GROWTH (CHERRY)

prominent, light veins

PROMINENT VEINS (RAULI)

hairy surface

WHITE UNDERSIDE (POPLAR)

paler outside

VARIEGATED (NORWAY MAPLE)

Margin and texture

Smooth, waxy leaves tolerate dry or harsh conditions, while others are coarse with rough surfaces. The great variety of leaves are adapted to different habitats.

LOBED (OAK)

COARSELY TOOTHED (HORNBEAM)

SMOOTH WAVES (BEECH)

SMALL TEETH (BIRCH)

CRINKLED (ELM)

SPINY (HOLLY)

NEW ENGLAND FALL

New England in North America is one of the best places to visit to see a spectacular leaf fall. Most leaves live for about six months, before dropping in a process called abscission, and are replaced every year. A large, mature tree may have around 250,000 leaves. Cold nights reduce the transportation of sugars around the tree and they become trapped in the leaves. Along with the lack of chlorophyll, this creates the reds and yellows of a glorious fall.

Look for maple trees: they create the most vivid colors.

Seasonal change

A new leaf is usually a vivid, light green. Weeks of hard work, plus the effects of wind, rain, and temperature fluctuations, gradually hardens the leaf and makes it duller and darker with age, until it finally begins to "turn" and decompose. Try photographing leaves from one plant throughout the year, to compare the colors as the year progresses.

LIFE CYCLE
Most leaves start life as bright green, but change color as they age and begin to degrade.

Forest floor

The forest floor in spring can be stunning, with swathes of flowers, while in fall, it is a scene of decay—yet still full of life.

Exploring leaf litter

Leaf litter is full to the brim with tiny animals such as insects, spiders, and salamanders. These are exploited by bigger ones, such as badgers, thrushes, and woodcocks. A careful look at the leaf litter will reveal a wealth of wildlife. Identifying leaf litter flora and fauna is a specialist's job, but you can get an idea of what is around in your local wood.

FINDING CLUES
Distinctive droppings or tooth marks on nibbled seeds offer clues to a woodland's inhabitants.

SNAIL TRAIL
Snails move on a muscular foot, coated with mucus to reduce friction and protect against sharp surfaces, leaving a slimy trail.

INSECT HUNTER
All kinds of insectivores, including shrews such as this pygmy shrew, can be found in leaf litter rich with insects, worms, and spiders.

MOISTURE LOVER
Small, slender, and moist-skinned, salamanders, such as this yellow-spotted variety found in North America, need a damp environment to survive.

Take a clear plastic box and a hand lens to examine small insects.

leaf litter spiders ambush prey, rather than relying on webs in this mobile environment

fallen leaves provide food, shelter, and a vital moist environment

beetles and their larvae feed in dead leaves

earthworms process vast amounts of soil and leaf matter

woodlice have tough, hard skins to retain moisture

USING A POOTER

The pooter has a short tube with gauze at one end, and a long open tube. Put the long tube over an insect, then suck sharply through the short tube. The insect should shoot into the cylinder. The membrane keeps you from sucking it into your mouth so you won't swallow it, but always make sure you're sucking the right tube.

BUG COLLECTOR
Pooters are devices for catching insects that let you identify them, then release them unharmed.

Forest flowers

Flowering plants face many challenges in woodland—trees demand a huge amount of water from the soil, and, when in full leaf, cast a deep shade on the forest floor. Flowers have evolved many ways to deal with such problems. Some, such as primroses, wood sorrel, and wood anemones, flower very early, before the trees are in full leaf. Others, such as toothwort and several kinds of orchids, parasitize other plants. Many simply grow on the sunny edges of woodland or forest glades.

slugs feed on forest floor debris and fungi, which helps disperse seeds and spores

saddle-shaped mantle has a respiratory opening

larvae developing underground are sheletered from cold winters

A small garden trowel will help lift a soil sample as well as leaf litter.

earthworms leave curly "casts" of decomposed matter

TROUT LILY

CREATING TOPSOIL
A cross-section of the leaf litter and upper soil layer on the forest floor reveals a host of animals and plants that help digest the fallen leaves.

Nature's recyclers

The world of rotting logs and leaves appears to be dead but is actually alive with miniscule animals, not all of them visible to the naked eye.

A wood is a celebration of life's abundance and even so-called "dead wood," such as this rotting log, is actually alive and important. The energy and nutrients that fuel life in the forest are broken down here, recycled, and made available for further use. Take time to examine fallen wood and you will see a host of creatures—insects, mosses, lichens, fungi, and ferns—that take advantage of this decay and in turn make a vital contribution to life in the forest by enriching the soil from which forests grow.

LICHENS AND BACTERIA
Both bacteria and lichens, those tangles of algae and fungi, thrive in areas of dappled shade.

CENTIPEDE
A centipede's soft, permeable skin loses moisture, so this tiny predator inhabits damp, sheltered places.

cavity in log becomes home for bees and wasps, even if made by other insects

loose bark offers shelter, food, and moisture

ivy growing over log provides shelter, and its berries are a vital food source in winter

INSECT LARVAE
Some fly and beetle larvae inhabit decaying wood; others feed on the fungi associated with it.

holly grows in shelter of oak trees—look for young plants on fallen oak

LONGHORN BEETLE
Some woodland beetles, such as this longhorn, develop their larvae in dead wood, where they are sheltered and can break down the rotting log into digestible materials.

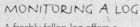

MONITORING A LOG

A freshly fallen log offers a habitat for wildlife for many years, but the creatures that exploit it change as time goes by. This is a perfect chance for you to watch and record what happens as a fascinating ecosystem develops. Keep a "log file" with notes, lists of wildlife inhabiting it, and photos—especially from a fixed position nearby—over several years.

firm, complete bark · shelf fungi
flexible twigs · fungus

NEWLY FALLEN
A fresh log with firm bark is a challenge for recyclers. Weak points allow beetle larvae and fungal spores to attack.

moss · red campion · frog
bark begins to break up

ONE YEAR ON
The bark begins to break up, and twigs become brittle. Mosses, lichens, fungi, and plants appear, and larvae, centipedes, and ants thrive in and around the decaying log.

wood sorrel · woodpecker
beetle hole · fungus

ABUNDANT LIFE
The log breaks up, while plants, mats of moss, lichen, insects, spiders, woodlice, and feeding birds thrive in and around it.

beech leaves cover fallen wood providing extra shelter and food for insects and their larvae

grasses set seed on patches of damp fiber and decaying leaves in open cavities

bore holes show activity of beetle larvae

fungi are found on rotting wood, from which they take nutrients

ferns are common in woodland and many grow on fallen wood

SPIDER WEB
Many spiders drape tangled sheets of web over stumps and logs, rather than creating the usual "cobwebs" across open spaces.

MOSS
The moist, sheltered habitat of a rotting log in woodland allows many moss species to thrive.

Bark life

Bark does far more than just protect the tree—it is also a vital lifeline for many insects, birds, and other wild creatures.

Examining bark

If you look closely at bark you will be able to spot the tell-tale signs of life—from insect trails and bore holes to cavities that provide homes for birds and spiders. Some insects lay their eggs in bark because it provides an insulating layer for larvae over the winter, as well as a good hiding place from predators. Birds, such as treecreepers or woodpeckers, feed on insects in and on bark, or store food caches within it. You may also see a well-camouflaged moth, blending in on a branch. Whether brightly colored, flaking or polished, scaly, smooth, or woody, bark is an ecosystem in itself.

BARK BEETLE
Lift a flake of loose bark and you may find a host of patterned lines. What looks like an abstract artist's design is in fact the work of beetle larvae, which burrow through the tree's surface.

TELL-TALE HOLES
Look for small holes on a tree trunk—this means a woodpecker has been active—in this case, a North American acorn woodpecker is storing nuts.

MOTHS
Many moths rest on trees. Some stand out, while some resemble pieces of bark.

SHELF FUNGUS
This fungus grows under tree bark as a parasite, taking nutrients from it.

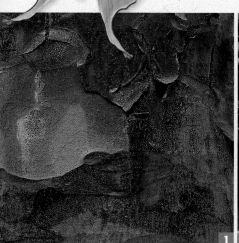

1

2

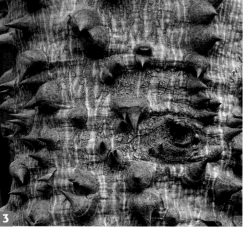

3

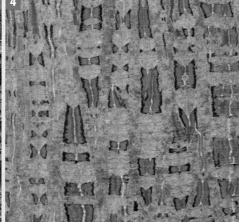

4

5

6

Bark types

Bark differs from tree to tree; on birches it is merely a thin skin, while on conifers it may be as thick as 12 in (30 cm) (see p.111). As the tree grows, a thin inner layer, called the cambium, continually produces new bark. The cambium grows either in large sheets, creating peeling or sheathlike bark, or in overlapping arcs, producing a cracked effect. Examine the colors, structures, and patterns and you will soon see that each type of tree has its own distinctive type of bark.

1 The paperbark maple's peeling bark reveals many different layers.

2 Wild cherry's bark forms a ringed or banded pattern.

3 The floss silk tree's bark is thorny, particularly when young.

4 The striped maple derives its common name from its bark.

5 English oak has rough and deeply fissured bark.

6 Sweet chestnut's bark becomes spirally ridged with age.

7 The smooth bark of birch is marked by raised pores (lenticels).

8 Sycamore bark can become gray-brown and flaky with age.

9 Marks and cavities give holly bark a calloused appearance.

10 Beech bark becomes mottled and fissured as it matures.

11 Plane trees have smooth bark that may flake in irregular shapes.

12 Chinese red birch has shiny bark with pronounced lenticels.

BARK RUBBING

You can study different types of bark by taking rubbings with sheets of thick, strong paper and a stick of wax crayon or charcoal. Bark rubbings reveal different patterns without the distractions of surface colors, moss, or other debris. Make your own carefully labeled collection to highlight the variety of trees you have discovered in a woodland in your local area.

BARK RUBBING

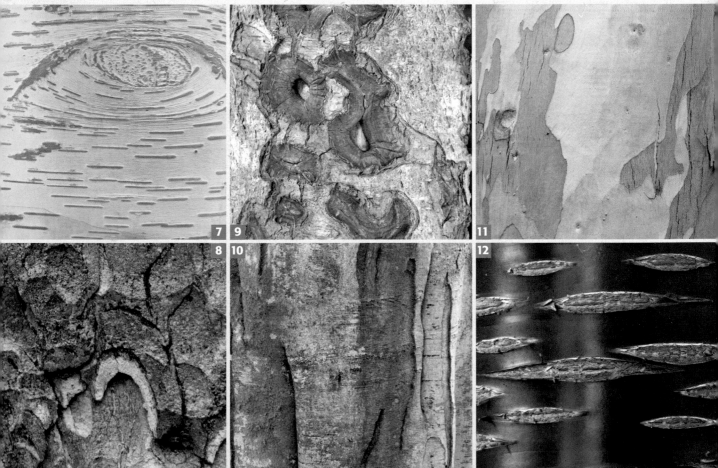

Looking up

Most of us forget to look up, but glance skyward in a forest and you will discover another layer of woodland activity to explore.

Pollination

Many trees can produce an identical version of themselves by sending out suckers. Flowers, on the other hand, exchange genes through pollination with another plant of the same species, creating genetically different offspring. Pollination is carried out by insects, such as bees or mosquitoes, by birds carrying pollen from flower to flower, or by wind. Look up in any woodland and you will often be able to see pollination in action.

SINGLE SEX
Male and female flowers appear on separate bay laurel, or sweet bay, plants.

MOSQUITO

MIXED BLOOMS
Both male and female flowers are found on each alder buckthorn plant, which are pollinated by mosquitoes.

Fruits of the forest

Trees are static and rely on external factors to help disperse their seeds. Forests are filled with all kinds of seeds, nuts, berries, and fruits that are eaten by all sorts of animals, from the smallest birds to the largest bears. These animals aid the plants by transporting seeds in their digestive tract and depositing them at a different location. Jays and squirrels bury acorns for later use, thus helping to spread oak woodland.

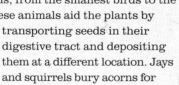
BLACK CHERRY

WALNUT

Never eat wild nuts or berries because they may be toxic.

SWEET TREAT
Juicy berries are packed with high energy and sugary nutrients that make them irresistible to bears.

ACORNS

Galls and miners

Close inspection of some woodland plants may reveal some odd-shaped growths. These galls are produced in response to parasites, such as fungi, bacteria, insects, and mites. Some insects use galls to provide food and protection for their larvae. The larvae of leaf miners create tunnels by feeding on the cells between the upper and lower surfaces of leaves.

GALL WASPS
Some wasps, such as this marble gall wasp, produce galls on oak trees. Gall wasps are tiny, and most have shiny red-brown or black bodies.

oak spangle gall
eggs laid by wasps

SPANGLE AND CHERRY GALLS
Most galls are produced by wasps—in this case creating red galls on the underside of a leaf.

"mines" show where leaf miners have tunnelled

LEAF MINERS
Some caterpillars, such as the horse chestnut leaf miner, injure leaves, but cause no lasting damage to trees.

FALLEN WONDERS

If you want to find out more about the variety of invertebrates that live in a healthy tree or shrub, carefully place a white sheet on the ground or hold out a rigid white board beneath it. Then, gently shake the branches above it to encourage insects, spiders, mites, and any other tiny animals to let go and fall onto the sheet or board. Beware of any fallen branches that may be dislodged by your movements. Identify what you can, record everything you find, and then leave the animals to return to their habitat.

LOOK AND LISTEN
Life in the canopy is best observed by lying down. Take time to relax, watch the action, and listen to birdsong and the hum of insects.

Forest birds

Birds are some of the most lively, colorful, and noisy forest inhabitants, yet they are apt to fly away at the least disturbance.

Woodland chorus

Getting to grips with woodland birds is difficult because many hide in the foliage, and some become very quiet in the summer. To get a better idea of what lives in a wood, and for the sheer enjoyment of hearing the birds at their best, try to hear a spring dawn chorus (see panel, below). Birds sing or call for a variety of reasons—to defend territory, ward off rivals, find a mate, warn of a predator, or locate their chicks. Over time you can learn to distinguish not only the calls of different species but also the types of calls.

RECORDING BIRDSONG

Distinguishing birdsong can be difficult but rewarding. Listen to birdsong CDs to prepare for when you are out in the field. Many field guides transcribe bird sounds into words such as *tiks*, *chaks*, and *tchuks*, which are very useful for identification. Try making your own notes when you're out—be creative with your descriptions.

chshree-up
schrree-eew
shrr-ooo

SOUND GUIDE
When transcribing bird sounds, the lines above the word are used to show variation in pitch.

SWEET SONG
American robins have several "call notes," but, like many other birds, its "song" is a declaration of territory.

THE DAWN CHORUS

This avian choir is at its best in spring, when males attract females and warn off rivals, but you will need to get up early to catch it—as early as 4am in some areas. Try to choose your location the evening before, because birds such as blackbirds often sing from the same song-post they settle on at dusk. Sit quietly, don't wear bright colors, and enjoy the performance.

Woodland birds

RED-EYED VIREO
More often heard than seen, North American vireos sing from forest canopies.

JACKDAW
The jackdaw is a noisy crow with pale eye, black cap, and gray hood. It is widespread in most of the Northern Hemisphere, where it is often found in flocks around old buildings, woods, or cliffs.

NORTHERN PARULA
A summer visitor to the eastern USA, the northern parula is one of North America's colorful "wood warblers."

Nesting

Birds' nests are not long-term "homes"—they are solely for hatching eggs and rearing chicks. We can learn much about birds from their nests, but take care to never disturb an active one. Over time, the average number of eggs, number of clutches, and chick survival rates give us vital data on the health of bird populations.

SONG THRUSH NEST

REDSTART NEST

BUILDING MATERIAL
Nests vary from mere scrapes in bare earth to extraordinary constructions, often with tough outer structures of twigs (top), roots, and grasses, lined with softer hair, moss, fur, or feathers (above, and left).

Migrants

Migration is one of nature's extraordinary events. In the Northern Hemisphere, birds head north in spring, to exploit a temporary glut of food, and return south in autumn, often sharing winter quarters with species that stay there all year. Some, such as geese, fly in families and learn routes; others migrate alone, like cuckoos, navigating by instinct (see p.15).

SUMMER MIGRANT
The wood warbler is a visitor to broadleaved woods in Britain and Europe during the summer. It winters in tropical Africa.

DEFIANT SONG
The robin, found widely throughout Europe, uses its elaborate song to defend a territory by warning off rival males.

WOODPIGEON
This is a big, colorful, bold, and abundant European woodland bird. It tends to be shy in farmland, where it is shot as a pest; it is often tame in town parks.

CHAFFINCH
A colorful European finch that is found in woodland, parks, and gardens. The female has the same white wing patches, but is much less pink than the male shown here.

CHIFFCHAFF
This small European warbler is typically rather plain, but can be identified by its *chiff chaff chaff chiff chaff* song.

Deciduous close-up

Deciduous woodlands around the world harbor an enormous diversity of life—including many flowering plants, mammals, insects, and birds—that varies according to its range and with the seasons. Get to know your local forest well, month by month.

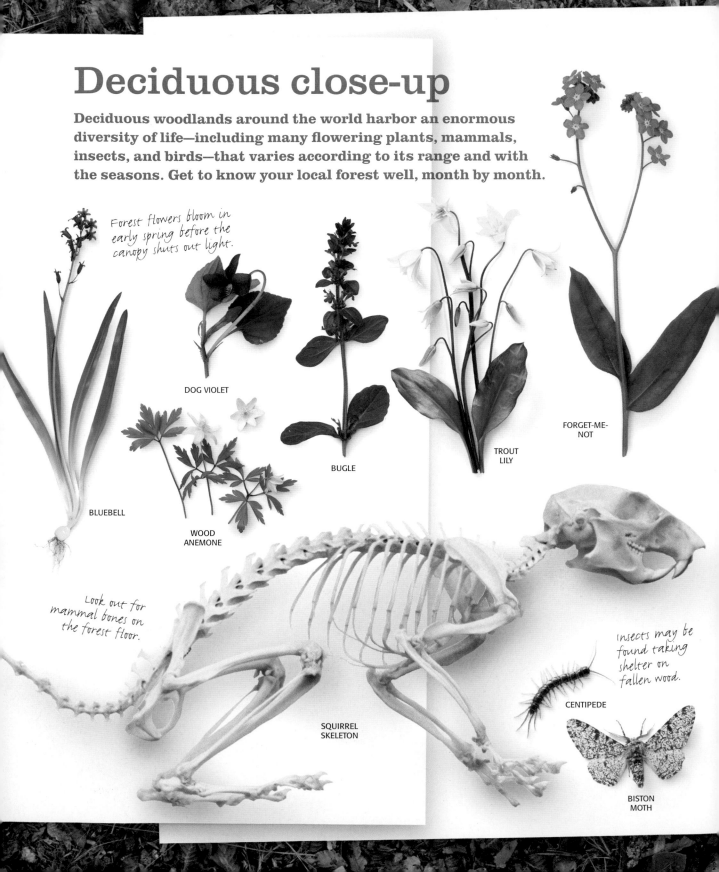

Forest flowers bloom in early spring before the canopy shuts out light.

DOG VIOLET

BLUEBELL

WOOD ANEMONE

BUGLE

TROUT LILY

FORGET-ME-NOT

Look out for mammal bones on the forest floor.

SQUIRREL SKELETON

Insects may be found taking shelter on fallen wood.

CENTIPEDE

BISTON MOTH

Nuts and seeds ripen and fall in autumn.

RED SYCAMORE WINGS

SYCAMORE KEY

SWEET CHESTNUT

Leaves of trees and shrubs provide shade in summer and carpet the floor in autumn.

BIRCH LEAVES

CANOE BIRCH LEAVES AND CATKIN

HORSE CHESTNUT

BLACK BRYONY

OAK GALLS

ORANGE PEEL FUNGUS

MOREL FUNGUS

HAZELNUTS

ACORNS

Many fungi live in close association with trees and are found at their roots.

FLY AGARIC

COMMON FROG

FIRE SALAMANDER

Look for amphibians near forest pools or decaying wood.

HONEY FUNGUS

The forest year

Few places reflect the changing seasons as well as a deciduous forest—its colors, sounds, and scents reveal the natural cycle of life.

Observing the changes

Appreciate the uniqueness of each season in a wood by keeping all your senses alert. Spring is the best time for listening to the birds, and the lush growth of summer provides great opportunities for plant hunting. Autumn brings with it the scent of rotting leaves and fungi, while the peacefulness of a winter wood should never be underestimated.

BRINGING UP BABY
Summer is the time when mammals are busy rearing young. Fox cubs may be seen playing outside dens.

spring flowers provide autumn fruit

CHERRY BLOSSOM

1 Spring stimulates new life. Longer days allow the increasing energy from a higher sun to pour through the trees. Woodland flowers thrive in the light, before the growing canopy casts deep shade.

2 Summer is a quieter time as animals and birds move on from the frenzy of courtship and defining territories to the hard grind of raising families. At this time of year, ferns and lichens become more obvious than flowers.

Examine plants to see insects feeding on them —many are camouflaged.

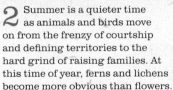

EATING GREENS
Caterpillars gorge themselves on lush, summer foliage.

ROOTING FOR FOOD
Wild boars turn over soil in their search for roots and invertebrates.

NEW SHOOTS
Conditions in spring—longer, warmer days with more sunlight —give plants, such as this hazel, the energy to sprout new growth.

SPRING TOADS

Common toads spend the winter buried in soft ground and emerge early in the year. They gather in shallow water in March, where females lay long strings of jelly containing three or four rows of black eggs—unlike the shapeless mass produced by frogs so they are easy to tell apart. Toad tadpoles often form dense schools, have flatter bodies, and are blacker than frog tadpoles.

TRACK A FOREST YEAR

Really get to know a particular wooded area, or even a single large tree, by visiting and recording it throughout the year. Choose somewhere close by and easy to get to so that you can visit every week. Note down anything that is new or has changed, and take photographs to compare at the end of the year. Identify and count all the trees in your chosen area, and as other plants begin to appear identify them and note their flowering dates. Listen for birdsong, try to identify it, and record it on a sound recorder if you can. Look closely for insects, fungi, and other wildlife of the wood.

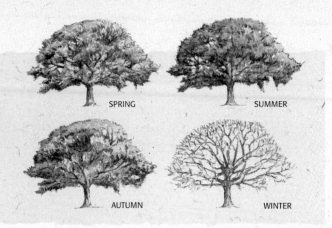

SPRING

SUMMER

AUTUMN

WINTER

earwigs burrow into the ground to survive winter

EARWIG

OUT IN THE COLD
Some mammals, including cottontails, stay active all winter.

3 Autumn sees a lowering sun, and with it, reduced light penetrating the forest. Insects decline and migrant birds leave, but the immense bounty of nuts, seeds, and berries that remains tempts some species to stay and begin storing food for the winter.

FALL FEAST
Rodents such as this North American chipmunk bulk up on autumn berries before hibernating.

Look for butterflies and moths in bushes and hiding on tree trunks.

FATAL FREEZE
As the weather turns cold some moths and butterflies hibernate while others die.

4 To survive winter, some animals hibernate, while birds roam in mixed, nomadic flocks for safety. A lack of foliage can make birds and animals easier to see at this time of year, and look for their tracks in mud and snow.

WINTER GREEN
Look up to see mistletoe clinging to bare winter trees.

Signs of life

Mammals are sometimes difficult to see in a forest, but finding evidence of their activities—dens, nests, and tracks—is often much easier.

Making tracks

Most tracks are left in mud, which can last a few days, or snow, which can be very short-lived. The best prints are those found in mud, which preserves details of the structure of the foot or paw. Snow tracks are far less well-shaped, unless they have been made in a thin layer of snow on soft ground, especially after fresh snowfall. Look for prints and tracks around muddy puddles, on wet trails in the wood, or near rivers and streams.

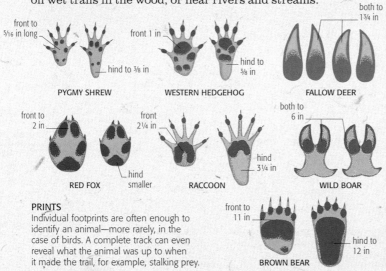

front to 5/16 in long
hind to 3/8 in
PYGMY SHREW

front 1 in
hind to 3/8 in
WESTERN HEDGEHOG

both to 1¾ in
FALLOW DEER

front to 2 in
hind smaller
RED FOX

front 2¼ in
hind 3¼ in
RACCOON

both to 6 in
WILD BOAR

PRINTS
Individual footprints are often enough to identify an animal—more rarely, in the case of birds. A complete track can even reveal what the animal was up to when it made the trail, for example, stalking prey.

front to 11 in
hind to 12 in
BROWN BEAR

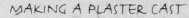

MAKING A PLASTER CAST

Good tracks are worth preserving. Photographs are valuable, but it's rewarding—and sometimes more informative—to make a plaster cast. First, spray the print with very light oil, such as cooking oil, then surround it with a "wall" made up of thin strips of wood, plastic, or cardboard, so that the plaster has a barrier and won't seep away. Carefully pour a runny plaster mix over the print. When it is set hard, lift it to reveal a "negative" cast. You can then make a second cast of the first to get back to the original imprint.

BADGER TRACK AND CAST
This broad, long-clawed print of a badger's foot has been preserved for future study in a plaster of paris cast.

1

4

5

Resting places

Most birds build nests for hatching eggs and raising their young, but mammals use their resting places as shelter for much longer. Some, such as a badger's set, are daily retreats; others, like a bear's den, are seasonal. Shelters can be found in all sorts of places: some are dug into the ground, while others might be nestled in a tree.

1 Look out for a loosely structured, roofed nest—this will be a squirrel's dray. A summer dray is used for resting, while a winter, or family, dray is stronger to provide better shelter.

2 This brown bear is hauling itself from its den under some rocks at the end of the winter. Brown bears put on fat, then sleep or while away the winter, eating little or nothing.

3 Fallow deer don't make dens, but leave their well-camouflaged fawns hidden in sheltered hollows where they keep still to avoid detection.

4 Foxes dig burrows called "earths." Simple ones are daytime or emergency retreats, larger ones for raising young.

5 Australia's nocturnal ringtail possum usually builds a daytime nest, but may also sleep in a natural tree cavity.

6 A badger sett looks like a large rabbit hole, but for the coarse gray hairs, tracks, piles of old bedding, and droppings.

Watching at night

Many animals are active at night, so an evening watch can yield amazing sights. You may be in for a long wait, so get comfortable. Nocturnal animals have poor vision, but hear and smell wonderfully, so sit still on a bank or tree above their level and downwind from them—keep quiet and don't smoke or wear perfume. Use a flashlight with a red filter—red light is at a wavelength that animals can't easily see.

Tips for your blind
1. Prepare a comfortable perch in advance.
2. Wear dull, dark clothes.
3. Turn off cell phones.
4. Cover your flashlight with red cellophane.
5. Always tell someone where you are going.

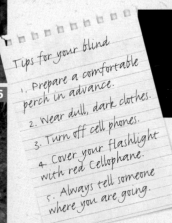

BADGER TRACK
Wait quietly and don't make a sound at a set and you may get a close view.

Pine plantation

Demand for lumber has led to extensive planting of conifers in stands of single species, such as sitka spruce. Young plantations are dense and dark, but thinning as they age creates a more natural condition. Before they are harvested, trees may lose branches or be blown over by gales. This creates space for wildlife, where fungi, such as morels may grow.

SITKA SPRUCE

MOREL FUNGUS

Coniferous forests

Conifer forests are not all dark swathes of "Christmas trees." While many plantations are poor habitats for wildlife, natural forests are home to a diverse range of plants and animals, many of them found nowhere else.

Redwood forest

Giant sequoias and redwoods grow in California. Sequoias thrive on high, snowy sierras and redwoods grow in the coastal fog belt. Coastal forests are often too dense for you to appreciate the trees' vast size. These giants act as multistory dwellings for wildlife ranging from small mammals such as chipmunks living on branches, to shrubs such as broom growing on the forest floor.

CHIPMUNK

BROOM

Scots pine forest

Scots pine forest grows from Scotland eastward across Siberia and stretches as far south as the Mediterranean on high mountains. The Scots pine was the only northern European pine to survive the last Ice Age and it has a fragmented distribution. Mature forests are home to predators, such as wildcats, and support rich plantlife, including heathers and cowberries.

COWBERRY

WILDCAT

Taiga

Taiga is the cold forest zone south of the Arctic tundra. Trees, such as the black spruce, have shallow roots to exploit the thin soil, downward-pointing branches to help shed snow, and dark needles to absorb weak sunlight efficiently. Ground beetles shelter in needle litter while wolverines have thick fur coats for insulation.

GROUND BEETLE

WOLVERINE

BLACK SPRUCE

BILBERRY

OWL FEATHER

Keep quiet and scan the canopy for shy animals such as squirrels and martens—watch for any movement against the bright sky.

Pinewood walk

With their year-round greenery, pinewoods have a characteristic beauty. There is a wealth of wildlife to discover—once you know where to look.

A walk through pinewoods can be a satisfying experience that engages all your senses. Experiencing the fresh scent of these evergreen forests is a distinctive part of any visit to this habitat, and like all forests, it can be a quiet, undisturbed place for a budding naturalist to explore. From insects scurrying on the forest floor to birds calling in the canopy, pinewoods harbor a wide range of animals, as well as plants and fungi.

MOSS

Search the undergrowth of open glades for colorful herbaceous plants, such as ling and other heathers.

LADY'S-TRESSES ORCHID

Listen for bird calls and other tell-tale noises. The sound of pine cones falling may indicate squirrels or birds, such as crossbills, feeding above.

Remember to keep one eye on the ground: here you might find ant nests, flowers, or fungi, or glimpse a basking lizard.

LING

LADYBUG

WOOD HEDGEHOG MUSHROOM

WOOD ANTS

Redwood inhabitants

CHIPMUNK
Rodents, such as the red-tailed chipmunk, nest on branches.

FERN
Licorice ferns grow on soil mats on branches of mature trees.

BAT
The nocturnal big brown bat hibernates in caves, but also lives in hollow trees, loose bark, and old buildings.

Coniferous trees

Conifers are handsome trees—richly colored and clothed in needlelike leaves. They vary in shape and adapt to different conditions.

Recognizing conifers

Conifers are fairly easy to identify. They are evergreen, which means they keep their leaves, or "needles," all year and shed them continually, rather than seasonally like deciduous trees. The most distinctive feature of most conifers is the fruit, or "cone," which is usually woody, but in some species, such as yew, it is more like a soft berry. The cones, leaf structure, and bark can help you identify different conifer types.

FIRS
Fir trees, such as the silver fir, have flattened needles and long cones that sit on high branches and break before they fall to the ground.

CONE AND NEEDLES

SPRUCES
The Norway spruce is the classic "Christmas tree." Spruce twigs are spiky and covered in tough, spiny needles in opposite bands.

CONE AND NEEDLES

PINES
Pines, such as the Scots pine, usually have thick, scaly bark, clustered needles. Cones vary widely between families.

CONE AND NEEDLES

CYPRESSES
Cypress trees, such as the Monterey cypress, have dark green scalelike leaves and small cones that remain on the tree for years.

CONE AND SCALES

ROOM FOR LIFE
A mature conifer tree provides many levels for wildlife to inhabit, from rodents, such as squirrels in the canopy, to fungus at its roots. A team of scientists climbed this 295 ft (90 m) giant redwood in the coastal forest of California, to map the complex structure of its crown.

WORLD'S OLDEST ORGANISMS

Trees are the oldest living things on Earth and the oldest tree—a spruce found in Sweden—has been dated at nearly 10,000 years old. Other ancient trees include the gnarled bristlecone pines (left) found high in California's White Mountains, where they are able to survive even the most severe drought. The oldest bristlecone is nearing its 5,000th birthday. Coastal redwoods (see main image, right) can reach 3,000 years old, and ancient yews can live for 1,500–2,000 years.

How conifers survive extremes

Unlike deciduous trees, conifers keep their leaves all year. The waxy, needle- and scalelike leaves minimize water loss to help the tree survive both drought and severe cold. Sap within the tree moves through much smaller cells than those in deciduous trees, which limits damage if the sap freezes in extreme cold. Some conifers, such as Scots pines, have shallow, wide roots to help them extract nutrients from thin, poor soil on rocky slopes.

THICK BARK
Most evergreens have thick, scaly, sometimes spongy bark, which offers protection for the sensitive layers lying just beneath.

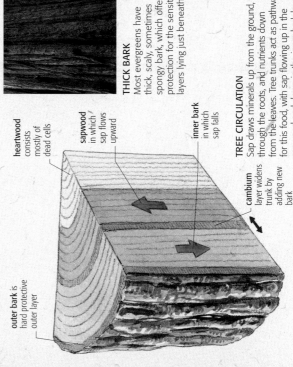

heartwood consists mostly of dead cells

sapwood in which sap flows upward

inner bark in which sap falls

cambium layer widens trunk by adding new bark

outer bark is hard protective outer layer

TREE CIRCULATION
Sap draws minerals up from the ground, through the roots, and nutrients down from the leaves. Tree trunks act as pathways for this food, with sap flowing up in the sapwood and down in the inner bark layer.

Forest fungi

Looking for fungi adds to any walk. You can find mushrooms and toadstools in a variety of shapes—but that's only one part of the story.

STRANGE FRUIT
Many fungi are poisonous and it is important to never pick or eat any mushrooms you find in the wild.

What are fungi?

Fungi are neither plants nor animals, but organisms that feed on rotting material, breaking it down to enrich the soil. The parts we see—from delicate toadstools to thick shelf fungi—are only the parts involved in reproduction, and they are known as fruiting bodies. Underground, threadlike filaments known as *hyphae* spread out to form a colony-like *mycelium*: a mass often many acres in size. Some can be thousands of years old.

MOLDY WOOD
Slime mold, which closely resembles fungi, can be found growing on rotting wood on the forest floor.

Fruitbody shapes

Most fungi have a stem topped by a cap. In puffballs, though, stems are almost invisible, while in others, such as stinkhorns, the stems are more striking than the caps.

PHALLIC

TRUMPET

CUP

CAP AND STEM

SHELF

BRAINLIKE

BALL

Cap shape and texture

Caps may be conical, domed, flattened, or dish-shaped and may open from round "buttons" into broad "dishes." They can be dry and flaky, silky, or greasy.

CONVEX

FUNNEL

GROOVED

DEPRESSED

CONICAL

LOOSE SCALES

A BENEFICIAL RELATIONSHIP

Many fungi live in close association with plants and algae, usually to the benefit of both; scientists estimate that more than 90 percent of plants need fungi for their own survival. Fungi help plants take up nutrients, such as nitrates and phosphates from poor soils, in a system known as "mycorrhizal symbiosis"—a partnership that benefits both parties. Fungi living in close association with algae form lichens, which are abundant in unpolluted forests, as well as on rocks, roofs, and walls. Some fungi parasitize animals, such as bees, while some ants and beetles cultivate fungi for food.

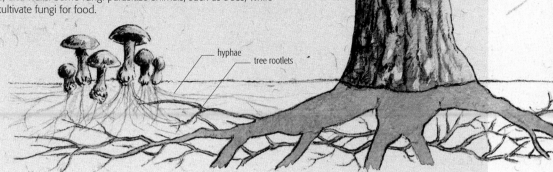

hyphae

tree rootlets

FUNGUS ROOTS
The word *mycorrhizae* means "fungus roots," and these colonize plant roots, helping the fungi access carbohydrates and the plant to absorb water and mineral nutrients.

Stem

The stem, called a stipe, raises the cap to allow a fungus to release spores to reproduce. In some species, the cap bursts open from a spherical shape, leaving a lower ring on the stipe.

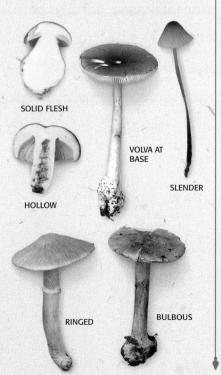

SOLID FLESH

HOLLOW

VOLVA AT BASE

SLENDER

RINGED

BULBOUS

Color

Color is important in identification but subtle shades of brown, pink, yellow, and orange can be difficult to describe. Find a color chart, or use your own terms for comparison.

RINGS OF COLOR

DARK CENTER

SPORE PRINTS

Spores are ejected from a fungus by a buildup of internal pressure or by the force of a raindrop. You can easily take a spore print to help identify a fungus. Put the cap on paper, place a glass over it, and leave it overnight. Then carefully remove the glass and fungus, and quickly spray the image lightly with hairspray to "fix" the print.

Gills

Some fungi have caps with fine plates or "gills" underneath—this is where the spores are produced. Learning the structure of the gills will help you identify the species of fungi.

UNEQUAL LENGTH

BROADLY SPACED

CROWDED

Coniferous close-up

Coniferous forests are widespread in the Northern Hemisphere and support an array of specialized flora and fauna throughout their range. The exact species of fungi, insects, and plants will depend on location, but all are home to a rich variety of wildlife.

PUFFBALL FUNGI

Insects and spiders inhabit the needle layer and thick tree bark.

WOLF SPIDER

GIANT WOOD WASP

Fungi thrives in the dark damp conditions of a pine forest.

CONIFER TUFT FUNGI

CUP MOREL

PURPLE AND ORANGE FUNGUS

skeletons and bones give clues to the mammals of the forest.

ANTLER FUNGUS

TUFTED BRITTLEHEAD

shrubs grow in the understory of fruits and in forest clearings.

Many moths are well camouflaged against rough pine bark.

EASTERN TENT CATERPILLAR MOTH

GYPSY MOTH

LOWER JAWBONE OF A DEER

GEOMETRID MOTH

IMPERIAL MOTH

BILBERRY

WINTERGREEN

SITKA SPRUCE
NEEDLES AND CONE

Lichens hang
from low
branches and
spread over
dead wood.

JUNIPER

WILD
RASPBERRIES

FOLIOSE
LICHEN

BELL
HEATHER

NORWAY
SPRUCE
CONES

Cones litter
the forest
floor.

SCOTS PINE CONES

Coniferous specialists

Cones solve problems for trees in tough conditions but can prove tricky for animals bent on eating their seeds.

The pine cone

Most pine trees bear both male and female cones. Male cones are small, with modified scales covering pollen sacs. Female cones are the more familiar large, woody cones containing ovules that, once fertilized by pollen, develop into seeds beneath tough scales. While their structure is similar, the size, shape, and woodiness of cones vary from species to species.

TOP OF CONE

BOTTOM OF CONE

tightly packed scales at base

cone tip

You can tell if humidity is high or low by whether a cone is open or not.

closed scale

algae

open scales release seeds

SCOTS PINE CONES
Rosy-pink female flowers turn purple in summer, with small scales that become bright green but woody the following year. The year after that, the cones are mature, and turn a dull gray.

branch

immature cones

clustered pine needles

attachment

CLOSED CONE
Female cones have seed scales, which open initially to receive pollen, then close tightly while the seeds mature. Later, they will also close in wet weather to protect and retain the growing seeds.

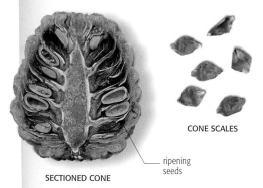

SECTIONED CONE

ripening seeds

CONE SCALES

Start a cone collection and look for clues to find out which animals opened them.

protrusion on scale

OPEN CONE
Mature cones open in dry weather—with reduced moisture content—ensuring that seeds are released in ideal conditions for wind dispersal.

Cone crackers

Seeds within pine cones lie deep between the scales at the base of thin, flat, winglike structures. They are nutritious but difficult to reach, and eating a whole cone, with its hard, rough, sharp-edged, woody scales, would be impossible or inefficient, so many animals have developed ways to get inside. In damp weather, scales close up tight— dry conditions open them—but this happens many times, even long after the seeds have been dispersed and long after the cone has fallen to the ground. Seed-eaters must first decide which cones are worth their attention.

1 Crossbills have evolved into many species, often in response to the size and shape of particular cones. They push their mandibles between scales, then close or twist their bills to open them. Seeds are then extracted with the tip of the tongue.

2 Squirrels simply bite the scales and gnaw their way into the seeds. You can easily tell cones bitten down by a squirrel from those worked on by a crossbill.

3 Woodpeckers often wedge cones into bark to make it easier to peck between the scales and extract the delicate seeds.

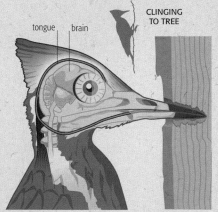

WOODPECKING

Woodpeckers chisel into living or dead wood; their long, sticky, spiny tongues (which wrap around the skull) probe deeply into holes in order to extract larvae. A woodpecker steadies itself with its stiff tail by using it as a prop, and grasps the tree firmly with specially adapted feet: two toes point forward, two point back. It also has sinewy attachments at the base of its bill and around its brain to reduce the shock of the fierce bombardment of bill on wood.

tongue   brain

CLINGING TO TREE

Forest

In a rut

Red deer make great wildlife-watching, and never more so than in fall, when stags fight for the right to mate.

Red deer are about the same size as the largest white-tailed deer: big males (stags) are more than 6½ ft (2 m) long and 3¼ ft (1m) high at the shoulder. Originally forest mammals, they are now also found on open mountains and moorland. The male red deer's bony antlers have several points, or "tines," and each year's antlers are bigger and more complex than those from the year before. Why antlers are shed annually—unlike horns, which grow continuously— is not obvious. Their growth requires a massive investment of energy, but, in winter, when food is short, the antler is simply "dead bone," making little demand on the deer. Stags are in their prime at eight years old; younger and older ones rarely secure a harem of females, or hinds. In fall, at the onset of the mating season (rut), males are very aggressive— keep your distance. Stags roar almost constantly, and walk together to assess each other's size and condition. Weaker males back down, but those of equal strength may fight. Females are attracted to the males with the loudest and most frequent roar.

AN ANTLER'S YEAR

A deer's antlers develop through the seasons. In spring a small, sensitive knob, or "pedicle," gives rise to the new antler; a covering of soft skin called velvet provides blood and oxygen, but gradually shreds and falls away when the blood supply to the antler ceases in autumn. The antler calcifies, becoming hard; then, at the end of winter, it falls away. Look out for shed antlers on the ground in winter or velvet in late summer.

pedicle
SPRING

growing antlers in velvet
MIDSUMMER

full grown, velvet slowly being shed
LATE JULY

HEAD TO HEAD
When two stags are evenly matched, they lock antlers and start a serious shoving match. Occasionally, a sharp antler point will cause damage, but this is rarely a fatal wound.

Elusive creatures

Red deer are so spectacular you can watch them from a distance, but most forest animals are shy and hard to find. In fact, finding some of them could take a lifetime.

PINE MARTEN
Shy pine martens are most easily viewed at nature reserves in North America and Europe.

WOLVERINE
This largely nocturnal animal of very northerly mountainous forest and marshland is rarely seen.

GRAY WOLF
The largest wolf is now scarce in both North America and its much-reduced European range.

LYNX
All four species of lynx are fairly hard to find. The European lynx (above) is one of the world's rarest large cats.

Bear country

Bears are very powerful animals and although encounters are rare, one needs to be aware in their habitats.

The most common American bear is the black bear: around 800,000 live in forests from Alaska to Mexico and they sometimes stray into suburbs. They are omnivores and eat fruit, seeds, bark, even moose calves, and occasionally raid beehives for honey and grubs. Smaller than brown bears, at 7 ft (2 m) when standing, they are still powerful beasts. The largest brown bears of North America, Europe, and Asia, at 220–1,500 lb (100–680 kg), match the polar bear as the world's largest land predator. American brown bears inhabit open, mountainous country, while Eurasian bears prefer dense forests. Standing upright at over 9 ft (close to 3 m), an adult brown bear is largely nocturnal, either by natural preference or through increasing fear of human predators. They pile on 400 lb (180 kg) of fat in summer, then retreat to a den where they are dormant for winter.

WILD BERRIES
Bears fatten up on berries, among other things, for their long hibernation between October and April.

CLOSE ENCOUNTERS

Black bears are more strictly forest animals. They seldom attack people unless they are threatened, wounded, or protecting their cubs. Yet the logging of forests and the growth of cities means that they are increasingly encountering humans. Bear attacks are relatively rare—they are more likely to seek cover if they see you coming—but the best way to avoid trouble is to follow some simple rules. Always explore bear territory with other people and avoid secluded areas or anywhere bears have been recently spotted. Make a noise as you walk, talking or whistling, so you don't startle any bears you might come across.

LOGGED OUT
Forest clearance forces bears to survive as best they can in less productive habitats.

SUPERIOR SMELL
Bears have a great sense of smell, which can lead them to human food. Always keep food in air-tight containers in bear territory.

Lowland rain forest

A constant growing season here results in a prolific plant life, including many types of orchid. There are more tree varieties in lowland rain forests than in any other habitat—more than 400 species per 2.5 acres (1 hectare) in some places. In South America inhabitants include tree frogs, jaguars, and tapirs, and rivers are home to giant otters.

CATTELYA ORCHID

RED-EYED TREE FROG

Tropical forests

Tropical forests are largely defined by high levels of temperature, rainfall, and humidity. Although they cover just five percent of the Earth's land surface, the forests are home to more than half the world's species.

Montane rain forest

Montane rain forest is found at altitudes above 3,280 ft (1,000 m). In Africa, it is home to mountain gorillas, colobus monkeys, and nectar-feeding birds. At the highest levels is cloud forest, where the trees are draped in moss and there is a profusion of ferns, orchids, and bromeliads.

CYATHEA TREE FERN

BLACK-AND-WHITE COLOBUS MONKEY

Monsoon rain forest

Whereas lowland and montane rain forest can receive rainfall at any time of the year, in monsoon rain forest there are clearly defined wet and dry seasons. Many tree species are deciduous, shedding their leaves during the dry months and coming back into leaf during and after the wet season. Monsoon forest is found mainly in India and Southeast Asia. Wildlife includes elephants, giant squirrels, and a variety of reptiles.

KING COBRA

INDIAN GIANT SQUIRREL

Layers of life

Tropical forests are made up of horizontal layers of vegetation that provide a variety of habitats for a huge diversity of wildlife.

The multistory forest

There are four main layers in a tropical forest. At the bottom, covered with fallen plant debris, is the shady and humid forest floor. Next comes the understory, consisting largely of palms, ferns, and vines; the plants at this level have larger leaves to compete for sunlight. Arching above is the main canopy that shields the lower levels from sun and lighter rain—this is the most wildlife-rich layer of all because food is abundant. The tallest trees protrude through the canopy into the top, emergent layer. Most wildlife stays in its own preferred story, with canopy inhabitants rarely, if ever, descending.

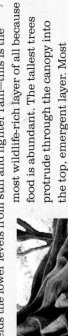

GIANT ROOTS
Huge buttress roots stabilize the tallest forest trees and provide a habitat for a wide variety of creatures.

MEAT EATERS
Pitcher plants are designed to lure and trap insects, which are then absorbed by digestive enzymes.

EXPLORING LAYERS

The sheer volume of plant and animal life in the forest can be overwhelming, so it is often best to focus on one layer at a time. Keep an eye on the forest floor for spiders, beetles, and millipedes, as well as fallen leaves and unusual fruits. Understory vegetation is particularly good for spotting butterflies and amphibians, so remember to look carefully at stems and under leaves for creatures at rest.

UP IN THE CANOPY
Aerial walkways offer the chance to experience canopy life and spot elusive birds and monkeys.

EMERGENT

Tropical inhabitants

MACAWS
Macaws are easy to spot in the emergent trees, where their bright plumage stands out. They often gather in fruiting trees and at sunset fly off in noisy flocks to roost.

SLOTHS
Slow-moving sloths are usually solitary and spend most of their time sleeping and eating leaves. They only climb down to ground level once or twice a week, in order to defecate.

TREE FROGS
Tree frogs are fantastic climbers and thrive in the canopy, finding shelter in leaves and plants. Food is so plentiful here that they rarely move far—some spend their entire lives in an area around 6 ft (1.8 m) squared.

BIRDS OF PARADISE

A relative of the crow family, New Guinea's male bird of paradise uses his extravagant plumage in an elaborate courtship display that includes bizarre calls and strange dances.

ORCHIDS

Rain forests are home to thousands of orchid species. Many are epiphytes that live on the trunks and branches of trees, although they are not parasitic and the host is not harmed.

TAPIRS

One of the rain forest's larger mammals, the tapir feeds mainly on vegetation and fruits and is a valuable seed disperser. It is also a good swimmer, and uses its prehensile nose as a handy snorkel.

CANOPY

UNDERSTORY

FOREST FLOOR

Mutual survival

The rainforest ecosystem revolves around a complex network of symbiotic (mutually dependent) relationships. For example, Brazil nut trees rely on ground-dwelling mammals to crack open the fallen seedpods and disperse the seeds to new areas away from the parent tree. Meanwhile some plants, such as orchids of the *Ophrys* genus, have evolved flowers with specific shapes that receive only particular insects. In return for the nutrients they receive, these insects then pollinate the plant.

RAIN FOREST FOOD CHAIN

Forest relationships are built upon a sequence of what eats what, with carnivorous predators, such as the jaguar, at the top and light-consuming plants at the bottom.

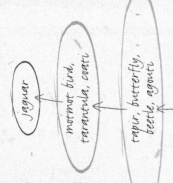

jaguar

marmot bird, tarantula, coati

tapir, butterfly, beetle, agouti

elephant ear, aroid vine, acacia tree, coccoloba tree, passion flower vine, strangler fig

WINGED GIANTS

The warm, wet conditions of tropical forests are so ideal for growth that some species of insect have grown far larger than any found in cooler, more temperate environments. With wingspans of up to 11 in (28 cm) birdwings are the world's biggest butterflies, dwarfing their counterparts elsewhere. The largest spiders are also tropical forest-dwellers and are powerful enough to catch small birds and rodents.

TROPICAL BUTTERFLY (CAIRNS BIRDWING)

TEMPERATE BUTTERFLY (POPLAR ADMIRAL)

Rain forest survival

To avoid the many predators of the rain forest, animals that are hunted for food have developed intriguing defenses to look and listen for.

Detecting camouflage

Many creatures use camouflage to blend into backgrounds and avoid detection. Look for anything that stands out from the normal outline or pattern of a patch of leaves or branches, and carefully check tree trunks for bark-colored moths and lizards. Context is everything: a jaguar's spotted coat may look out of place in a wildlife park but is ideal camouflage in the dappled sunlight of the forest.

OUT ON A LIMB
Chameleons vary in size, some are hard to find at just 1 ¼ in (3 cm), others can be as large as a domesic cat.

CHANGING COLOR

If you watch a chameleon for long enough it may change color. This is due to special cells that contain the pigment melanin, which is redistributed under the skin. When the melanin is concentrated, the skin's yellow cells dominate, turning the chameleon pale. When the melanin disperses within the blue scattering layer, the creature becomes darker and its color changes accordingly.

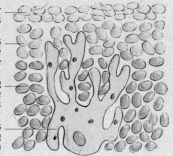

outer layer of skin cells

yellow cells turn the chameleon pale

blue scattering cells turn the creature dark

inner cells containing melanin

Warning signs

Camouflage is not the only defense strategy.
Other ways of repelling an attack include spraying
foul-smelling secretions, releasing irritating
spines or scales, and displaying rear parts with
markings to look like the front end—predators are
often reluctant to take on a creature face-first. If
you spot a creature with vivid colors it may be a
warning to steer clear.

PREDATOR BEWARE
Many butterfly and
moth caterpillars rely
on bright colors and
body protrusions to
avoid being eaten.

FOREST SENTINELS
One of the best ways to find forest
animals is to listen for their calls,
but this can work both ways if the
howler monkeys see or hear you
first. They act as an early warning
system for the whole forest, issuing
bellowing roars to tell other forest
dwellers that an intruder or potential
predator is at large.

FATAL FROGS
Poison dart frogs are highly
toxic. Some contain poison
that can be deadly to
humans if it enters through
broken skin or the mouth.

DESPERATE MIMICRY
Some harmless insects, such as the
moth on the left, imitate the warning
colors of poisonous species, such
as this actinote butterfly (right),
to deter would-be predators.

Getting around

Forest animals move around in a variety
of ways. Well-worn corridors in the
undergrowth are evidence of ground-
dwelling mammals walking or running
around, while shaking branches may
indicate that monkeys or lemurs are
jumping about within the canopy. If you
can see through the trees you might catch
a glimpse of birds of prey gliding above the
canopy and searching for a potential meal.

GLIDING AWAY
Flying lemurs, or colugos, can
be seen gliding from tree to
tree using special flaps of skin
that stretch between their legs.

MASTER OF DISGUISE
Some grasshoppers, such
as those from the Acridida
family, use ingenious forms
of camouflage or disguise to
escape detection, resembling
leaves, bark, and even
colorful flowers.

**GENERATES
POWER**

**SHIFTS
BODY WEIGHT**

**CONTINUES
MOMENTUM**

**MOVES TO
NEXT SWING**

SWINGING ALONG
Gibbons can move at
great speed through the
canopy and can cover
a span of around 25 ft
(7.5 m) in a single swing.

Conservation

The fate of the world's tropical forests and their wildlife is one of today's most important conservation issues.

A wealth of wildlife

We still do not know how many different plant and animal species rely on tropical forest, but the total could be more than 30 million. Such remarkable abundance is the result of having all the ingredients for a profusion of life—light, warmth, water, and food—in one place. The diversity of the rain forest is further boosted by the vast range of different mini-habitats that it contains. Some species of wildlife are so specialized that their only home on the entire planet might be a tiny area of rain forest.

EXTINCT IN THE WILD
The rate of rain forest destruction is so fast that species disappear every day. Specialized amphibians, such as this Panamanian golden frog, are especially vulnerable.

Why are forests still being destroyed?

Rain forest is cut down in order to extract valuable hardwoods, such as teak and mahogany. The remaining vegetation is usually burned so the land can be turned over to agricultural use. Palm oil is used in many household products and is a key ingredient in fuels made from plant material, called biofuels. Palm oil plantations now cover vast expanses of former rain forest, as do cattle ranches. Such practices offer no refuge for forest wildlife, which is either displaced or killed.

LOGGING PROFITS
Illegal logging is responsible for the depletion of large areas of the Amazon rain forest. Environmental organizations are trying to educate people on buying wood products from responsible sources.

Sustainable forestry and tourism

Tropical rain forests can have longer-lasting economic value to the world if they are retained and their products harvested sustainably. This can be achieved through agro-forestry, where trees are replanted and harvested at appropriate intervals, often combining livestock grazing in the same area. Low-scale tourism also raises awareness, especially when indigenous communities are involved in hosting and guiding tourists. If you want to visit a rain forest, an eco-tour is the best option. It will offer you a unique chance to learn about the forest from those who know it best, and the money generated will improve living standards for local people and support conservation.

JUNGLE TOURISTS
Trekking in hot and humid rain forest can be hard work, but it can offer the opportunity to experience, at first hand, the world's greatest show of biodiversity.

VOLUNTEER PROGRAMS
Get directly involved in rain forest conservation by volunteering. You could focus on the rescue and rehabilitation of endangered forest primates, such as chimpanzees and orangutans.

saving forests from home
1. Only buy furniture made from tropical hardwoods with a Forestry Stewardship Council (FSC) logo.
2. Always use recycled paper.
3. Never buy animal products from forest sources.
4. Sponsor tree-planting programs in logged forests.
5. If you visit a rain forest, travel with a responsible firm that works with local people.

Protecting forest habitats

The best way to conserve forest wildlife is to protect its home. Most species depend on primary forest, with plenty of mature trees, an intact canopy structure (see pp.124–25), and a diverse understory. Secondary forest, where the largest trees have been removed for timber, supports far fewer species. One of the most urgent problems is fragmentation: when parts of a forest are cleared and the surviving trees become isolated from each other. Planting forest "corridors" to connect these patches is vital to enable wildlife populations to reconnect and maintain their genetic viability.

1 Mountain gorillas inhabit forests in East Africa. Only a few hundred survive in an area that is inaccessible and difficult to monitor.

2 Duikers are small antelopes that are hunted for human consumption—a practice that has led to widespread extinction of species in African forests.

3 Large birds of prey such as the harpy eagle are highly sensitive to disturbance. As a result, they are one of the first forms of wildlife affected by logging.

4 The forests of Central Africa are home to many thousands of African forest elephant, but they are a constant target for ivory poachers.

5 The tiger has been brought to the brink of extinction in Southeast Asia due to habitat loss and poaching, to supply body parts for traditional medicine.

BIRDS AT RISK
These magnificent hornbills of Africa and Asia boast a large bill, used to catch prey and handle food. Unfortunately they are often shot for food.

Scrubland and heath

Most scrublands and heathlands are not naturally permanent habitats; without the maintenance of grazing or fire they would soon become woodland. Exceptions are those where altitude, nutrient poverty, or wind prevent the climax community from succeeding. These are open, hot, and dynamic places where communities "boom and bust" in rapidly changing conditions, and in the modern world they are sadly often endangered by human activities such as clearing for agriculture or fragmentation through development. For this reason they are frequently rare, their species component exotic and exciting—and naturalists love them!

Lowland heath

Originally woodland cleared by prehistoric humans, lowland heath is found mainly in north western Europe. It is defined by short plants and shrubs, such as heather, gorse, and types of grasses, and is home to a range of specialized animals, including birds such as the woodlark and nightjar. When left to its own devices, without being controlled by grazing and fire, lowland heath reverts to woodland.

YOUNG NIGHTJAR

BELL HEATHER

Scrublands and heaths

Heaths and scrublands are habitats in transition. They are usually found on nutrient-poor soils and are shaped by factors such as grazing and fire. Their unique conditions provide a home to many interesting types of wildlife.

Moorland

Moorland is wetter and colder than lowland heath, and it occurs at higher elevations, usually 985 ft (300 m) or more above sea level. It also has fewer shrubs than lowland heath, and plants such as heather are more prominent, alongside other low-growing species such as bilberry and bog myrtle. Upland birds, such as grouse, thrive here, as do birds of prey, and reptiles such as adders.

ADDER (COMMON VIPER)

BOG MYRTLE

Garrigue and maquis

Found around the Mediterranean, these two habitats are closely related. Maquis is dense scrub, containing dwarf oak, strawberry tree, and broom. Garrigue is more open, dominated by rosemary, lavender, and cistus, and with areas of pine and cork oak trees. Reptiles are common in both habitats, alongside mammals such as wild boar and deer.

WILD BOAR

ROSEMARY

Chaparral

Chaparral is a type of scrubland found across the western USA, its age and extent determined by the periodic fires that sweep the area. The dense undergrowth of chamise and toyon shrubs shelters birdlife such as quails and wild turkeys, while predatory mammals include coyotes, bobcats, and even mountain lions.

WILD TURKEY

Fynbos

The term given to coastal scrub in southern Africa, fynbos is one of the most important botanical habitats in the world. It is home to more than 7,000 species of plants, including types of lily and heather, as well as the proteas for which the habitat is famed among botanists. Birds like the cape sugarbird are found nowhere else but here.

CAPE SUGARBIRD

CORK OAK
LEAVES

SPANISH FESTOON
BUTTERFLY

CLEOPATRA BUTTERFLY

Find a sunny spot where you can watch butterflies as they fly around searching for flowers to extract nectar from.

Garrigue walk

The scent of aromatic plants and the trilling sound of insects are the essence of the Mediterranean garrigue, especially in the heat of high summer.

The garrigue is a habitat full of subtle sounds. Muted birdsong and the scuttling noises of rodents and lizards are clues to the diversity of wildlife that lives here. Insects are particularly abundant, and sun-loving species seek out open areas of bare soil and exposed rocks. These are also good places to search for lizards and other reptiles.

Listen for the rustle of reptiles, including tortoises as they bulldoze their way through the vegetation in search of plants to eat.

MYRTLE

STRAWBERRY
TREE

LAVENDER

Where shrubs such as myrtle and strawberry trees start to dominate, the open character of the garrigue gives way to maquis.

ASCALAPHID

TONGUE
ORCHID

Summer is a great time for plant hunting, with many types of heather coming into bloom. Look out for their flowers, which can be seen in varied shades of purple, pink, and red.

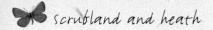

Chaparral cycle

Natural wildfires are an essential part of the chaparral, heath, and grassland ecosystems, bringing about a period of regrowth.

Tinder dry

High summer temperatures and prolonged periods of drought are normal in the California and Mexico chaparral. With the vegetation so dry you can hear it cracking, late summer and early autumn are the natural peak seasons for fires. Certain plants and animals depend on these fires, including the fire beetle, which flies to a blaze site so it can mate and lay its eggs in the fiercely hot conditions they need for hatching.

FIRST ARRIVALS
Lizards are the first creatures on the scene after a fire. Spot them hunting returning insects and basking on still-warm branches.

OPPORTUNISTS
Very flexible in terms of what they eat, coyotes soon start scavenging in burned areas. Their howls, yips, and barks are audible at night.

1 After a fire the chaparral is charred and seemingly dead, yet the renewal process has already begun. Seeds start to germinate in the warm ash and a variety of creatures soon come to forage in the newly created open areas.

2 Encouraged by winter rains, green shoots emerge through the ash, and shrubs regenerate from roots and stumps. Deer and rabbits return to graze on new growth, followed by predators such as coyotes.

TRACKING WILDLIFE

As animals return to the changed landscape, their tracks become visible in the cooled ashes of the fire. Coyote and fox prints are easily identifiable, but the large, rounded paw marks of a mountain lion or cougar are more elusive. Birds make tracks too—ground-hunters, such as roadrunners, prefer open, burned areas because they can see their prey more easily.

FRONT

COYOTE
PAW PRINTS

HIND

LOST IN THE FIRE
Some animals inevitably perish in the flames. This coyote skull may have belonged to an older or injured animal unable to flee.

ADAPTED FEET
Part of the cuckoo family, roadrunners are well known for sprinting across open ground in pursuit of reptiles. Their feet are flexible enough to allow them to perch, and they nest in bushes, relying on the regeneration of shrubs.

GROUND FEEDERS
Quail move around in small groups, keeping in touch with each other with low clucking sounds.

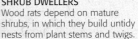

SHRUB DWELLERS
Wood rats depend on mature shrubs, in which they build untidy nests from plant stems and twigs.

3 The first summer after a fire, you can see well-established ground plants. Mature shrubs may not have survived, but a new generation starts to replace them, attracting ground-feeding birds and small mammals.

4 Within three or four years the vegetation has recovered well. Maturing shrubs eventually shade out the smaller plants that appeared immediately after the fire.

FORAGERS
Listen for noisy, inquisitive scrub jays as they hunt for acorns, seeds, bugs, and lizards in new scrub.

Heat-loving plants

Fires bring both death and life to the plants of the chaparral. The clearance of thick and aging vegetation offers a lifeline to long-dormant seeds and bulbs in the soil below. Some species rely on the intense heat of a fire to spark their germination. These so-called "fire followers" make a colorful, but temporary, display in the spring after a fire, while regenerating shrubs such as manzanita and evergreen oak are more permanent features.

first blossom creates a nectar source for insects

WILDFIRES

Fires can occur either naturally through lightning strikes or, unfortunately, as a result of accidental or deliberate human activity. Flames sweep across the chaparral faster than a person can run, often causing loss of human life and property. Such sites should always be visited with the greatest of caution and preparation.

bright colors contrast with charred landscape

MANZANITA

CALIFORNIA POPPY

EVERGREEN OAK

SAGE

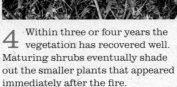

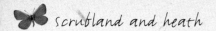

Life in the scrub

Scrubland creatures are engaged in a constant battle to survive. Small insects are preyed on by larger ones, which in turn are eaten by birds, reptiles, and mammals.

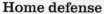

BURROWING SCORPION

Home defense

Insects occupy all levels of the heathland and scrubland habitats, and competition for a desirable spot can be intense. Look for territorial tussles between beetles, and for male butterflies chasing away intruders. Also keep an eye out for insect-hunting birds—warblers move through the scrub, searching for spiders and caterpillars, while shrikes perch prominently, scanning for large beetles and lizards.

MEGA PREDATOR
Tarantula hawks are top predatory insects. They can even overcome a large spider with their deadly sting.

SOUNDS OF THE SCRUB
In the heat of summer, an orchestra of crickets, grasshoppers, and cicadas produce a constant trilling, chirping, and rasping. Look for cicadas on tree trunks.

SPIDER TACTICS
While some spiders hunt their prey by chasing it, others use webs or lie in wait in holes, jumping out to grab passing insects.

Underground life

From ants to scorpions, a huge variety of small creatures use underground burrows for safety and to breed in. They either excavate their own accommodation or take over a home that originally belonged to something else. Watch holes in the ground carefully to see what species emerge. Evidence of mining bees is easy to spot—look for tiny, volcano-shaped mounds of spoil in areas of exposed soil. The dirt is carried up by the bees as they excavate their chambers, and they leave it piled around the shaft entrance.

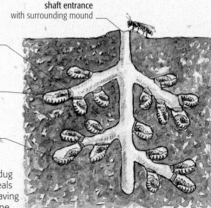

shaft entrance with surrounding mound

chamber seal is closed by female with wax

side chamber contains small larva feeding on stored pollen

small larva develops into pupa in chamber

LEFT ALONE
Each mining bee nest is dug by a single female that seals the entrance and dies, leaving the young to develop alone.

Rearing moths and butterflies

Search for caterpillars on plants such as sages and brambles, then transfer them to a secure but ventilated transparent container. Put a little soil and dead plant material at the bottom, and each day provide fresh supplies of the same type of leaves you found them on. Eventually, the caterpillars transform into cocoons. Release the adults when they emerge after a few weeks (longer with some species).

A SHORT LIFE
Emperor moths are easy to rear from caterpillars, but live only a week or two until they find a mate, breed, and die.

PHEROMONE TRAP

Some moth species locate each other using chemical signals (pheromones), including those given off by females to attract males. Watch this behavior by rearing moths such as emperors. Place a newly emerged female in a pheromone trap made of plastic or netting, folded or stitched into a tentlike shape and suspended from a branch. Watch males arrive and whirl around as they try to reach her.

ATTACK FROM ABOVE
Burrowing solitary wasps can be
found worldwide. They swoop
down and paralyze their prey
before carrying it off to their
nests as food for their larvae.

Scrublands close-up

Dry, scrubland habitat is home to an array of hardy plantlife, insects, and mammals. The actual species will vary, depending on where you are in the world.

LARGE BLUE BUTTERFLY

Insects occupy all levels of scrublands—in winter, look for moth cocoons on the ground.

MOTH COCOON

CYTISUS BROOM

ZEBRA SWALLOWTAIL BUTTERFLY

EMPEROR MOTH

PRAYING MANTIS

short plants and shrubs, including herbs, characterize the transient scrublands.

FALSE DEATH CAP MUSHROOM

PENNY BUN MUSHROOM

OLIVE TREE LEAVES

YELLOW-GIRDLED WEB CAP MUSHROOM

search through areas of dense shrubs and plants, which provide shelter for fungi species.

FLAT MUSHROOM

PELARGONIUM WEBCAP MUSHROOM

CRAB RUSSULE MUSHROOM

TREE
ECHIUM

HAIRYBROOM

CHILEAN
FIRE BUSH

HAREBELL

skeletons may indicate
animals that have
not been able to flee
from wildfires, which often
affect scrublands.

OWL
PELLET

COMMON
SAGE

VOLE
SKULL

SPHAGNUM
MOSS

DEER
SKULL

SHREW
SKULL

Heathland

The open, exposed character of lowland heath means that much of the wildlife lives on or near the ground.

A changing habitat

Lowland heath is a constantly evolving habitat found in Europe. If it is left unmanaged by humans and unaffected by natural events, such as fire, the open heather habitat is rapidly replaced by scrub, which in turn becomes woodland. In the past, heathland was valued for what it produced, and managed by grazing and the cutting back of invasive gorse and birch. After decades of decline, such activities are being used again today to keep lowland heath in the condition required by the specialized wildlife that lives there.

A VERSATILE PLANT
People in Europe traditionally used heather to stuff pillows and mattresses, for insulation, roofing material, and making brooms, as well as in the production of ale and honey. Older plants were burned periodically to promote growth.

HEATHLAND POOLS

Wetland areas are home to species that otherwise could not survive in the heathland environment. Find a suitable pool and try pond-dipping for amphibians such as frogs, toads, and newts, and look out for aquatic invertebrates, such as raft spiders. You can also find damp-loving plants, such as bog bean, bog asphodel, and sundew, growing at the water's edge, and see dragonflies and damselflies hunting overhead.

RAFT SPIDER

SOUTHERN DAMSELFLY

BOG BEAN

COMMON TOAD

SPECIALIST SONGSTER
Dartford warblers are found in gorse scrub. In spring, look for males on a prominent sprig as they sing their buzzy, chattering song.

BUTTERFLY BEHAVIOR
Lowland heath butterflies can be seen flying low over heather and feeding on its nectar.

stems were dried and bound together for thatching and broom-making

flowering heads were used like hops to make ale

heather was considered by some to be lucky, and dried sprigs were bunched and sent for sale in the cities

MOVING IN
Thorny gorse readily colonizes open areas. The young plants soon develop into thick patches of scrub and eventually crowd out the heather.

NEW SHOOTS
Heather seeds can lie dormant for decades, but they start germinating as soon as the scrub above them is cleared and light floods in.

SUN LOVERS
Lizards bask in sunny patches of soil between heather. Find a sheltered location and wait quietly for them to emerge.

FINDING SNAKES
Early morning is the best time to spot adders; look under discarded sheets of plastic or iron. Take care because adders are venomous.

ROOTS FOR FUEL
Slabs of matted heather roots, known as turves, are traditionally dug and burned for fuel during the winter.

HEATHLAND KILLER
Ground beetles, such as the green tiger beetle, can be spotted chasing down prey on areas of exposed soil.

heather has
tightly bunched flowerheads

BLOOMING HEATHER
Heather flowers provide nectar for bees, butterflies, and moths, while the leaves are eaten by caterpillars, birds, and livestock.

Grassland

The acacia-freckled African savanna, the silver seas of the high Andean páramo, the endless, rolling prairies of North America, or the flower-rich downlands of southern England all have an enduring appeal—perhaps because the first is our own species' primal home. They are all open and warm habitats that are highly productive, supporting a large number of herbivores, and in turn, a range of carnivores, from lions and maned wolves to foxes and coyotes. Meanwhile, at ground level, the constant grazing gives non-grass species a chance: flowers prosper, and with them, insects. For all these reasons, grasslands are a great foraging ground for naturalists.

Downland

Found mainly in Britain and Western Europe, downland is characterized by chalky soil and depends on grazing to avoid being invaded by scrub. Downland is also notable for its abundance of wildflowers—early spring displays of pasque flowers give way in summer to orchids, thistles, and daisies. Insects are abundant, and mammals include rabbits, brown hares, and predatory stoats.

BROWN HARE

PASQUE FLOWER

Grasslands

The wide open spaces of the world's grasslands are dominated by herbaceous plants and grasses, and kept in their natural state by grazing, fire, and long spells of dry weather. Most are home to large herds of herbivores.

Prairie

North America's prairies are home to herds of bison, as well as elk and pronghorn antelope. The grasses that characterize the plains are sustained by vast root systems that withstand both fire and drought. Predators include grey wolf and birds of prey, and among the many wildflowers is milkweed, the foodplant for the caterpillars of monarch butterflies.

MILKWEED

MONARCH BUTTERFLY

Savanna

Dotted with acacia trees, savanna is a classic African landscape, but this mix of open grassland and scattered thorny scrub is also found in other continents. The diversity of vegetation supports a wide variety of wildlife, from large grazing mammals, such as wildebeest and zebras, to browsers, such as giraffes, which tackle the scrub.

ZEBRA

Pampas

The windswept pampas are found in South America. They are prone to wildfires, and so larger forms of plantlife, such as trees, struggle to survive there. As a consequence, almost all the birds and animals of this habitat live on the ground. The maned wolf preys on smaller mammals and has evolved long legs to see over tall grasses.

MANED WOLF

Steppe

Dry areas of grassland plain, known as steppe, can be found in parts of Mediterranean and eastern Europe, and in Asia. These habitats are known for their contrasting hot summers and harsh winters. After a long winter, the arid steppes come alive in spring, as crocuses and tulips burst into bloom. Birds such as cranes are found here, along with grazing mammals, including saiga antelope.

SAIGA

WILD TULIPS

CRANE

CINNABAR
MOTH

GREAT GREEN
BUSH CRICKET

BEE
ORCHID

Visit downland on a sunny day, when insects become active in the warmth. You will see butterflies feeding on flower nectar.

Downland walk

A dramatic display of flowering plants makes chalky downland the perfect habitat for a wealth of wildlife, with an especially diverse and noticeable array of insects.

In summer, the sky above flower-rich downland is full of flying insects and the sound of birds singing. Small mammals, such as voles and shrews, run through tunnels in the grass, always on the lookout for a predatory stoat or weasel. At ground level, the plants themselves are teeming with life, from tiny ants to bumble bees, while beetles and crickets can be seen perching on stems and leaves.

Keep an eye out for beetles in the grassland turf. Their boring and burrowing activities help keep the grassland ecosystem in good shape.

DARK GREEN
FRITILLARY BUTTERFLY

CENTAURY

Always examine flowers carefully. You may spot a crab spider or ladybug hiding among the petals or in the center of the flower.

DOR BEETLE

CHALKHILL BLUE BUTTERFLY

Lie down carefully on the grass to see flowers at close quarters and enjoy the scent of herbs such as thyme.

WILD THYME

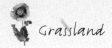

In the grass

A variety of smaller habitats within grassland support interesting insects and invertebrates, all of which thrive among the rich diversity of plants.

Life in the wild

Insects live in all layers of the grassland, from the turf that is kept cropped by rabbits and other grazers, through the tangled jungle of grasses and herbs, up to the flowering heads of taller plants, where many beetle species can be found. Each species has its own special requirements and many live within a surprisingly small area. Some are fiercely territorial, defending their patch against intruders, while others are more nomadic, constantly on the move to find food or a mate. When exploring grassy slopes and banks, look closely for ground-foraging beetles and spiders' webs among the grass stems. Also check for snails that thrive on chalky grassland soils and don't forget to look up—the air will be full of butterflies, day-flying moths, hoverflies, and bees.

SPOTTED BEETLE

SINGING INSECTS

Male crickets and grasshoppers use their body parts to "sing." Crickets rub their wings together, while most grasshoppers chafe their hind legs against their forewings. This is known as stridulation and is the characteristic sound heard in grasslands during warm weather. Its purpose is to attract potential mates, who detect the singing via special receptors.

hind leg acts as a rasp   **forewing** creates noise

GRASSHOPPER

NIGHT LIGHT
Glow-worms can be found worldwide in grassland, and are most visible after dusk. The flightless female attracts males with a light made by a chemical reaction within her body.

SPIDER RELATIVES
Look for harvestmen as they scramble through lower vegetation. They have no silk or venom glands (unlike spiders), so use their long legs to find and trap insects.

BUTTERFLY WATCHING

Although certain butterflies will fly in overcast conditions, most only come out in the sun. The peak time for butterfly activity is mid-morning to mid-afternoon. Choose your site carefully: a sheltered location is best, with plenty of flowering plants to attract the butterflies and warm rocks and grassy banks where they can bask in the sun. Try to get a close look at them as they rest.

BUTTERFLY

BUTTERFLY NET

Making mountains

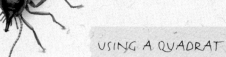

TERMITE

Termite mounds can be found in South America, Australia, and Africa. The mud towers act as protection and create the correct conditions for the colony's queen to breed. Various chambers inside include the royal cell, where the queen and king reside, and the fungus gardens that nourish the colony. Animals, such as anteaters and aardvarks, have adapted powerful claws to penetrate the mounds.

TERMITE SKYSCRAPER
Mounds can reach heights of more than 20 ft (6 m) and house several million individuals, with roughly equal numbers of males and females.

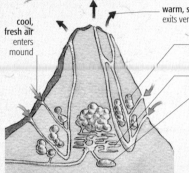

cool, fresh air enters mound

warm, stale air exits ventilation shafts

fungus garden

living chambers and nursery areas

royal cell

VENTILATION SYSTEM
A network of shafts ensures cool air reaches the internal chambers, and rising warm air leaves the mound through the top.

USING A QUADRAT

To get a good idea of local plant and invertebrate diversity drop a sampling square, known as a quadrat, randomly on the ground. Note the number of plant and ground-dwelling insect species in each square of the frame.

STRIDULATING GRASSHOPPER
Different species of crickets and grasshoppers make distinctive sounds that often follow the same pattern—a series of chirps repeated about every two seconds. Use their song to track down the elusive insects on grass stems and flowerheads.

Grassland close-up

Grasslands around the world provide a rich habitat for plants and insects. The species will vary with location, but study the ground and grasses to see what you can discover.

GULF FRITILLARY BUTTERFLY

Look around flowering plants for butterflies—you may also see their pupae hanging from leaves, twigs, or stems.

SMALL COPPER BUTTERFLY

LARGE WHITE BUTTERFLY

SILVER-SPOTTED SKIPPER BUTTERFLY

OX-EYE DAISY

A closer look through dense grass will reveal that it is also made up of wildflowers, which come into bloom in springtime.

Check grass stems for perching insects and invertebrates, such as grasshoppers.

HARVESTMAN

TERMITE

TIGER BEETLE

Take care when walking through long grass—snakes and worms may be sheltering there.

GIANT GRASSHOPPER

SLOW WORM

YELLOW CHAMOMILE

SAW WORT

BURDOCK
SEED HEAD

REST-
HARROW

YELLOW
BEDSTRAW

MUSK
THISTLE

TUFTED HAIR
GRASS

QUAKING
GRASS

COUCH
GRASS

GREEN-WINGED
ORCHID

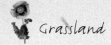
Life on the plains

With extreme weather and little in the way of shelter, wildlife of the plains needs to be tough and resilient. Animals here spend most of their lives out in the open.

DISAPPEARING DOG
Wild dogs once thrived on Africa's open plains, but are now under threat due to persecution, habitat loss, and disease.

The great herds

The grassy plains of North America and Africa are home to herds of plant-eating animals such as antelope and bison, which are constantly on the move in search of fresh pasture and water. Young calves must be able to run within minutes of birth so they can keep up with the others and avoid the predators that follow the herd, hoping to pick off the weak. In the past, the herds contained many millions of animals. While you can still see impressive gatherings of certain species, their numbers and the area they roam over are greatly reduced.

GRASSLAND CONSERVATION

The flat, open nature of grassland makes it vulnerable to conversion for agricultural land. Crop farming and livestock ranches squeeze out wildlife, which comes under further pressure from urbanization and other activities, such as recreation and mining. Many grassland species are now endangered, so protecting the remaining undamaged habitats is vital.

PRAIRIE FARMING
Less than one percent of native prairie remains, largely due to farming.

ON THE MOVE
One of the world's last great wildlife migrations takes place in Africa every year across the plains of the Serengeti. Up to 1.5 million animals are involved, mostly wildebeest, zebra, and gazelle.

LIVING SIDE BY SIDE
Antelope often wander the North American prairie in the company of bison—similar to the way in which African gazelles graze alongside wildebeest.

LOSING GROUND
Gamebirds such as prairie chickens struggle to survive where grassland is farmed.

Refined predators

A healthy grassland ecosystem can support enough prey for predators to occupy specific niches. While conflicts sometimes arise, different species have evolved in ways that help ensure that they are not often in direct competition. On the African savanna, for example, the lion is king, preying primarily on buffalo and zebra and usually seen hunting in family groups. Leopards, meanwhile, hunt alone and prefer to take smaller antelopes, while hyenas and wild dogs will tackle almost anything.

STALKING SERVAL
By moving slowly through long grass, servals first use their large ears to listen for rodents and ground-nesting birds, before pouncing on their prey.

CHASING CHEETAH
Cheetahs hunt by sight, which means they prefer short grass and rely on their amazing speed to chase down their prey.

BURROWING DOWN

Highly social prairie dogs are a
type of ground squirrel that live in
colonies. They dig a system of
underground chambers, tunnels, and
escape routes, lining the chambers
with grass to help insulate them. In
deep soils their burrows can reach
depths of 13 ft (4 m) or more.
The small humps outside burrow
entrances—spoil heaps from the
prairie dogs' excavations—provide
elevation points from which the
rodents can keep guard. Each colony
is usually home to a mature male
and his harem of up to four females.

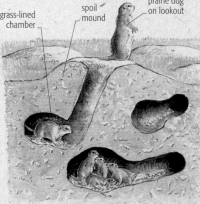

grass-lined
chamber

spoil
mound

prairie dog
on lookout

STATE OF ALERT
Prairie dogs are native to
North America and can often be
spotted on lookouts outside their
burrows. Their once vast territories
have been hugely reduced,
mostly due to prairie farming.

Mountain and hillside

Those of us with a hunger for wilderness gravitate to these environments because their slopes often have restricted cultivation, so they seem less "bruised" by the hand of man. But our perception of what appears natural is often skewed by idealized landscapes. If we really want to explore these habitats, perhaps we should revel in an exploration of the ecologies and behaviors of the unique assemblage of specialized plants and animals that live in these precipitous places: species for which the edge—and sometimes the void beyond—is a comfortable home.

Plateau

These bleak, windswept places are covered with snow for much of the year and have a similar climate to the Arctic tundra. The plants that thrive here, such as purple saxifrage, grow close to the ground in thick mats and have small leaves to reduce water loss. Plateaus have few predators, making them a haven for animals that can endure the conditions, such as the ptarmigan with its thick, downy plumage.

PURPLE
SAXIFRAGE

PTARMIGAN

Mountains

The world's highest places present formidable challenges, with scorching days, fiercely cold nights, and some of the most extreme weather on Earth. The plants and animals that live here need to be superbly adapted to survive.

Pinnacles

Even the bare rock of mountain pinnacles can support life. Freezing and thawing creates cracks in rocks, where you can find plants like camelids or slipperworts growing. Several species of cats hunt for prey among the rocky ledges, such as the extremely rare snow leopard in Asia, and the mountain lion, whose habitat ranges from Canada to the southern end of the Andes.

DARWIN'S
SLIPPERWORT

MOUNTAIN
LION

Forested peaks

Tropical mountain forests are almost permanently cloaked in clouds. The near constant rainfall leaches nutrients from the soil, so many plants have adapted to get their food from other sources. Some bromeliads do not root in soil but attach themselves to trees and other plants, catching nutrients and water in overlapping leaves. Because of the dense vegetation, many forest animals, such as the tree kangaroo, spend much of their time up in the trees.

BROMELIAD

TREE KANGAROO

Volcano

If you visit an extinct or dormant volcano you will notice that the rich soils surrounding it are flushed with life, but some specialists can live in areas with an active volcano. Volcano hummingbirds disperse but soon return after an eruption, while other species make practical use of the heat. Some New Guinean megapode birds incubate their eggs in hot volcanic sands, while alligator lizards from Central America warm up on hot, volcanic rocks.

VOLCANO HUMMINGBIRD

ALLIGATOR LIZARD

159

Living with your head in the clouds

Mountainous areas are home to a range of diverse habitats, with very specialized plants and animals exploiting every niche.

Mountain zones

Because of their vast range of elevations and temperatures, mountains have numerous microclimates, home to very different plant species. At the base of the mountain, a deciduous woodland gives way to a line of conifers, which thrive in the cold. Above this treeline, the alpine tundra, which receives intense sunlight and wind, is home to small-leaved, low-growing plants. In some sheltered areas of tundra, wildflowers take root, forming alpine meadows. The tundra finally merges into the scree and rock of the higher slopes, where only lichens grow.

MOUNTAIN PINE
In Europe, the altitude to which trees can successfully grow is marked by a distinctive line of mountain pines.

DIETARY SUPPLEMENTS

"Rain deserts" are common in mountains. So much rain falls in these areas that it leaches all the nutrients out of the soil. Plants that grow in such environments need to supplement their nutrient intake, and some do this in a very unusual way. The nepenthes pitcher plant produces a sweet nectar and has a brightly colored rim to entice insects, and even animals as large as frogs and rats, to investigate their vase-shaped pitcher. Unlucky victims lose their footing on the slippery rim surface, fall inside, drown in the fluid that collects in the pitcher, and are slowly digested by the plant.

Life on high

HIMALAYAN BEES
These bees can nest as high as 13,100 ft (4,000 m). Their furry bodies help maintain their core temperature.

MARMOTS
Large rodents of the squirrel family, marmots hibernate through the winter in large burrow systems. They have a loud, piercing whistle.

MOUNTAIN CAPRIDS
Nimble and sure-footed, caprids such as Dall sheep live on steep slopes and rugged ground, where they can outrun predators.

MOUNTAIN BUTTERFLIES
Only seen flying for a few weeks in the summer, butterflies, such as the mountain ringlet, overwinter as larvae, buried deep in grass tussocks.

ALPINE NEWTS
Look for these in the grass and around water on mountain heaths in the summer. You won't find any in snowy winters though, because they will be hibernating.

WOODLANDS

MONTANE

Life at high altitude

Life above 9,800 ft (3,000 m) has the added challenge of a lack of oxygen. Mountain animals like the pika and some migrating birds, such as bar-headed geese, have various adaptations to get around this problem. They have more efficient hemoglobin in their blood, and special sacs that direct air back through the lungs before it is exhaled, to extract as much oxygen as possible. These adaptations allow mountain animals to live normal lives in as little as one third of the oxygen found at sea level.

LIVING THE HIGH LIFE
The pika has a thin pulmonary artery wall, to allow more efficient uptake of oxygen into the blood.

GETTING AROUND THE MOUNTAIN ZONES

The most important thing to remember about exploring the mountains is to be prepared. The weather is not only more severe, but it can change very suddenly and catch you unaware. Always tell someone where you are going and when you will be back, take a map and compass, and keep abreast of weather forecasts. It is also important to know your limits: set a time by which you need to turn back in order to make it back down safely before dark. Unless you are an experienced mountain climber, it is not advisable to attempt hiking in steep or rocky terrain outside of marked paths.

HAVE FUN UP HIGH
Hiking or mountain biking are great ways to get around the mountains, but always remember to stick to designated paths.

Mountain plants

Mountain winters are long and severe; the short summer months bring an explosion of color as plants rush to grow and flower while they can.

Life above the treeline

The small alpine plants that grow above the treeline have adapted to low temperatures and humidity, frost and ice, increased winds, and a short growing season. Where there is enough soil, tussock grasses, shrubs, and low trees dominate—larger plants with bigger leaves cannot tolerate the dessication caused by the high winds. Some plants in this zone have tough, hairy leaves; this reduces moisture loss and minimizes the effects of frost and ice. Others have special red pigments that can convert the sun's light into heat.

MOUNTAIN LAUREL
This shrub grows on rocky mountain slopes. The leaves are retained from year to year and are quite toxic, which prevents them from being eaten by passing animals.

RHODODENDRON

Despite their huge success as garden plants around the globe, the rhododendron is an alpine plant with most species originating in the Himalayas. Rhododendron flowers attract scarce mountain pollinators with a spectacular array of colors—white, yellow, pink, scarlet, purple, and blue. In cold conditions, the leaves of certain species roll in on themselves creating a cigar shape. As it gets colder they roll even tighter, protecting themselves, and reducing water loss.

Mountain meadows

Look around you in the mountains and you will see that the various habitats often occur in a patchwork. This is due to prevailing winds, exposure to the sun, hillside location, soil consistency, and underlying rock type, all factors that affect plant growth. Alpine meadows grow in the most favorable habitats, where sediments from weathering rocks create soils capable of sustaining grasses and wildflowers. Most of them store up energy to last them through the harsh winters and flower briefly. Many are dwarfed and stunted by their environment.

RECURRING BLOOMS
Some meadow flowers, such as the Indian paint brush, are perennials, meaning that a new plant grows from the existing root every year.

ALPINE MEADOW
Alpine plants have a short flowering season. It may take some years to build up enough energy to flower, but when they do it can be a spectacular sight.

RED HELLEBORINE

LESSER BUTTERFLY ORCHID

creeping mazus grows "prostrate" or in flat mats

garland flower is a smaller version of the shrub daphne

Keeping a low profile

Maintaining a low profile is a common strategy for plants above the treeline. If you kneel down for a closer look you will see that many of them grow in a creeping fashion, creating thick cushions or mats that are woven tightly together to provide a trap for precious soil blown around by the wind. By hugging the ground they are less exposed to the elements and they also provide shelter for insects and small animals. In turn, the insects help pollinate their protectors.

alpine moltkia has small leaves that reduce water loss

alpine phlox attracts insects with bright flowers

st. john's wort is a smaller version of its lowland cousins

HIGH AND DRY
Perfectly adapted to withstand drying winds, this mountain kidney vetch is highly drought tolerant.

SYMBIOSIS
Many rock roses form a relationship with root fungi (see p.113) that help the plant absorb minerals and water.

SHADY BLOOM
A classic alpine flower, the rock jasmine flourishes in the cold, in partial shade, and in rock crevices.

REGENERATION

The sight of plants growing from volcanic ash may be surprising, but it is not unusual. In the short term, the layer of ash ejected by a volcanic eruptions kills vegetation, but over time, this layer breaks down into soil. Depending on the original volcanic material, this soil can be incredibly rich in nutrients, such as potassium and magnesium, as well as scarce trace elements. Loose seeds blown across the mountain quickly take root in the fertile soil. In Sicily, the benefits of volcanic soil are well-known—the lower slopes of Mount Etna have been farmed for centuries.

Scaling the heights

Mountain mammals inhabit a precarious environment. However, they are protected by its remoteness.

Survival in the mountains requires athletic sure-footedness and an ability to survive in one of the most extreme habitats in the world. In return, the environment offers protection, a potential lack of competition, and even an escape from parasites and biting insects. For example, Dall sheep migrate to higher altitudes in the summer months to escape the black fly. Mammals that rely on the mountains are highly adapted and therefore particularly at risk from the effects of climate change. As temperatures increase, they are forced higher and higher up the slopes and may eventually have nowhere left to go. The best way to see mountain mammals is with a good pair of binoculars. Find a safe, comfortable spot with a good view and slowly scan the mountainside. Look for any sudden movement or for an ibex or mountain goat balanced on a knife-edged ridge.

MOUNTAIN PREDATORS

The hunters of the heights have to be exceptionally gifted to catch their nimble prey. Cats, such as North America's mountain lion and the snow leopard of the Himalayas, can bound great distances—their broad paws with furry undersides provide great traction and their long tails help them balance. Coat thickness varies from winter to summer, with waterproof outer fur and dense underfur providing insulation against the wind and snow.

The snow leopard is secretive and very rare, you'll be lucky to ever see one in the wild.

SURE-FOOTED SHIFTERS
Mountain caprids have hooves with sharp rims for lodging in small footholds, and a small rubbery pad between them for improved grip.

Mountain birds of prey

Birds of prey can be found in a variety of habitats, but they are nowhere more at home than in the skies above mountain ranges, soaring on the strong currents of air.

Mountain hunters

Look up while you are hiking in the hills and mountains and you might see a large bird of prey (raptor) soaring high up in the sky. While it may seem effortless, it actually takes a huge amount of energy to get their bulky bodies airborne. Raptors get around this problem by nesting on rocky ledges, and can launch themselves into the air using gravity to give them momentum and then lift. Their keen eyesight means they can scan vast areas of land for prey or carrion—a great advantage on a mountainside where food may be scarce.

THERMALS
Raptors ride thermals in tight upward circles. They may need to flap their wings to move to the next current.

Mechanics of flight

The key to soaring flight is rising columns of warm air called thermals. They are created when warm air from the ground rises. Large birds of prey, such as vultures, look for smooth, dark areas, such as plowed fields or roads, which absorb more heat and thus create more dramatic thermals. In turn, updrafts occur when winds hit the mountains and are forced up. Using both, raptors can soar for hundreds of miles, hardly using any energy at all.

FINE FEATHERS

A remarkably versatile body-covering, the feathers of raptors are adapted to a wide range of purposes. Primary flight feathers are the largest, outermost feathers of the wing—they propel the bird forward then provide lift to keep it aloft. Contour feathers give the bird's body an aerodynamic, streamlined outline, while down feathers provide insulation.

DOWN FEATHER

CONTOUR FEATHER

FEATHER COLLECTION
Look for discarded feathers, they will tell you about the area's birds even when none can be seen.

FEATHER STRUCTURE
Flight feathers have a central, hollow shaft and many side branches called barbs. These hook together to create a solid surface.

each barb has hundreds of barbules

barbules "zip" together

FLIGHT FEATHER

Mountain birds in flight

Andean condors can have a wingspan of 9¾ ft (3 m)

VULTURES
Some vultures and their relatives, such as this Andean condor, have the largest wingspans of all raptors. They wheel in circles looking for carrion.

primary feathers bend up at the tip

EAGLES
Fierce hunters, eagles capture prey by approaching it from behind. Golden eagles are recognizable by the shallow v-shape in which they hold their wings.

FALCONS
Many falcons such as the peregrine (pictured) and the North American prairie falcon live in mountainous landscapes. The fastest of all raptors, peregrine falcons can attain speeds of 200 mph (320 kph) when diving.

narrow, tapered wings enable rapid flight

BEARDED VULTURE
Also known as the lammergeier, its diet includes bones that it carries up high and drops onto rocks below to smash apart for the marrow inside.

Mountain close-up

Mountain wildlife will vary geographically, but you'll also notice a change in plants and animals as you move from one mountain zone to the next.

COULTER PINE NEEDLES

A line of conifers marks the highest point at which trees can grow.

APOLLO BUTTERFLY

Mountain butterflies migrate to higher elevations daily, returning to the lower slopes at night.

HERMIT BUTTERFLY

COULTER PINE CONE

PINE CONE AND SEEDS

SLATE

HORSEFLY

Mountain insects and spiders seek shelter among low-growing plants.

LICHEN

Rocks and fossils provide a glimpse into changes in Earth's geology.

SCAPHITID AMMONITE

COMMON WASP

ORB SPIDER

WHITE GRANITE

RED GRANITE

GRANITE WITH LARGE CRYSTALS OF QUARTZ, MICA, AND FELDSPAR

ALDER

Deciduous trees populate mountain foothills.

LAVENDER

ROWAN

Smaller conifers, such as juniper, sometimes form a second belt below the treeline.

JUNIPER

THISTLE

Wildflowers and grasses grow in alpine meadows.

RED HELLEBORINE

SEDGE

Animal remains reveal mountain species even when none can be seen.

RED DEER ANTLER

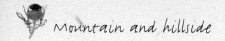
Life in the underworld

MOUSE-EARED
BAT

Caves are particularly prevalent in limestone mountains, formed by chemical action and erosion. The conditions inside are usually fairly constant, and they provide shelter for a multitude of unusual creatures.

Cave dwellers

Animals that live within caves fall into three categories. Troglobites live their whole lives in caves and never come out. Troglophiles, such as the cave salamander, favor caves, but may also live elsewhere. Trogloxenes use caves for shelter or for certain parts of their life cycle, but also venture out into the light. Classic trogloxenes include a huge number of bat species that roost and hibernate in caves.

CAVE VISITORS
Some animals end up in caves by accident, perhaps swept in by flash floods. Frogs have been found deep underground, apparently thriving!

STALACTITES AND STALAGMITES

Look around a cave and you might notice what look like "stone icicles." These are formed by acidic water, carrying dissolved limestone, dripping through the roof of the cave. Some of the dissolved minerals are left behind and eventually form stalactites, hanging from the roof of the cave, and stalagmites, growing up from the floor where the drips land. This may take tens of thousands of years, and the two may eventually connect as a column.

ANCIENT STALACTITES AND STALAGMITES

SPIDERS
Some cave-dwelling spiders, such as European cave spiders, are though to be photophobic—averse to the light.

MOTHS
While many moths overwinter as pupae, some, such as the herald (pictured) and tissue moths, hibernate as adults in caves.

CAVE ARTHROPODS
Arachnids such as this pseudoscorpion do well in cave environments. Unlike true scorpions, they do not have a tail with a stinger.

EXPLORING CAVES

Caving (spelunking) is one of the most exciting realms of exploration in nature. Often a tiny entrance will lead to vast systems with miles of passageways and rooms as big as a sports stadium. However, caves can be very dangerous places—it is easy to lose your footing on loose or uneven rock, and heavy rain can lead to flash floods. Make sure you're fully prepared, and check weather conditions before any expedition into a cave system. If you are new to caving, only attempt it with an experienced guide.

Creatures of the deep

The world's deepest, darkest places are inhabited by some of the strangest-looking animals on the planet. These creatures have adapted to live in the darkness and have evolved to suit their surroundings with useless eyes, extended tactile limbs, antenna for feeling their way around, and an increased sensitivity to air pressure and temperature. Because food and oxygen can be scarce underground, troglobites often have low metabolisms and long lifespans. Some cave crayfish can live to be over 100 years old.

CAVE CRAYFISH

WINDOW TO THE WORLD
While much of the world underground is barren, cave entrances are a veritable haven for life—sheltered and safe, but with easy access to the outside world.

PLANTS
The cave systems themselves are too dark to support plant life, but cave entrances are often alive with shade-loving plants, known as sciophytes. Sheltered from the wind, they thrive in moist conditions.

OPPOSITE-
LEAVED
SAXIFRAGE

HERB
ROBERT

WOOD
SORREL

Lake, river, and stream

There is an almost incomprehensible range of scale in these habitats. Some lakes are sea-sized, and some massive rivers invisibly merge with oceans, yet they also vary throughout their latitude and altitude, as well as in response to the environment beyond their banks. No matter what the location, however, the thirst for a freshwater lifestyle has led to a wonderful richness of species—and for many of us, the humble garden pond forms a perfect doorway to the discovery of this abundance. Lie on your belly and you can peer into the process of metamorphosis, marvel at a web of life linking predators, prey, and plants, and simply enjoy a range of species very alien from yourself.

Upland streams

These turbulent, rocky waterways flow quickly in places, but most have quieter stretches as well. Waterfalls and runs are interspersed with pools, which are home to stonefly and caddisfly larvae, as well as small fish. Birdlife includes wagtails and diving specialists, such as dippers. Few plants can grow in the fast water itself, but ferns and mosses cling to the banks.

AMERICAN DIPPER

Lakes, rivers, and streams

Freshwater habitats are some of the richest in terms of wildlife. The animals and plants that live in them vary, not only according to geography, but also to water chemistry and the speed of water flow.

Lowland rivers

Lowland rivers flow more gently than upland streams, and host a greater range of species. Plant life often grows thickly in the water and on the banks. Mayflies can be seen swarming around the water and laying their eggs on its surface, and mammals, such as beavers, make their home at the waterside in dams made of branches and mud.

MAYFLY

EUROPEAN BEAVER

Ponds

Ponds are usually abundant with nutrients, such as nitrogen and phosphorous, and often full of plant life. Many ponds are cut off from streams or rivers, and the animals that live in them are often either seasonal visitors or are introduced. Most insects, such as water striders, have wings.

CANADIAN PONDWEED

WATER STRIDER

Lakes

Lowland lakes are full of nutrients and support a variety of animals, including dragonflies, which lay their eggs in and around the water, and bottom-feeding fish, such as carp. In upland lakes the water contains fewer nourishing elements and fewer species of fish. However, diving birds and ducks do make these lakes their home.

MALLARD

DRAGONFLY

Swamps, bogs, and fens

These waterlogged habitats are found in upland and lowland areas. Swamp describes a wetland with continuous water cover. Bogs and fens have peaty soil—bogs are acidic and fens are neutral or alkaline. Vegetation in these habitats includes mosses, sedges, and reeds. Inhabitants range from frogs, snakes, and waterbirds to animals as large as alligators in the swamps of North America.

COOT

AMERICAN ALLIGATOR

BLACK-HEADED
GULL EGG

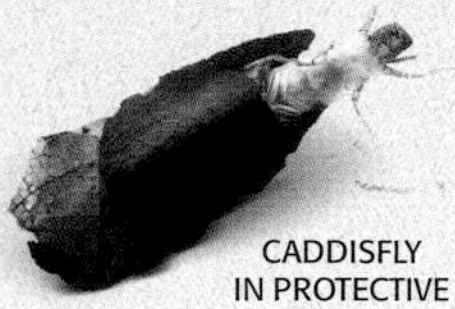

CADDISFLY
IN PROTECTIVE
CASE

*Keep an eye out
for water bird
nests. If you
find one, keep
your distance
and never collect
bird eggs.*

Lakeshore walk

**Try visiting a lake regularly to see how the freshwater
wildlife changes through the year. The still water of
lowland lakes is particularly rich in plants and animals.**

In winter lakes may freeze over, but
waterfowl, such as ducks, may be
seen in patches of open water or on
the ice. Look out for grebes and their
elaborate courtship displays, and
kingfishers shooting over the water.

Visit the lake again in summer and
there will be less waterfowl, but look
out for the grebes with their young,
and for dragonflies patrolling or
laying eggs on the water's surface,
or into plants just beneath it.

MAYFLY

*Find a spot where you
can look into the
water for fish. If you
are lucky, you may
even see a lurking pike.*

FLOWERING
RUSH

HAWKER
DRAGONFLY

EMPEROR
DRAGONFLY

Check the surface
for damselflies and
dragonflies laying
eggs. Mating
damselflies may be
seen on waterside and
emergent vegetation.

CATTAIL

Take a closer look at
aquatic plants and
you might see a
dragonfly perched
on a stem or leaf.

Life of a river

From their small streams to vast coastal estuaries, rivers carve the landscapes through which they flow.

Stream to river

Many rivers are born in higher areas of land, or uplands. Rainwater, melting snow, and water oozing out of bogs trickles into streams. As they flow downhill, these streams meet other streams and a river is formed. Farther downstream, a river may join other rivers. Some rivers begin in the lowlands; their water comes from natural springs that rise from subterranean water stores, such as chalk formations. Most rivers make their way to the sea, or into a lake, changing their character—and the animals and plants that depend on them—along the way.

Upland streams and rivers

Nutrients, such as phosphorus and nitrogen, are harder to come by in these bubbling, rocky waters than in the lowlands, so you will see fewer plants and animals here. But keep a lookout for dippers—these short-tailed birds "dip" and will go underwater, searching for food.

WATER WALKER
Dippers are well adapted to upland river life. This plump white-throated dipper is found throughout Europe.

Middle reaches

Here, you should notice calmer water, intermittent rocky stretches, and a greater variety of plant and animal species. Try to see diving ducks, such as the merganser—a duck with serrated bill edges that help it grip slippery fish. On sandy, muddy, or gravely sections, look out for the white flowers of water crowfoot, floating on the water's surface. In Europe, you might see beautiful demoiselle damselflies—although only between May and September, during their flight period.

BOTTOM-DWELLER
A sleek, silvery fish with a colorful dorsal fin, the grayling searches riverbeds for larvae and other food.

FLYING JEWELS
Demoiselles are exotic-looking damselflies with tinted wings, which live by rivers and streams.

BRINGER OF LIFE
Australia's Adelaide River reveals how water enriches an otherwise barren landscape. Note how green vegetation lines the river's meandering banks.

FISH-WATCHING

Fishermen wear polarized glasses to make it easier to see fish in the water. Try wearing a pair to help you see what's living in your local rivers. Similarly, polarized filters for camera lenses will help you better record what you see.

POLARIZED LENS

Lowland rivers

Nutrient-rich lowland rivers typically support more species than higher stretches, and these are the rivers most of us know best. The type of species that live in and around them is influenced by chemistry—more alkaline waters can be especially rich. Pollution from farming or sewage works can reduce the diversity and number of species a river supports.

SWIMMING SNAKE
Grass snakes are good swimmers. They can reach lengths of 4 ft (1.2 m) or more, and feed mainly on toads and frogs.

PATIENT HUNTER
You will often see herons, such as this gray heron, waiting or wading slowly, while looking for fish to eat.

Estuaries

Large rivers flow into the sea at estuaries. At low tide, mudflats are loaded with tiny snails, crustaceans, and other invertebrates that provide rich pickings for shorebirds and wildfowl (see pp.226–27). Estuaries are not always easy (or safe) to explore, so take great care when watching from the edges.

EXPERT FISH-CATCHER
Cormorants are skilled fishers, on estuaries and elsewhere. You can often spy them spreading their wings to dry off after a dive.

LIFE CYCLE OF A SALMON

Atlantic salmon lay their eggs in gravel on stream and riverbeds. The fish that emerge stay in fresh water for one to five years, sometimes more. Then they head downstream to the North Atlantic, where they remain for about one to four years. To spawn, they leave the sea and head back upriver. Most returning salmon find their birth stream, using their sense of smell to help find their way. Most spawn just once in their life, but a minority repeat their journey, spawning up to four times in total.

INCREDIBLE JOURNEY
On their way to spawn, salmon jump weirs and waterfalls, and clear heights of over 9¾ ft (3 m).

179

Riverbank

For the best riverbank experience, try a quiet walk, or just sit and watch—preferably when there aren't any other people around.

Wet and woody

The saturated soil of a riverbank supports an abundance of plant life, which in turn provides protected areas for insects and invertebrates to reproduce. Mammals, such as otters, also make the waterside their home, living in well-hidden "holts" within the dense vegetation. Willow and alder trees can be seen along riverbanks. Alders are the only broadleaved trees with cones, and their seeds provide food for many birds. Weeping willows, with their drooping branches, are easy to spot by European and Asian rivers.

WILLOW
There are many willow species, and some trees are hybrids. Telling them apart isn't easy.

ALDER
Long male catkins (flower clusters) hang from alders in winter, while shorter cone-shaped female catkins can be seen in spring.

Riverbank-dwellers

Rivers mean fish, so predators, such as small mammals, thrive here. These mammals all have various adaptations for life at the riverside, such as webbed feet and whiskers, to help them navigate through murky waters. You may see an elusive otter—but don't confuse it with the smaller mink. Seeing a beaver is very rare, but you might make out their lodges or dams, made from nearby trees.

SKILLED BUILDER
Beavers are expert tree-fellers: just one family can cut down several hundred trees in a single winter for dams, lodges, and food.

Riverside fishers

Fish-eating birds have two main methods of hunting—stalking and diving. You can see herons stand patiently, or stalk, when hunting. Fish are their main prey, but they will also eat amphibians, reptiles, and insects. Kingfishers perch, watch, then dive in to grab a small fish.

QUIET HUNTER
Heron species vary in size, but all use the "stalk-and-stab or -grab" approach when feeding.

fish swallowed head-first

ragged crest

RAPID DIVERS
You may spot a kingfisher, such as this belted kingfisher, gliding. It dives at speed to catch a fish, then bangs it on a branch before swallowing.

1 ADULT BREAKS FREE
The nymph hauls itself out of the water and the new adult breaks out of its final larval exoskeleton.

2 FLUID ENTERS WINGS
Body fluid pumps into the new adult's wings by contractions, to give them their full form.

3 MATURE ADULT
A damselfly may take a week and a half or longer to become fully mature and ready to mate.

LIFE OF A DAMSELFLY

Damselflies and dragonflies spend most of their lives underwater. Eggs are laid by adults and develop into aquatic nymphs, or larvae. These are fierce predators. To grow, they must shed their skin and may do this more than ten times before they emerge. Some spend five years underwater. Adults may live less than two weeks, but some survive for two months.

WATER VOLE
Water voles are small rodents found in Europe and Asia. They feed on plants and grasses along the water's edge and also use this material to line their burrows.

DANUBE CRESTED NEWT
This newt lives in rivers, ponds, and lakes in central and southeast Europe. It can reach 5 in (13 cm) in length, sometimes more.

NIGHT-HERON
This black-crowned night-heron is the world's most common heron species. It feeds mainly between dusk and dawn on a varied diet, ranging from fish and reptiles to bats and small birds.

WATER SHREW
The water shrew can be found throughout much of Europe. It swims very well and, unfortunately for its aquatic-invertebrate prey, has poisonous saliva.

WEBBED PREDATOR
All freshwater otters eat fish as their main food, but some will take birds, small mammals, or frogs. The webbing between their toes helps make them superb swimmers.

Pike

A ferocious predator, this common fish can grow to vast sizes. It is found in North America, Europe, and Asia.

Pike are found mainly in fresh water, such as pools, lakes, canals, and rivers, although some have been seen living near the coast of the Baltic Sea in Northern Europe. They prefer well-vegetated habitats that provide plenty of cover to hunt from, as well as places for their vulnerable offspring to hide. Pike can grow up to 5 ft (1.5 m) long and are top predators. They loiter among weeds, well-hidden by their olive-green coloration, and wait for their prey to come to them. A single high-speed lunge propels the hunter out of cover and onto its victim. Mostly, pike eat fish—including other pike—but frogs, newts, unsuspecting ducklings, insects, crayfish, and water voles are also taken. They typically live alone and are very territorial. During the breeding season the male woos a female by poking her with his "muzzle" and releases his sperm, which fertilizes her eggs in the water, outside her body.

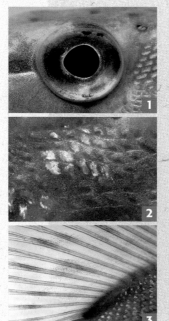

FISH ANATOMY

Most fish are shaped to move efficiently through water. An internal skeleton provides support, and gills take oxygen from the water and supply it to the body. Shifts in water pressure, and vibrations, are sensed by a system of sensory organs known as a "lateral line" running along each side of the body. Some fish have whiskerlike chin barbels to feel for food—these appendages contain their taste buds.

1 Fish require no eyelids as the surface of their eyes is always kept moist. In habitats where visibility is poor, fish often have larger eyes.

2 Most fish have scales and in the majority of species each scale is a thin layer of bone. Scales provide protection without hindering flexibility.

3 Fins propel and steer the fish and help it hold its position in the water. Some fish use them for display in courtship or territorial defense.

HEAVYWEIGHT HUNTER
A northern pike has tipped the scales at 77 lb (35 kg), and the biggest individuals are females. Pike may live to be 30 years old.

Water birds

Swans, geese, ducks, and grebes are just some of the fascinating birds you may see on larger areas of open freshwater.

Waterfowl and other birds

Wetlands attract all types of bird life; many come to feed, or to nest and raise their young within the dense vegetation. Some of the most common birds are known as "waterfowl," a group that includes swans, geese, and ducks. However, this is not the only group of birds that live in this habitat; others include storks and herons. Diversity is the name of the game here—some species build floating nests, others nest in tree holes. Some eat fish, while others feed on invertebrates or plants.

TAKING OFF
Some water birds, such as this trumpeter swan, need plenty of space for takeoff. Watch them run over the water's surface to help get the required momentum for flight.

long, slender neck

AGGRESSIVE SHOW
Birds like the mute swan make threat displays, including wing flapping and "busking"— where a swimming birds pulls back its neck and lifts its wings.

UPENDING
Many water bird species have long necks to allow them to reach underwater plants far down, especially when they upend.

SWAN FOOD
Dabbling birds feed by skimming in shallow water and sieving food and water through filters in their bills.

SNOW GOOSE
Snow geese in North America come in two colour forms – this one is white, but the "blue" snow goose is mostly gray-brown.

GRAYLAG GOOSE
Most farmyard geese are descended from graylags. Different subspecies have different bill colors.

Geese

They may have webbed feet like ducks and swans, but geese are adapted to eat plants on land. Their bills suit their tough vegetarian diet, and they walk well because their legs are central on their bodies. Like swans, male and female birds look alike. Usually, they mate for life, breed in the far north, migrate in family units, and winter further south. In some areas, however, Canada geese and the UK's feral graylags can be seen all year round. You will see geese flying in the "V" formation, which is also characteristic of ducks.

WHITE-FRONTED GOOSE
Like all true geese, white-fronts are found only in the Northern Hemisphere. They breed at high latitudes, but wintering birds can be seen in Europe and the USA.

white patch at base of bill

orange legs and feet

orange
chest-band

Ducks

Ducks can be divided into divers and dabblers. The mallard is a dabbler, the tufted duck and scaup are divers. Diving ducks propel themselves underwater to feed. To help them swim, their legs are positioned towards the rear, which makes walking awkward. You are less likely to see divers on shallow water than dabblers, as the latter typically skim for food at the surface of shallow waters, or a little lower when they upend. Dabblers' legs are positioned farther forward, so walking is easier. Male ducks in decent plumage are usually fairly easy to identify and distinguish from females. Be warned, however—when males moult their flight feathers they adopt a more cryptic plumage, and may look similar to the females.

COMMON SHELDUCK
This large, boldly marked bird is easy to see in parts of Europe. Males are larger, brighter, and have a red bulge on their bill.

WOOD DUCK
A North American bird that nests in tree holes. The drabber, mainly brown females look very different to this male with its patterned head and shiny, green crest.

RAISING YOUNG
As is typical among dabbling ducks, this female mallard has sole responsibility for looking after her ducklings. The male probably left when she was brooding her eggs.

Grebes

Grebes are striking birds. Males often resemble females, although some species look very different when they are not in breeding plumage. A grebe's feet are set at its back end, making them superb swimmers when hunting fish, but vulnerable on land. They have lobed toes rather than webbed feet. Floating nests are common, and adults transport their chicks on their backs. It is unusual to see a grebe fly, although most of them can.

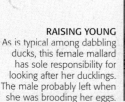

GREAT CRESTED GREBE
This European grebe is now fairly common. In the 19th century, its feathers adorned women's clothing and numbers plummeted. Flooded gravel pits provided new habitats and helped its UK population recover.

GREBE COURTSHIP

Finding a partner is something grebes do with style, putting their attractive head ornamentations to good use. These European great crested grebes are performing the "weed ceremony." Partners ascend from the water face to face, then swing their weed-laden bills from side to side. Courtship begins in winter, and also includes head-shaking, which is fairly easy to observe. The North American western grebe is famous for its "rushing ceremony", where birds rush side-by-side and upright over the water's surface.

chick
rides on its
parent's back

WESTERN GREBE
This North American species has a strong, sharp bill that it thrusts forward to stab prey and other birds.

On the surface

Look carefully at the water in freshwater habitats and you will see that the surface can be alive with a variety of creatures.

Animal adaptations

The water surface is an unusual and fascinating microhabitat that is inhabited by a variety of specially adapted animals. Water striders feed on animals that have fallen in and become trapped. They live up to their name by walking quickly across the surface film; their long legs distribute their weight over the water. Water snails also move across the surface film, but they cling to it from beneath the water. Beetles and water boatmen use the water surface as a temporary filling station, taking on air before and after diving into the water.

SURFACE INHABITANTS
Some animals, such as this water boatman, have special adaptations like long legs and sensitive water-repelling hairs to help them move on water.

SEMIAQUATIC SPIDER
The European raft spider has water-resistant hairs on its legs to enable it to detect vibrations and run over the water surface after its prey.

TRANSPARENT FLEA
There are many species of water flea, which are crustaceans. Some use their branched antenna as oars to swim around under the water surface, filtering microscopic organic food particles out of the water.

SENSITIVE HAIRS
Water-repelling (hydrophobic) hairs stop water striders from getting wet and sinking, making walking on water seem effortless. They are common and easy to spot—look carefully for the tiny depressions its feet make on the water surface.

middle legs provide thrust

front legs used for seizing prey

back legs used to change direction

TESTING SURFACE TENSION

The water surface is like a very thin, transparent film that is strong enough to support a small amount of weight before it gives way—this is called surface tension. Watch soap bubbles and you will see clearly the surface layer of a liquid. You can test surface tension with a simple experiment. Put some water in a bowl, take a small sewing needle, and try to float it on the surface. If you are having problems, try floating a small piece of tissue on the water and putting the needle on top of it—it might be easier if a small part of the needle projects over the edge of the tissue. Push the tissue down and away from the needle and, with practice, the needle should float, supported by surface tension. Animals, such as water striders, raft spiders, and water measurers, are very light and their long, hairy legs allow them to use surface tension to walk on water.

Surface predators

Insects that don't normally live on water, such as flies, can become caught on the surface if they fall in. This is good news for water striders, whirligig beetles, water crickets, and raft spiders that all hunt their prey at surface level, and can move across the water at quite a speed to catch it. Great water boatmen also hunt at the water surface, but attack their prey from beneath the water.

NASTY BITE
Great water boatmen should not be handled—they can bite. These predators sense vibrations on the water's surface and attack fish and tadpoles with their penetrating "beak."

OPPORTUNIST
Water measurers catch water fleas that live beneath the water and also eat insects that are trapped on the surface.

PREDATORY FLY
Some brightly colored, long-legged flies live on the surface film and feed on mosquitoes and other small insects.

SPEED SKATING
Whirligig beetles whizz in circles on water. Their eyes are divided to see predators and prey above and below the water line.

WATER HUNTER
Look out for water crickets' orange markings and watch these insects hunt. When chasing food, they can move at great speed.

Pond dipping

A healthy pond will be teeming with life; pond dipping is a simple and rewarding way to get a closer look at nature.

Viewing pond life

Find a safe, stable spot on the edge and always supervise children closely. Try to use a long-handled net with a fine mesh. Make sure you catch a variety of specimens—don't just dip into open water, because some creatures live around plants and in mud at the bottom.

VIEWING JAR
Put some pond water in a clear glass jar or bucket and empty the contents of your net into it. Let it settle and see what you have caught. Always return your catch to the pond.

caddis flies come out at dusk or night and are often mistaken for moths

oar-like hind legs

water boatmen are predatory bugs, they should not be handled because they can bite—their usual prey include tiny fish and tadpoles

frogs need to lift their head above water in order to breathe

webbed hind foot for swimming

water scorpions have large front legs for catching prey, such as small fish and tadpoles

freshwater snails graze on underwater plants, but they need oxygen and return to the surface to take gulps of air

damselfly nymph

caddis case of plant material

caddis fly larva surrounded by a protective case that is built with sand and stones

A COURTSHIP DANCE
Red-spotted newts live in North American wetlands and ponds. During the breeding season the female is lured in by the male's spots and fanning movements.

Breeding season

If you visit a pond during the breeding season of April and May, and shine your flashlight into the shallow water at night, you might be lucky enough to see courting newts. Pond newts do not spend all their life in a pond, but do return to the water to breed. You may be able to pick out a courting male, as he is typically more "crested" and colorful than the female. He uses his tail to waft pheromones (chemical signals) through the water to the female, and then drops a spermatophore (packet of sperm) near her.

Tadpole development

The transformation from frog spawn to froglet is fascinating to watch and is an activity you can encourage. The shallow, unpolluted water of a garden pond is ideal to raise tadpoles. Keep the pond well vegetated to provide food and places to hide for the froglets.

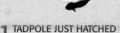

1 TADPOLE JUST HATCHED
Tadpoles emerge from the spawn after 30–40 days. They begin by eating the spawn then algae. You can also give them chopped lettuce in ice cubes.

2 TADPOLE WITH HIND LEGS
Between six and nine weeks, the tadpole grows hind legs. Provide plants, such as lilies, and branches and rocks as cover for hiding spots.

3 TADPOLE WITH ALL LEGS
By week 11, the front legs are fully developed. Provide plenty of rocks, or a sloped piece of wood, so that they are able to climb out of the water.

4 FROGLET
By week 12, metamorphosis is complete. The froglet will now eat small invertebrates. It could be two or three years before the frog breeds.

fringes on legs propel beetle through water

strong, grasping front legs

great diving beetles are fierce predators that can be up to 1½ in (3.5 cm) long—their diet includes newts, frogs, and fish

dragonfly eggs

male sticklebacks are aggressively territorial and build nests they attract females to for egg laying

throat and belly turn red in spring

dragonfly nymph

Swamps, bogs, and fens

If you want to encounter a variety of species in a truly wild setting, try spending some time in one of these fascinating wetland habitats.

Insect-eating plants

The best places to see sundews are waterlogged habitats, such as bogs, which are nutrient-poor because water cannot flow to, or from, them easily. These remarkable plants get the nutrients they need by catching insects. The "hairs" on a sundew's leaf have a gland at each end that secretes a sticky substance. Once an insect is caught, the edges of the leaf gradually curl over, and enzymes help break the insect down. Sundews aren't the only carnivorous plant—in North American bogs you can find pitcher plants (see p.160), cobra lilies, and venus flytraps.

WATER WORLD
You will find plenty of plants even in the soggiest swampland. Reed swamps are dominated by reeds and bulrushes, while cypress trees flourish in swamp forests.

DEADLY VARIETY
There are about 150 sundew species. The great sundew has a large range, and grows in habitats in North America, Europe, Japan, and Hawaii.

fairly long, reddish bill

SMOOTH MOVER
Watch the edge of a European reed bed and you might see a slim water rail. Listen carefully for its shrieks, squeals, and grunts.

Reed-bed birds

Some bird species have adapted to life in reedbeds—wetlands dominated by reeds. Many rails, such as the water rail, are surprisingly slim, enabling them to get through dense vegetation, and the plumage of bitterns provides great camouflage. Reed warblers weave their nests around reed stems, and as the plants grow, the nest goes up with them.

male shows black stripes

REED RESIDENT
Look for colorful bearded tits in European and Asian reedbeds, where they eat reed seeds during the winter. Their *ping ping* calls might help you find them.

SILENT HUNTER
Bitterns, like this American species, are in the heron family and breed in marshes. They move quietly around the water's edge preying on fish, amphibians, and insects.

PRODUCTS FOR PEOPLE

While reeds are still used for thatching, they aren't the only wetland plant to have been exploited by humans. Sedge is also used in thatching, and in some areas, peat is still used as a fuel. Cranberries were originally bog plants, but are now grown commercially in North America. The cranberry harvest involves beating the beds, and then gathering the floating berries for juice and food.

Wetland inhabitants

Swamps, bogs, and fens provide a home for many plants and animals. Those shown here are just a few of those you might encounter on a wetland visit. You won't find all of them at every site, of course, but if you go with open eyes and an enquiring mind you should see something special.

1 Bog asphodel flowers in acidic European bogs between July and September. It is a short plant that produces orange fruits.

2 The common reed is a grass found in Europe, the USA, and Asia. It can grow to heights of 9¾ ft (3 m) or more. In bloom, it reveals purple flowers.

3 The cranberry is found in North America, Europe, and Asia, and has pink flowers, which can be seen between June and August.

4 The yellow or flag iris is a distinctive plant that grows in Europe, northwest Africa, and parts of Asia. It flowers between June and August and can be over 3¼ ft (1 m) tall.

5 The European common lizard is found in a wide variety of habitats. Look for it soaking up the sun on warm summer days.

6 An infamous snake of the eastern USA, the venomous water moccasin eats a wide range of prey, but frogs and fish are its usual food.

7 The marsh frog is found in Europe and Asia. This large amphibian can grow to 6 in (15 cm), and sometimes more. Look for frogs on lily pads.

8 American alligators live in the swamps of the southeastern USA. An adult male can be over 13 ft (4 m) long.

9 The snipe is a wading bird that can open the tip of its long bill independently of the rest of it. The sensitive tip is used to feel for food.

BOGBEAN
This attractive plant is found in North America, Europe, and Asia. Its pink-and-white flowers bloom between April and June.

191

Coast

The interfaces between land and sea are among the richest habitats on the planet at any latitude, because the mix of the terrestrial and marine generates opportunities for an immense diversity of life. Combine this with a multitude of geological and geographical variables, as well as the resulting range of coastal types, and that diversity expands even further. From mudflats to mangroves, sand to shingle beaches, towering cliff-sides to tidal pools, there is a fabulous array of species living on the edge of land and sea. It's also the place where you can safely explore part of the marine environment without getting too wet!

Sand

Sand forms a range of habitat types. Specialized creatures inhabit tide-washed sand, drawing birds such as sanderlings in to feed on them, while dry sand can blow into vast dunes that, when colonized and anchored by plants such as sea holly or marram grass, form a rich but environmentally challenging habitat for wildlife.

SEA HOLLY

SANDERLING

Beaches

At the front line between land and water, beaches are created and shaped by the actions of the sea, which erodes and deposits sediment. The nature of a beach, however, depends on the geography and geology of the land nearby.

Rock

Waves are a potent force of erosion, wearing away even the hardest of rocks where they meet the sea. On one hand this creates cliffs, but the other result—a rocky beach at sea level—is equally dramatic and the source of endless exploration and inspiration for any naturalist. Each rock pool is a miniature ocean, home to a variety of accessible marine life such as mussels, anemones, and seaweeds.

MUSSELS

WRACK

SEA-ANEMONE

Coral

The gleaming white sand of many tropical beaches is formed from the broken and bleached remnants of coral of shallow-water reefs. At higher latitudes, similar types of beaches are built from crushed seashells or the remains of chalk-encrusted seaweed. Both are local beach types that reflect local sources of sediment, as revealed by the shells and bits of coral that wash up on them. All are rich in bird life. Some, like terns, feed offshore and nest on shore.

FAIRY
TERN

CORAL REEF

MUREX
SHELL

Gravel

Gravel is also a product of erosion. Pebbles are deposited as a fringing beach along an exposed coastline, sometimes thrown into ridges by storm waves. While the seaward zone supports annual plants, whose life cycle takes place in summer, more stable gravel supports drought-tolerant perennials such as sea kale and stonecrop. Ground-nesting birds, such as terns, thrive within the mosaic of pebbles and plants.

SEA KALE

STONECROP

SEA BUCKTHORN

Find a patch of sea buckthorn in autumn and you may see birds such as thrushes gorging on the energy-rich fruits to sustain them on their migration.

BUMBLEBEE

Pollinating bees may be scarce in such exposed habitats, so large flowers are needed to attract them. Watch and wait to see what arrives.

Beach walk

Bleak and windswept, a beach in winter resonates with the cries of seabirds. And summer brings a whole new set of sights, scents, and sounds.

Whether made up of sand or gravel, all beaches drain freely, and plants here must be able to cope with drought. Gently squeeze and stroke the leaves and you'll find coatings of wax or hairs and succulent, fleshy stems—all part of the plants' adaptations to preserve water. Large, showy flowers attract pollinating insects, which lure in dragonflies and other predators from their freshwater breeding sites.

YELLOW HORNED POPPY

SOUTHERN HAWKER DRAGONFLY

VIPER'S BUGLOSS

Check out nectar-rich flowers for hawk moths and hoverflies. They provide a vital meal for these migrating insects.

RED VALERIAN

CABBAGE WHITE CATERPILLARS

Tread carefully! Ground-nesting birds such as plovers lay their eggs directly on the beach, relying on camouflage for protection.

PLOVER EGG

SOW THISTLE

Delve into foliage, or search by flashlight at night, to find insect larvae. Susceptible to drought and predation, they hide deep within the undergrowth.

Turning tides

A knowledge of tides is crucial to the exploration of coastal habitats, both for safety reasons and because tides affect everything that lives within them or nearby.

Understanding tides

As the Earth spins on its axis, each point on the planet's surface passes through two high tides every 24 hours. These bulges of water are formed by the gravitational pull between the Moon and the Earth. High tides occur twice a day at intervals that are a little over 12 hours apart, due to the Moon's orbit changing its position relative to the Earth.

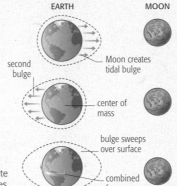

EARTH   MOON

second bulge

Moon creates tidal bulge

center of mass

bulge sweeps over surface

combined forces

MOON'S PULL
Once the Moon's gravity pulls a bulge of water toward it, a counterbalancing bulge forms on Earth's opposite side as the planet rotates.

READING A TIDE TABLE

Tide tables tell you when high and low tides occur on any particular day, and they normally give the predicted heights of those tides. Learn to use them—they could save your life. But remember that these are only predictions; both the timing and height of tides can be affected dramatically by weather conditions and atmospheric pressure, so remember to keep checking tides visually, too.

TIDE TABLES

4

3

4 Spray zone

This area beyond the tide's reach is still strongly influenced by the sea. Wind-driven salt spray means that the animals here, such as sea slaters, must tolerate a salty environment. On exposed coasts, the spray zone may extend hundreds of yards inland.

SEA SLATER

PERIWINKLE

3 Upper tidal zone

Survival in the upper tidal zone necessitates an ability to tolerate exposure to air and varying salt levels. In hot weather, seawater evaporates and becomes saltier; in wet weather it is diluted. A few species, such as channelled wrack, tolerate these extremes; others such as anemones retreat into pools.

CHANNELLED WRACK

BEADLET ANEMONE

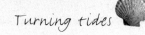

Tidal cycle

In most places, the high to low tide cycle takes a little over 12 hours, but there are also longer-term tidal cycles. At full and new Moon, high tides are higher and low tides lower ("spring tides"), with "neap tides"—lower high and higher low tides—in between. And even longer cycles occur: the highest tides of all occur around the spring and autumn equinoxes.

STRANDED JELLYFISH
When a high tide recedes, it may leave behind some marine animals, like jellyfish.

Take a close look, but don't touch—it can still sting!

HIGH AND LOW TIDE
The constant ebb and flow of tides changes the land- and seascapes of our coastlines. Animals and plants in tidal zones must move or adapt to ever-changing conditions.

POWER OF THE TIDE

The shape and orientation of certain tidal inlets sometimes produces a powerful bore or tidal wave on the rising tide, which may be several yards high and push far upstream. Although a potential pollution-free, renewable energy source, harnessing this power can seriously harm wildlife dependent upon the natural tidal progression.

SURFERS ON A TIDAL BORE

2 Middle tidal zone
In addition to constant wave action, the middle tidal reaches are subject to alternate dousing with seawater and exposure to air. Brown seaweeds dominate this zone on rocky shores, and you will find animals such as crabs, whelks, and barnacles here.

EDIBLE CRAB

BROWN SEAWEED

DOG-WHELK

BARNACLES

1 Lower tidal zone
Here, seawater dominates and wildlife needs to cope with only short periods exposed to the air. However, wave action is constant, so any seaweed is tough and leathery. Animals such as lugworms survive in burrows, and sea stars anchor themselves with tube feet.

SEA STAR

LUGWORMS AND CAST

Sand and gravel

Coastlines are shaped by the sea. Tides, waves, and currents erode, transport, and deposit material, sculpting diverse landscapes.

Cliffs are eroded by the action of the waves. Rocks are then worn down into ever smaller fragments, which can be picked up by currents and transported along the shore until the strength of the current is no longer able to support them. In this way, transported sediments are sorted into different sizes—the smaller the particle, the farther it is carried from where it eroded. Each sediment type supports distinct habitats, and each has a characteristic range of plants and animals.

LONGSHORE DRIFT
You can work out in which direction sediment is being transported by the sea by looking for a build-up of material on one side of a spit of land or barrier.

Examine boulders on the upper shore for barnacles, taking care to avoid unstable rock surfaces.

pebbles are deposited in areas of high current strength, and can be thrown up into ridges by storm waves

coarse shingle is highly abrasive when carried by sea—shingle foreshores are often devoid of life

BOULDERS
Angular chunks of rock that fall from a cliff gradually become rounded, worn down by the sea's continued erosive action as happened to these boulders off the coast of Maine.

SEDIMENT
Sorted into size classes by coastal currents, different sediments are deposited in different environments. The finest particles of all, called silt, are laid down only in the most sheltered conditions, such as in the lee of an offshore barrier or in the heart of an estuary, forming mudflats and salt marshes.

2½–½ in (64–16 mm) diameter

½–⅛ in (16–4 mm) diameter

ROCK FORMATIONS

Erosion not only produces sediment, but also creates cliffs and other distinctive geological features. Cliffs are rarely uniform—the rocks that are exposed vary in composition. Some are more vulnerable to erosion than others, and different erosion rates can produce large landscape features such as headlands of harder rock. On a local scale, a small weakness in the rock may be attacked by waves, forming a cave and eventually extending right through a headland in the form of an arch. Once gravity takes over, the roof collapses to leave a stack.

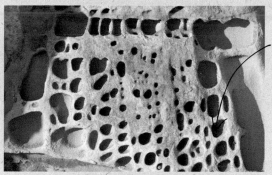

Look for pockets of erosion where the rock was softer.

HONEYCOMB ROCK
Sedimentary rocks vary in hardness as a result of their formation. Water or wind-blown sand often scours the weak points, creating remarkable, almost artistic erosion features.

fine shingle particles hold water and organic matter, which allows invertebrates to move in

sand is the foundation of some of our best-loved habitats—dunes for wildlife and beaches for our enjoyment

SPIT
Sand and gravel extends as a spit across the mouth of an estuary in southwest England.

4–2 mm diameter

2–0.125 mm diameter

DUNES
Carried first by water and then blown by the wind, sand can pile up and form large mobile dune systems, such as the Dune du Pilat in France.

BLACK SAND
Sand is the same color as its parent rock. The black sand found on Fuerteventura, in the Canary Islands, formed from volcanic lava.

Between the tides

Tidal pools are a window into a rich underwater world of marine life, otherwise visible only to the diver or snorkeler.

Anything you lift out of a tidal pool must be put back.

STAYING SAFE
Take care on the shore. The rocks can be slippery, the pools deep, sometimes hidden by seaweed—and always keep an eye on the tide.

Types of tidal pool

Tidal pools of all shapes and sizes are revealed when the tide recedes. Deep pools, with overhangs and crevices, have more niches for different plants and animals, and provide shelter from the action of the waves. Shallower pools are easier to investigate, but contain a more restricted range of life.

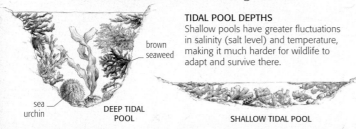

sea urchin

brown seaweed

DEEP TIDAL POOL

SHALLOW TIDAL POOL

TIDAL POOL DEPTHS
Shallow pools have greater fluctuations in salinity (salt level) and temperature, making it much harder for wildlife to adapt and survive there.

Life in a tidal pool

Every pool is a marine microcosm, home to plants and animals, both predators and prey. The mini-dramas of everyday life and death play out before your eyes, as you peer into the pools at low tide. But with predators around, it pays to be well hidden—you will find much more by exploring among the seaweed fronds and holdfasts, under the boulders, and deep into crevices. Watch rocks closely as some animals, such as crabs, are masters of camouflage.

MAKING A VIEWER

Light reflecting off the surface of water and ripples caused by the wind can make it difficult to see what lies beneath. Sunglasses with polarizing lenses help reduce glare, but better still, a simple underwater viewer will reveal all—especially in bright conditions.

1 Take a plastic ice-cream carton and cut out the bottom with a sharp craft knife.

2 Carefully cover over any sharp edges with strips of waterproof tape, such as duct tape.

3 Tightly roll plastic wrap over the bottom of the carton and fasten it in place with an elastic band.

4 Put the covered end of the viewer just under the water's surface, and peer through the box.

Survival strategies

tough ridged surface

twin shells close tightly

Pools of water at low tide allow marine animals to survive higher up the shore than would otherwise be the case, by protecting them from drying out in the air. But animals on the menu of predators such as starfish must take other defensive measures, including living at the edge of the pool where these predators cannot reach, at least not until the tide comes in.

SHUT TIGHT
Out of the water, mussel shells close to protect the animal inside. However, this behavior is no defense against the stabbing bill of an oystercatcher.

DRAWING IN
The stinging tentacles of anemones open only underwater. At low tide, they are withdrawn into the body, leaving a round, jellylike blob.

red seaweeds attach to rocks or kelp at lower tidal pools

wracks cover rocks at low tide but use gas-filled sacs to float on surface at high tide

limpets withstand crashing waves by clinging firmly to rocks

Tidal pool inhabitants

STARFISH
Feeds on mussels and other bivalves, pulling the shells apart with its multitude of sucker feet.

GOBY
Mottled markings can make it hard to see as it scours deep pools for small invertebrate prey.

PRAWN
With a translucent body, a prawn blends into its background—until it moves.

HERMIT CRAB
Protects itself by squeezing its soft body into an empty seashell.

SEA URCHIN
Although mainly subtidal, may be found in deep, lower-shore pools.

shell covered in spines

crabs shelter, scavenge, and hunt in deep tidal pools

topshells graze algae on the surface of rocks

starfish roam walls and floor in search of prey

anemones are fiercely territorial, stinging neighbors who get too close

TIDAL POOL NICHES
Each part of a tidal pool is home to something. Look around the edges for limpets and barnacles; in deep water for anemones and fish; or among seaweeds for crabs.

LIMPET SCARS

When the tide comes in, limpets glide over rocks, grazing on algae. Unable to tolerate exposure to the air and vulnerable to predation by birds, they return as the tide falls to their home patch. Repeatedly "sticking like a limpet" creates a shallow depression, or scar, on the rock—visible long after the animal has died.

circular depression left by limpet

Look for limpet scars at the edges of tidal pools.

Shorebirds

Wherever you are in the world, some of the greatest concentrations of bird life can be found along shorelines, attracted by abundant food.

Shoreline specialists

Birds gather wherever there is food. The twice-daily tides that wash our shores bring in nutrients that support a rich and diverse food chain. At the top of this food chain are birds. As the tide retreats, waders and gulls throng the shoreline probing beneath the surface for invertebrates. Many waterbirds breed around the coast—sometimes in vast colonies—while others make use of shorelines as part of their annual migrations.

STIFF COMPETITION
To reduce competition for food resources, different bird species vary in their structure and behavior so that each has its unique feeding niche.

Gulls

The generalists of the bird world, gulls feed upon a vast range of foods, from fish to earthworms, and carrion to domestic refuse. Their stout bills and robust digestion allows them to feed opportunistically, which makes many gull species highly adaptable. Hence the fact that the name "seagull" is now quite inappropriate: they are found almost everywhere, from city rooftops—in effect, man-made cliffs—to the open oceans.

gray above and white below, for camouflage against sea and sky

short, often powerful bill

webbed feet

FOOTPRINTS IN THE SAND
Until erased by the tide, soft sand and mud can reveal the passing of birds, in the shape of footprints and pellets, the indigestible remains of meals.

Terns

Built for precision flying, terns feed by hovering, then plunge-diving on their fish prey, caught with the daggerlike bill. Food is carried back to the chicks until they can fly, so breeding colonies are close to rich feeding grounds. When not raising young they stay farther out to sea. The arctic tern has the longest migration of any bird, flying an average of 1.5 million miles (2.4 million km) –equivalent to three round trips to the Moon—in its lifetime.

black cap

long, pointed bill

long wingtips

short legs

IN FLIGHT
A forked tail, long and pointed wings, and an acrobatic flight have given rise to the alternative name for terns of "sea-swallows."

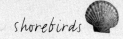

Waders

A combination of long bill and long legs makes waders well adapted to feeding on invertebrates in soft mud. But the whole story is far more complex— different bill lengths and shapes give access to different foods, while longer legs allow feeding in deeper water. Waders congregate mostly outside the breeding season, and especially in high tide roosts when their feeding grounds are unavailable.

IN FOR THE KILL
The oystercatcher's bladelike bill can pry open bivalve mollusks such as cockles and mussels.

largely black feathers above

stout, orange bill

long legs

OYSTERCATCHERS

small black eye

long, pointed bill

strongly barred, brown plumage

CURLEWS

long, stout legs

sleek, slender body

straight bill

SANDPIPERS

large eye

head and breast markings

short bill

PLOVERS

piebald plumage

fine, upcurved bill

very long legs

AVOCETS

HOW WADERS FEED

The length of a wader's bill is a factor in determining its diet. Some use visual clues to find their prey, picking at surface food, turning over stones, or probing siphon holes in the sand. Others rely on touch, often using a regular "sewing-machine" action and specialized muscles that allow them to open the tip of the bill deep in the mud and capture their prey. Watch carefully—often the bird will bring its food to the surface to wash it, giving us the chance to see exactly what it is eating.

FEEDING HOLES

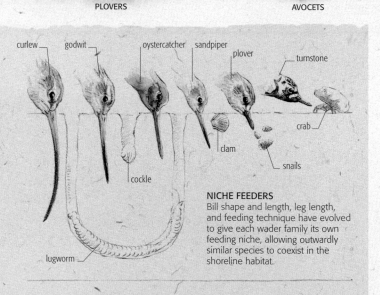

curlew godwit oystercatcher sandpiper plover turnstone

crab

clam

snails

cockle

lugworm

NICHE FEEDERS
Bill shape and length, leg length, and feeding technique have evolved to give each wader family its own feeding niche, allowing outwardly similar species to coexist in the shoreline habitat.

Seal colony

Although they spend a lot of time in the water, all seals need to come ashore to breed, and many gather in colonies.

Seals and sea lions both belong to a group of aquatic, warm-blooded mammals called pinnipeds. Pinnipeds live part of their lives in water and part on land—their flippers and torpedo-shaped bodies make them well suited for diving and moving gracefully in water. The group is split into three families: walrus, eared seals, and true seals. True seals include the harbour (or common) seal, which is widespread in the Northern Hemisphere. In the North Atlantic, harbour seals often form mixed colonies with gray seals, however, the two species have different characteristics. Courtship and mating by harbour seals takes place in the water; they come ashore to rest and to pup. The pups can swim as soon as they are born, so breeding colonies can be on sand banks and flat beaches. In contrast, gray seal colonies are more active and mating takes place on land. Bulls fight to secure the best areas of beach and with them the most females. Their pups cannot swim for the first few weeks of their life, until the first white coat is shed, so they are born on rocky islets or pack ice, above the reach of tides.

VISITING A SEAL COLONY

Seal colonies can often be seen easily from land or sea, but care must be taken when viewing them not to cause disturbance. Pups may become separated from their mothers if a colony is spooked. Each species has a distinct breeding season: harbour seal pups are born during the summer months, while gray seal pups tend to be born in the winter. Timings vary across their geographical ranges however, so do take advice from local experts.

BOAT TRIP
Seal colonies provide the basis for many ecotourism initiatives—approaching by boat allows close viewing with minimal disturbance.

GRAY SEALS
Gray seal pups remain out of the reach of the tide for several weeks after birth, but storm waves may sometimes wash them out to sea.

Beach close-up

Walk along a tideline anywhere in the world and you'll find the remains of coastal and marine fauna and flora, which have washed ashore or drifted from the ocean.

DRIFTWOOD

GOOSE-BARNACLE

SCALLOP SHELL

SPONGE

PEBBLES

Stones are smoothed by the sea—some may contain fossilized remains.

AMMONITE FOSSIL

MERMAID'S PURSE

WINKLE SHELL

shells litter some beaches, many more may lie buried under sand.

LIMPET SHELL

WHELK EGGS

SAND-DOLLAR

MUSSEL SHELL

OYSTER SHELL

RAZOR-SHELL

STARFISH

BROWN SEAWEED

seaweeds are torn from rocks by rough waves despite their strong holdfasts.

SEA BEAN

Partial or whole skeletons and cases of sea animals are washed ashore or dislodged from tidal pools.

RED SEAWEED

GULL FEATHER

CUTTLEFISH SKELETON

GREEN SEAWEED

SEA-URCHIN TEST

CRAB

JELLYFISH

Sandy beach

Sand is a hostile habitat for many plants and animals. All dune inhabitants must have adaptations to cope with difficult conditions.

How a dune forms

Onshore winds pick dry sand from the beach and blow it inland. Out of reach of the tide, sand mounds can be colonized by drought-tolerant plants—their roots help stabilize the surface, while their shoots interrupt the wind flow, leading to further buildup of sand. This process continues until dunes are formed, sometimes more than 325 ft (100 m) high in favorable locations.

SANDY HOME
Mounds of vegetation interspersed with bare sand create microhabitats in which many animals thrive.

Try to avoid trampling the plants that help stabilize the sand.

prickly saltwort

sea rocket

common orache

sea sandwort

sea couchgrass

lyme grass

dune slacks are wind-scoured depressions reaching down to the water table; they are wetland oases, and home to a unique mix of plants and animals

sea spurge

Embryo dune

Low dunes on the seaward fringes are colonized by salt-adapted annual plants, which can complete their life cycles rapidly between the upheavals caused by storms.

PRICKLY SALTWORT

SEA ROCKET

Foredune

A short distance from the tideline, a range of creeping plants can get a roothold. Most of these have fleshy leaves for storing water in hot weather, and waxy leaf coatings or silvery hairs to reflect intense summer sunlight.

SEA SANDWORT

LYME GRASS

TURTLES

Ocean-wandering sea turtles come ashore on sandy beaches in warmer tropical and subtropical areas to bury their eggs in deep holes, which they excavate in low dunes. Incubated by the warmth of the sun, the hatchlings emerge at night in an attempt to reach the relative safety of the sea before dawn brings the risk of predation.

Dune builder

With its almost unlimited ability to grow both horizontally and vertically through depositing sand, marram grass forms the backbone of most large coastal dune systems. To survive drought, it has wax-coated leaves that roll up in dry weather, reducing the loss of water from its breathing holes on the upper surface of its blades.

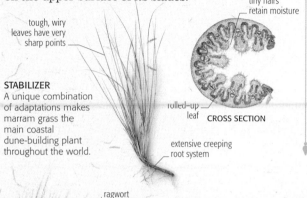

tough, wiry leaves have very sharp points

tiny hairs retain moisture

rolled-up leaf   **CROSS SECTION**

extensive creeping root system

STABILIZER
A unique combination of adaptations makes marram grass the main coastal dune-building plant throughout the world.

Dune dwellers

Unlike plants, animals can move or hide to avoid intense summer droughts. Reptiles, insects, and snails, for example, take refuge in the tussocks of marram grass, where they can take advantage of shade and trapped moisture. Amphibians, such as natterjack and spadefoot toads, bury themselves in moist sand, and sit out the drought until the rains return. Ghost crabs burrow all year round for safety.

DUNE DIGGER
Translucent ghost crabs inhabit deep burrows in sand, emerging at night to forage safe from gulls.

NATTERJACK TOAD

ragwort

marram grass

wild thyme

sand fescue

sea bindweed

Yellow dune

Marram grass adds stability to foredunes, promoting further dune growth. Other largely drought-tolerant plants follow, but yellow dunes still have a high proportion of bare sand. A lack of organic matter creates the sand's color.

RAGWORT

SEA SPURGE

WILD THYME

Gray dune

More mature dunes are stable enough to support a greater diversity of plants. Dead leaves and other organic matter incorporated into the sand give it a grayish colour, which is often enhanced by extensive patches of lichen growth.

SEA HOLLY

211

Coral reef

The largest structures made by living organisms, coral reefs support a vast number of species, yet they are one of Earth's most fragile habitats.

Reef formation

Coral reefs are formed by groups of invertebrates called polyps, which deposit a hard outer skeleton of calcium carbonate as they grow. Corals get some nutrients from the water, but gain as much as 90 percent from algae called zooxanthellae. These live in coral tissues and use photosynthesis to convert sunlight into carbohydrates. This process limits the growth of reefs to areas where sunlight can penetrate the water, mainly in the tropics.

EXPLORING REEFS

Diving or snorkeling over a tropical reef, such as the barrier reefs of Australia and Belize, can feel like flying over a rain forest, with an incredible diversity of life to absorb. Be warned, however—coral heads are remarkably fragile, and any foreign substances or materials that breach the coral's protective mucous membrane can compromise an entire coral head that may have been alive for hundreds of years. Take great care not to handle corals, and certainly never consider removing anything from the reef as a souvenir.

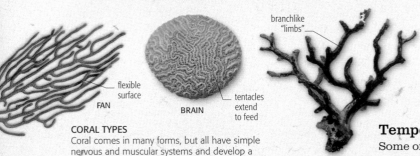

FAN — flexible surface

BRAIN

BRANCHING — branchlike "limbs", tentacles extend to feed

CORAL TYPES
Coral comes in many forms, but all have simple nervous and muscular systems and develop a rigid calcium carbonate skeleton.

Living together

The vast number of species living in close contact on the reef has led to a variety of interesting and useful relationships. Symbiosis is a process where two organisms interact, often over a source of food. Mutualism is a kind of symbiosis where both animals benefit, as in the examples below. In commensalism, one animal benefits while the other is barely affected.

CLEAN SWEEP
Cleaner wrasse pick parasites and damaged scales off larger fish at "cleaning stations." In return, the wrasse can rely on a constant source of food.

FOOD FOR SAFETY
Clownfish gain protection from an anemone's stinging tentacles, and the anemone eats food discarded by the clownfish.

Temperate reefs

Some of the world's most spectacular reefs are actually found in cold, temperate waters, with luridly colored sponges, soft corals, and similar marine creatures anchoring themselves onto rocks and other hard structures. In addition, giant kelp forests provide stunning habitats for marine wildlife. The kelp itself grows as much as 20 inches (half a meter) a day—one of the world's fastest-growing plants.

SLY SWIMMERS
Seahorses inhabit seagrass beds and coral reefs. Slow movers, seahorses swim in an upright position, allowing them to easily hide behind vertical corals and grasses.

curled tail for gripping plants and rocks

UNDERWATER FORESTS
The giant kelp beds of temperate climates resemble sunlit forests. Their dark corners are full of life, and are hunting grounds for seals and otters.

Tropical reef species

PEACOCK MANTIS SHRIMP
Not a true shrimp, the peacock mantis punches its way through marine snail shells that it encounters on the reef.

MIMIC OCTOPUS
This octopus survives by mimicking other species in and around the reef, impersonating their movements and shape.

STARFISH
The crown-of-thorns starfish is a chief coral predator. It throws its stomach onto the coral head to digest the polyps.

TITAN TRIGGERFISH
One of the most territorial reef animals, titans have been known to bite divers, even chasing them back to the boat.

CORAL REEF LIFE
The nooks and crannies are home for thousands of different fish, such as these blue-lined snappers, and offer an infinite hunting ground for those higher up the food chain.

Limestone

Usually pale gray or yellowish in color, limestone is a very variable rock—a result of the variety of ways in which it was formed. Although often hard, leading to erosion structures such as platforms, it is vulnerable to weathering by acid rain. Many types of limestone contain the fossilized remains of animals that inhabited the prehistoric seas when the rocks were formed.

WAVE CUT PLATFORM

LIMESTONE

Cliffs

Wherever rocks meet the sea, cliffs evolve. Their size and slope are dictated by the rock type. Erosion features such as caves, arches, and stacks reflect weaknesses in the rock that are more vulnerable to wave attack.

Chalk

A pure form of limestone, chalk is generally gleaming white and relatively soft. Under attack from the sea, it usually erodes into near-vertical cliffs. Each layer of the rock becomes visible as a ledge, which is often used as a nesting site by seabirds. In a chalk cliff, look for seams of flints. These glassy nodules formed the basis of the earliest human industry —the shaping of stone tools.

WHITE CHALK

NATURAL ARCH

Granite

WHITE GRANITE

Granite was formed by the cooling of molten volcanic rocks beneath the Earth's surface. This extremely hard, crystalline rock contains minerals that give it distinctive colors. Because of its makeup, it erodes very slowly, which is why granite cliffs are often stepped and well-vegetated—usually with few sheer drops and littered with large, rounded boulders.

STACK

Sandstone

A common sedimentary rock in which grains of sand are visible, sandstone ranges in color from pale whitish to red, or even green. Sandstone cliffs often show layers that allow you to track environmental conditions present during deposition. Erosion acting upon these features may create many natural sculptures, including caves.

RED SANDSTONE

SANDSTONE CAVE

Volcanic

VOLCANIC ROCK

Throughout Earth's history, volcanic lava flows have solidified into a range of blackish rock types, commonly including basalt. The crumbly (friable) rocks in places of recent volcanic activity, such as the Canary and Hawaiian islands, form some of the most impressive, barren cliff landscapes in the world. In such places the first stages of colonization by flora and fauna are visible.

BLOW HOLE

Look behind rocks or shrubs for more delicate plants such as maidenhair ferns, which take advantage of the natural shelter.

MAIDENHAIR FERN

SPRING SQUILL

SIX SPOT BURNET MOTH

Cliff view

Carved and molded by wind and salt spray, the plants and animals that inhabit a clifftop can be as dramatic and beautiful as the steep, rocky slopes themselves.

Crashing waves and the cries of seabirds lend an air of wildness to cliffs, where life clings to a precarious existence in the face of often harsh elements. Revel in the grandeur by all means, but don't overlook the small stuff. Take time to look at the windswept summer turf and you'll see that it is studded with an array of beautiful plants and miniature flowers, which in turn host an array of insect life.

Look out for a frothy mass of plant sap—or "cuckoo-spit"—on cliff plants and you'll find froghopper nymphs inside. They secrete the sticky stuff to hide in for protection.

ROCK SAMPHIRE

CUCKOO-SPIT ON PLANT IN BUD

Holes in leaves are a sign of plant-loving insects. Turn over the leaves to find butterfly and moth caterpillars.

WILD CABBAGE LEAVES

HOTTENTOT FIG

Bees and wasps visit nectar-rich cliff flowers in the summer. Look for their nesting burrows in sun-warmed patches of bare soil.

SEA MAYWEED

BURROWING WASP

Cliff colony

Sea cliffs, especially in northern temperate and Arctic regions, are often home to large colonies of seabirds. Here, their nests are relatively safe from predators.

nest of mud and seaweed

adult kittiwake incubating its eggs

STICKY NESTS
Seaweed, mud, and droppings (guano) create a nesting platform for gulls, such as kittiwakes.

Living on the edge

Cliffs provide an excellent location for seeing a large number of different seabirds in summer. They provide a wide range of niches for seabirds to use as breeding sites, from the very top to just above tide level. Different species prefer different places, but all share one common requirement: the need to be close to the sea, the source of much—if not all—of their food.

POINTED EGGS
Ledge-nesting birds, such as murres, have pointed eggs that roll in circles—not off the ledge.

pointed tip

GANNET COLONY
Gannets live in large colonies. The safest spots are in the center; younger birds nest at the edges where gulls take eggs and chicks.

Sea watching

Cliff tops provide an excellent vantage point for scanning the ocean for birds and marine mammals, such as porpoises. Watching the sea takes patience— for much of the time there may be little to see. Make sure you have a sheltered place to wait, warm clothing, and good binoculars. The rewards will come when you spot something, perhaps a frenzy of gannets diving on a school of fish or a pod of whales passing by.

COASTAL VISITORS
Promontories such as cliffs give you the chance to watch dolphins as they pass close to shore.

Watch birds from a boat to avoid disturbing them.

BIRDWATCHING
Viewing cliff birds requires great care. Make sure you remain behind any safety fences or, better still, take a boat trip to view the spectacle from below.

What nests where

SKUAS
Skuas nest on the ground on cliff tops, close to other birds from which they steal food and often their chicks.

KEEPING COUNT

Monitoring seabird colonies helps measure the health of the marine environment. Recent declines in many areas have raised issues of overfishing, pollution, and climate change. Accurate counts are tricky, especially when some birds are away fishing. Photographs can be used to record changes over time.

PUFFINS
Although their numbers are in decline in places, puffins are easy to spot, with their unusual beaks. They dig burrows in soil on upper slopes and cliff tops.

MURRES
Lining the ledges, in close-knit ranks, murres and razorbills are among the most numerous of all the cliff-nesting seabirds.

CORMORANTS
The large, untidy nests of cormorants are usually found in caves or crevices near the foot of a cliff, just above the waves. The droppings show their location.

Cliff close-up

The wildlife found on cliffs varies depending on location and the geological makeup of the habitat. Most cliffs will have low, matted plantlife, while sandy cliffs facing the sun are rich in insects.

SEA BEET

Clifftop flowers often grow in mats to reduce exposure to high winds.

STONECROP

ROSEROOT

TREE MALLOW

BUCK'S HORN PLANTAIN

ROCK SEA LAVENDER

COMMON BLUE
BUTTERFLY

PROVENCE
BURNET MOTH

RED
ANT

Insects and snails feed
on plants and some
make their homes in
the loose soil.

LICHEN-COVERED
ROCKS

KIDNEY
VETCH

Lichen thrives on
rock faces exposed
to sunlight and
sea spray.

BANDED
SNAIL

CLADONIA
LICHEN

Rocks can reveal
the remains of
sea life that
lived thousands
of years ago.

CARLINE
THISTLE

COLT'S
FOOT

FOSSILS IN
LIMESTONE

BIRD'S FOOT
TREFOIL

AMMONITE
FOSSILS

THRIFT

Estuary

Where a river meets the sea, the resulting estuary becomes a fluctuating mix of fresh- and saltwater. Interlaced with a range of other wetland types, such as salt marshes and mudflats, this mosaic of shallow, open water channels can harbor underwater sea-grass meadows—food for waterbirds and vital habitats for creatures such as sea horses and other fish.

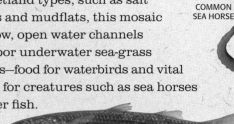

COMMON SEA HORSE

EEL GRASS

GRAY MULLET

Coastal wetlands

On low-lying coastlines, the boundary between land and sea is blurred by the presence of coastal wetlands. Influenced by salt water and tidal movements, they make up some of the richest wildlife habitats in the world.

Salt marsh

Where a mudflat surface is exposed for a sufficient part of the tidal cycle, salt-tolerant plants take hold to form salt marshes, providing swathes of color as they bloom during the summer months. Due to their deep tidal creeks, they aren't easily accessible to people, which adds to their attraction to birds, such as gulls, and other wildlife species.

BLACK-HEADED GULL

SEA PURSLANE

SEA LAVENDER

Mudflat

Extensive mudflats, washed by every tide, are at the heart of many coastal wetlands, and are home to a vast range of invertebrates, including mollusks such as cockles and clams. These in turn attract wading birds such as sandpipers when the tide is out, as well as fish when the tide floods in. Largely featureless, apart from shallow creeks and pools, mudflats play host to some remarkable concentrations of species on a global scale.

CURLEW SANDPIPER

COCKLE SHELL

Mangroves

The tropical counterpart of salt marshes, mangroves are found in sheltered, muddy tidal waters. These swamps are formed when salt-tolerant trees gain a roothold. Many fish and crustaceans such as crabs rely on the shelter of their root systems and the upper branches provide feeding and breeding sites for water birds, reptiles, and other animals, protected by a natural moat.

FIDDLER CRAB

MANGROVE SNAKE

Tidal marshes

Washed by the highest tides, salt marshes are dynamic habitats of low-lying coastlines, abounding in specialized plants and animals.

Salt-marsh strategies

Protecting the land by absorbing the energy of the sea like a sponge, salt marshes are nature's own sea defenses. All the plants that make up these marshes must be able to thrive in salty water. Many have desalination cells, which strip salt from the water, leaving freshwater for the plant's use. Other adaptations in these plants include some way to get rid of excess salt—you can see the crystals of excreted salt on their leaves—and succulent tissues in which to store available freshwater.

MARSHLAND SAFETY

Deep creeks and pools, soft mud, and the relentless tides, can make exploring a salt marsh treacherous. Luckily, salt marshes are flat, so much of their fascinating wildlife can be viewed from the safety of nearby higher ground— binoculars are essential.

STAND TOGETHER
Local knowledge is invaluable. Walking with a guide is the safest way to explore marshes.

STRIPED BASS
Salt marshes support spawning and nursery areas for many fish species like bass, which move in at high tide.

Submergence marsh

Each tide brings in a fresh supply of silt. As this silt is deposited, the mud surface rises, and eventually plants begin to germinate and colonize. The lower submergence marshes are washed by every tide, but plants like cord grass and sea aster have air spaces in their tissues that allow them to survive the time they spend underwater. Animals here include fish and crabs, which take advantage of the rich food supplies.

BLUE CRAB
Marine creatures such as crabs remain in the marsh at low tide, taking refuge in pools or burying themselves in the mud.

Emergence marsh

Midlevel marshes are covered by the higher tides of the monthly cycle (see pp.198–99), so salt is a an ever-present challenge, which is why salt marshes are rarely as diverse as their freshwater counterparts. But many salt-marsh plants have attractive summer flowers, such as the vibrant, purple sea lavender, and these in turn attract insects.

GROUND BEETLE
Some insects such as beetles can live in leaf litter on the marsh surface.

Salt-marsh birds

Regular soaking by the tides prevents birds from breeding on all but the highest-level marshes. Above the reach of summer tides, however, waders and gulls nest, sometimes in large colonies. In winter, many species of birds use all areas of the salt marsh—which makes it a great place to view them from a safe distance in a hide. Waders roost on the high marshes, safe from ground predators, and feed in the muddy creeks; ducks and geese graze at all states of the tide; and large flocks of finches and buntings make use of the abundant supply of seeds produced by the salt-marsh plants.

MARSH DABBLER
Many ducks, such as this teal, head for salt marshes in winter, where they graze and dabble for the nutritious, oil-rich seeds.

WETLAND FISHER
Even at the lowest tide, the network of creeks and pools in a salt marsh provide very rich pickings for birds like herons and egrets, such as this great egret, which feed on crustaceans and fish.

ARROW GRASS
The fleshy leaves of sea arrow grass can be distinguished from true grasses by their sweet, aromatic scent when crushed.

Upper marsh

Above the level of all but the highest tides, the upper marshes are often dominated by low shrubs, typically members of the spinach family. Infrequent tides followed by evaporation in sunlight can produce extremely high salt concentrations, however, so most plants have fleshy leaves that can store rainwater and help buffer the effects of salt at their roots. Insects such as crickets are common here.

MARSH MALLOW
At home in salt- or freshwater, the mallow can be found in damp marshes and tidal river banks.

BUSH CRICKET
Safe from the risk of frequent flooding, a wide range of insects can be found in the upper marsh zone. Some, like the bush cricket, are almost invisible in the green foliage.

Mudflats

Found in sheltered areas, such as estuaries, mudflats are made up of very fine particles of material deposited by the sea and river water.

MUDDY MOSAIC
Estuarine mudflats form an intricate mosaic with water channels and salt marsh.

How mudflats form

As soon as the fine particles, or silt (see p.200), settle out, plants begin to colonize it. Firstly, microscopic algae called diatoms start to grow on the surface, helping to "glue" the silting together and make it more stable. The seeds of salt-tolerant plants, carried by the tides, can then germinate—their roots give even more stability to the mud and their shoots help to slow down water movement, which means that even more silt is deposited when the sea washes over it.

LIFE IN SALTWATER
Glasswort has a range of adaptations for life in saltwater, including fleshy, cylindrical stems for storing freshwater.

What to spot

At first glance, mudflats may seem bleak and devoid of life, but take a closer look and you will notice an abundance of marine creatures and plants. This rich habitat is reliant on twice-daily tides that supply the mudflats with food as well as fresh silt. Even when the wildlife is not visible, it is often possible to see evidence of their activities, such as worm casts and feeding tracks. If you decide to visit a mudflat, keep an eye on the sea and be careful not to get cut off by the rising tide (see pp.198–99).

1 Gulls and other water birds that feed on the flats leave their tracks in soft mud.

2 A gull's pellet is the indigestible remains of its last meal—handle with care and be sure to wash your hands after touching it.

3 Cockles and other filter-feeding shellfish form dense beds on the surface or in the top layer of mud.

4 In shallow water, fan-worms extend a crown of feathery feeding tentacles from their rubbery mud tubes.

5 The shells of mussels are attached by strong threads to stones and other hard structures that are buried in the mudflats.

6 Dog-whelks leave feeding tracks as they move over the surface, feeding on dead organic material.

7 Algal mats provide food for grazing wildfowl and snails.

8 Mud-snails are tiny but numerous and provide miniature morsels of food for throngs of wading birds.

9 A shallow depression marks the inhalent end of a lugworm's u-shaped tube, through which it draws water and food.

10 Lugworms feed on organic matter within mud and sand, excreting the indigestible remnants as worm casts.

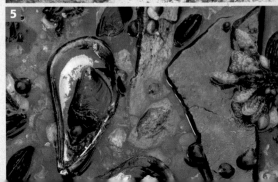

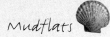

What lies beneath

To get a true picture of mudflat life, you cannot just look at the surface. Buried in the mud, sometimes at considerable depth, is a range of burrowing and tube-dwelling invertebrates. Some filter food from the sediment, while others prey on the animals around them. They stay in their burrows, where they are protected from drying out when the tide recedes, and only show themselves at the surface of the mud when it is covered with water. At high tide, they are preyed upon by fish, but at low tide wading birds take their toll. The length of wading bird bills determines the range of prey available to them (see pp.204–05).

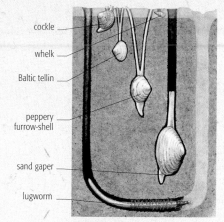

cockle
whelk
Baltic tellin
peppery furrow-shell
sand gaper
lugworm

BURROWERS
Each type of burrowing animal lives at a particular depth within the mud.

PEACOCK WORM

RAGWORM

BOOTLACE WORM

BURROWING MUDSHRIMP

MUDDY DWELLERS
Whether pushing through the mud or inhabiting a tube, the hidden riches of a mudflat add three-dimensional complexity to a hugely diverse ecosystem, as productive as any other habitat on Earth.

SIEVING FOR LIFE

To fully appreciate the richness of mudflat life, you need to get your hands dirty. Dig up a small sample of mud with a trowel and put it through a series of strainers, starting with the largest mesh. This will retain the larger shells and lugworms, while a finer mesh will hold back mud-snails and smaller worms. Even mud that has passed through both strainers will still have life in it, including larvae and nematodes that are only visible through a microscope.

CLEAN SWEEP
A garden riddle, strainer, and brushes are the basic tools to tease apart any specimens.

Mangroves

Mangrove swamps are dominated by a range of salt-tolerant trees that grow in relatively sheltered estuarine conditions.

Trees from several families have adapted to living with their roots in salty water. Although not closely related, these species are all called mangroves. Each displays one or more of a set of adaptations, including breathing tubes in the roots, impermeable root surfaces to limit salt uptake, and the ability to excrete excess salt through their leaves. These adaptations have enabled mangroves to flourish in places where few other plants could survive. Mangroves play host to a vast range of wildlife, both above and below the water. Depending on the region—mangroves are found in the Indian, Atlantic, and Pacific oceans— scarlet ibises, proboscis monkeys, and mangrove snakes may be found breeding or feeding above the water line, while the underwater zone harbors numerous crabs, oysters, and other crustaceans and mollusks, often important as a food resource for local communities. The sheltered water among mangrove root systems also makes them important nursery areas for many types of fish and other animals that spend their adult lives out at sea.

FRAGILE HABITAT

Despite their extensive root systems, mangroves are vulnerable both to human influences—pollution, shrimp farming, and coastal development—and to natural erosion by the force of the sea. However, where they do survive, their ability to absorb wave energy plays a vital role in protecting coastal settlements from storm waves and tsunamis. Board walks and boats are the safest way to visit mangroves without harming them.

MANATEE
Large, slow moving, aquatic herbivores, manatees are found in mangrove swamps in the Atlantic. The closely related dugong inhabits coasts from East Africa, through southeast Asia, to Australasia.

SALTWATER CROCODILE
The saltwater crocodile is the world's largest living reptile and is found in coastal habitats from India to Australia. Juveniles feed largely on fish and are major predators in mangrove swamps.

All at sea

Most of the oceans' depths have never been explored, but you can watch many species from the surface of Earth's last great wilderness.

Exploring the big blue

Over 70 percent of the world's surface is covered by seas and oceans, which have an average depth of over 2 miles (3 km). Most ocean depths are beyond the reach of all but the most specialized submarine, but you can explore coastal seas—both above and below the waves—with relative ease. Many types of animal life are within easy reach of the seashore, and taking a boat trip can provide an insight into the lives of seabirds, seals, whales and dolphins, and other mammals such as sea lions and sea otters. Under water, diving or snorkeling can bring you into contact with another experience—ocean wildlife—and give you a totally different, more intimate encounter with many types of marine animals.

SWIM WITH DOLPHINS
Dolphins are naturally inquisitive and highly intelligent mammals, and may approach visitors in their environment.

BOAT WITH A VIEW
Take a ride in a glass-bottomed boat in areas with clear seas, and you can get a close-up view of sea life.

IDENTIFYING FINS AND TAILS

The shape and marks on the dorsal fins of cetaceans allow scientists to recognize individual animals. The challenge is to identify species by fin profile as they surface to breathe. The very tall, curved dorsal fin of a killer whale is unmistakable, as is the curved back of a humpback and its tail silhouette before a dive. Porpoise sightings, however, are more fleeting; look for a straight, leading edge to their dorsals instead of the curve of a dolphin's. Narwhals lack a dorsal fin, but their tails have a distinct notch in the middle.

ORCA (KILLER WHALE)

HECTOR'S DOLPHIN

HUMPBACK WHALE

NARWHAL

WHALE-WATCHING
An encounter with any type of whale is unforgettable. In this orca pod, you can see the huge dorsal of an adult male.

Taking the bait

Many marine animals rely on speed to escape predators, but small fish such as anchovies or sardines gather in schools for protection. Large schools can also form at an upwelling, where smaller fish gather to feed on plankton. Just like large flocks of birds, a school of fish can move as one, whirling and changing direction so rapidly that it is difficult for a predator to pick off any one fish. However, when many predators come together, the odds change, and a wildlife spectacle unfolds as the school changes from a safe haven into a "bait ball." In this situation, attackers strike from all sides; the fish are driven toward the surface by dolphins, whales, or sharks, where they are picked off by waiting seabirds, such as gannets.

DIVING GANNETS
Plummeting from a great height, gannets can penetrate deep into the water to spear their prey.

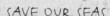

BAIT BALL
Clumps of fish such as sardines attract predators from above and below—sharks, tuna, whales, and diving birds.

STRANGER TO THE GROUND
Most albatross species spend almost their entire lives at sea. The wandering albatross has the largest wingspan—nearly 11½ ft (3.5 m).

SAVE OUR SEAS

Modern fishing methods, climate change, and pollution are stripping oceans of life and upsetting their natural balance. We can take practical steps to lessen our impact on the oceans by keeping beaches clean, supporting marine sanctuaries, and safely disposing of harmful pollution.

POISONOUS OIL
Oil spills destroy the waterproofing on seabird feathers and the fur of seals and otters, then poisons them as they preen or clean themselves. It also affects the entire food chain.

DANGEROUS GARBAGE
Any garbage in the sea is gathered by currents. The North Pacific gyre, about twice the size of Texas, contains millions of tons of plastic—toxic to marine life.

Tundra and ice

Freezing temperatures present life with problems. Combine these with high altitudes, extreme weather, or long periods without sunlight, and you have one of the most challenging environments on Earth. Yet if there are resources available, no matter how sparse or apparently remote, life will reach for them and adapt to take advantage of them. The barriers of glacial cold, unremitting darkness, or thin air have been breached by a guild of specialists that thrive where we would shiver to a fatal standstill. And of course, the fate of these remarkable communities is now under serious scrutiny as these fragile habitats succumb to climate change.

The Arctic tundra

The treeless Arctic tundra is a great place to see wildlife such as elk, musk ox, and polar bears, from the comfort of a guided tour.

What is the tundra?

The Arctic tundra is a vast landscape north of the tree line (see pp.160–61), extending through Canada, Alaska, Siberia, and Scandinavia. It is a habitat shaped by extreme cold. For much of the year, it is snow-covered, dark, and windy. Soil in this region is almost perpetually frozen and is called permafrost. This limits the growth of roots, so the only plants that survive there are small shrubs, mosses, and lichens. In summer the upper permafrost melts, transforming the tundra into a marshy bog that supports a host of wildlife.

SOLID GROUND
Permafrost is soil that remains below the freezing point of water. Plant life blooms in summer when its upper layer thaws.

What you might encounter

Since few animals can tolerate its harsh, cold conditions, the tundra is a place of low biodiversity. However, you may see caribou (also called reindeer) and musk ox grazing on small plants and lichen. Predators include Arctic foxes and wolverines, and smaller animals include Arctic hares and lemmings.

ICE SURVIVOR
Lemmings survive the cold by burrowing underground. They migrate when their numbers swell, but many drown in rivers and lakes.

SUMMER VISITOR
The polar bear isn't just a creature of the ice. In summer they move into the Arctic tundra, where in North America they may be seen on a wildlife tour.

THREATS TO THE TUNDRA

Tundra all over the world is under threat. Mining and drilling for oil, and the 800-mile (1,288-km) long Alaska pipeline, directly impacts the environment, but the most severe threat is global warming. Polar temperatures are rising faster than average. This melts permafrost and releases greenhouse gases such as carbon and methane, which could have damaging results for the planet as a whole.

THE ALASKA PIPELINE

CARIBOU OR REINDEER?
Caribou and reindeer are two names for the same species. In winter they migrate to graze in forested areas, feeding on lichens and grasses.

What to see in the summer

Winters are cold, windy, and harsh, but visit the tundra in summer and you'll see a transformed landscape. Long days of almost 24-hour sunlight warm the topsoil, melting the surface layers and turning the environment into a lush, boggy marshland where many plant species can grow. Summer is a good time to see animals that migrate to this region; they do so to avoid predators as well as to feed on abundant insects and fish. Caribou are just some of the migrants, roaming many hundreds of miles to graze on the summer plant life. You can also see bird species such as snow geese, which gather in massive flocks, raising their chicks in the marshlands.

FLOCKS RETURN
Snow geese arrive in the tundra in summer, ready to lay eggs and raise their young. They feed on tundra vegetation in such large flocks that they are depleting the habitat used by many other species.

SUN FOLLOWER
The Arctic poppy is a miniature version of its relative in temperate regions. Its tiny flowers turn their heads to follow the Sun.

SILENT HUNTER
Snowy owls prey on small animals such as lemmings. With no trees available in the tundra, the owl makes its nests on the ground.

Even the snowy owl's huge talons are feathered to help it cope with the cold.

WATCH OUT FOR MOSQUITOES

We may think of mosquitoes as tropical insects, but the summer tundra teems with them. Because tundra is flat with frozen permafrost below, meltwater from the surface has nowhere to go. Stagnant puddles are warmed by 24-hour sunlight, making them ideal for mosquito larvae. This is good news for waterfowl, which feed on the larvae, but less good for caribou, and human visitors, who are plagued by the blood-sucking insects. Take your insect repellent!

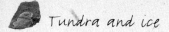

Arctic fox

In the tundra the change between seasons is extreme and the animals that live there must adapt to survive.

The Arctic fox lives in some of the coldest parts of the planet. The fox stores heat within its body by exposing little of its surface to the cold, with stout legs, a short muzzle, and small rounded ears. Its chief adaptation for dealing with the cold in the icy Arctic winters is its fur. The Arctic fox is the only member of the dog family to change the color of its coat with the seasons. In spring, the fox is tawny brown but as winter comes, thick white hair grows through. The hairs of its winter coat are almost double the length of those of its coat in summer, and the thick, deep fur provides warmth. Every part of the animal's body is covered in fur—even the pads on the soles of its feet, helping it walk on ice. The reason for the fox's color change is to blend in with the white of the environment. This allows it to sneak up on its prey and avoid larger predators. The Arctic fox preys on small rodents, such as lemmings. It has such sharp hearing that it can hear them rustling and pounces on them through the snow.

SEASONAL FUR

Both hunter and hunted employ similar strategies to avoid detection. Arctic foxes prey on Arctic hares, although their large size makes them intimidating game. By blending in with its surroundings the fox can use stealth to approach its quarry. The hare's white color helps it avoid its predators, which also include Arctic wolves and snowy owls.

CAMOUFLAGE COLORS
The Arctic hare in winter (left) and summer (right). In winter its white coat usually blends with snow to avoid the eyes of predators.

HIDE AND SEEK
In winter the thick coat of the Arctic fox turns white, blending with the snow and ice. This camouflage helps it sneak up on rodents, birds, and occasionally ringed seal pups.

Life on the ice

The Arctic and Antarctic are among Earth's last wildernesses. Although these areas are changing fast, wildlife thrives there.

Visiting the ice

Visiting a polar region can be the most exciting trip you'll ever make, yet due to the sensitive nature of these fragile environments, tourists must respect them. Antarctica can only be visited by ship from November to March. Many Arctic destinations, such as the Norwegian island of Spitzbergen, are also best seen from the water; ideally between May and September. Remember that these are remote, pristine, and extreme locations. Listen to your guide, respect the animals and the ice, and you can have some of the most memorable wildlife encounters of your life.

DISTANCE FLYER
Arctic terns winter in Antarctica, but breed in the Arctic, so may travel up to 25,000 miles (40,000 km) a year.

What you will see

Habitats are similar at the poles, but the wildlife in each area is different. On an Antarctic cruise, several penguin species are the main attraction. Penguins are curious and largely unafraid of humans, so you can spot them on sea ice and rocks all around the continent. In the Arctic, expect to see whales, walruses, and polar bears. While the latter are top predators with little fear of man, cautious encounters from a safe distance can be magical.

What to pack
1. Binoculars, for spotting birds and whales.
2. Sunscreen to protect your skin—the ozone layer is thin at the poles.
3. Sunglasses to cut glare reflected from the ice.
4. Camera to record what you see.
5. Warm clothing, especially for hands and feet.

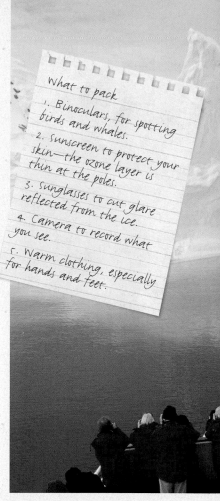

POLAR CRUISE
Most polar trips include a cruise to see the beautiful and ever-changing natural sculptures carved by the ocean from floating ice.

LIFE UNDER THE ICE

At both poles, the foundation of the food chain is made up of tiny crustaceans called krill, which feed on algae growing under the ice. In Antarctica alone, an estimated 500 million tons of krill provide food for penguins, seals, and whales.

KRILL

1 The world's largest penguin, the emperor, is the only penguin to winter in Antarctica. Adults come onto the ice to raise gray, fluffy chicks.

2 Masters of the sub-Antarctic islands, elephant seals are true giants, and viciously defend their harems of females from other males. You can spot them on rocks and sea ice from your boat.

3 Belugas are one of the so-called Arctic "ice whales." They travel long distances beneath the ice, using holes and cracks to surface and breathe.

EARTH'S VITAL ICE

Climate change is drastically affecting polar regions, which must be conserved for all species—not just those that live there. Average Arctic temperatures have risen at twice the rate of those elsewhere, while the Antarctic Peninsula has risen to five times the average. This has profound implications for the planet. An increase in the Earth's temperature causes icebergs to melt, raising sea levels. The Greenland ice sheet is the area scientists consider most at risk: if it melts, sea levels could rise by up to 23 ft (7 m), bringing flooding to many coastal areas.

The wandering albatross has the largest wingspan of any bird, reaching 11 1/2 ft (3.5 m). This enables it to travel great distances.

Ice structures

"Ice" describes a range of different forms of frozen water, as varied in shape and size as snow, icicles, glaciers, pack ice, icebergs, ice caps, and ice sheets. The Antarctic ice sheet is the largest single mass of frozen water on Earth and contains about 61 percent of the planet's fresh water. Glaciers—giant, slow-moving masses—often end in the sea, where they may "calve" icebergs. Ice attached to land is called "fast ice" while drift ice is free-flowing; a good example of the latter is the Arctic ice pack, formed when the surface of the sea freezes.

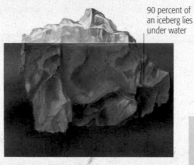

90 percent of an iceberg lies under water

HOW ICEBERGS FLOAT
Ice floats because it is less dense than water, thanks to open spaces formed between the hydrogen molecules when water is frozen.

MELTING ICE
Pack ice (above, right) refers to a body of drifting ice, which is carried along by wind and surface currents. Icebergs (below) are carved by the sea and sun into various organic shapes and sizes.

Desert

For the human species, this hostile, parched habitat has proved a challenge simply due to the inaccessibility of water and, despite modern technologies, deserts remain sparsely populated. However, time has allowed other animal and plant species to evolve adaptations not only to survive, but also to prosper in the searing heat, bitter cold, and months or years without renewed moisture. Although there isn't normally a huge diversity of these desert specialists, and many never flourish in massive numbers, the forms and behaviors that allow them to function here, such as the nocturnal habits of desert spiny mice, are fascinating— and from our envious perspective, admirable.

Sand dunes

Vast seas of sand, sculpted by winds into dunes over 1,000 ft (304 m) high, characterize the deserts of Africa, Australia, and the Arabian peninsula. Creatures such as sidewinding snakes have adapted ways of moving easily over the sand of this shifting habitat. Plants here are largely restricted to grasses, while birds include scavengers such as ravens.

SPINIFEX GRASS

SIDEWINDER

WHITE-NECKED RAVEN

Deserts

From hot deserts like the Sahara to the cold uplands of the Gobi, deserts cover almost a fifth of the world's land surface. Defined by their aridity, deserts contain many different habitats and highly specialized wildlife.

High, arid plateau

High-altitude cold deserts have some of the most extreme conditions anywhere. Mammals such as yaks and bactrian camels must be able to withstand the bitter winter temperatures and frequent snow, while vegetation is sparse and highly seasonal. Predators such as eagles soar overhead, looking for weakened prey.

GOLDEN EAGLE

YAKS

Seasonal lakes and salt pans

Water is always scarce in the desert, but heavy rainfall often forms temporary lakes. These can spread over huge areas, providing a lifeline for amphibians, visiting birds, and other animals. Salt pans are more permanent, and are often home to specialized feeders like flamingos, which rely on the brine shrimps that thrive there.

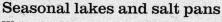

BRINE SHRIMP

CHILEAN FLAMINGO

Gravel and stony plains

Expanses of gravel, stones, and sand—one of the most inhospitable desert habitats—are often prehistoric seabeds. With little or no shade, creatures such as scorpions seek shelter under rocks, while birds like the sandgrouse search for food in the open. In spring, however, these seemingly lifeless plains can burst into a blaze of color as annual flowers bloom after winter rains.

DESERT SCORPION

Bajada

The bajada occurs where open plains abut mountains, and is made up mainly of slopes of rocky debris. Water often gathers here, which allows many cacti and other plants to flourish. This diverse habitat supports a range of wildlife, from reptiles such as rattlesnakes and gila monsters to specialized birds like the gilded flicker. Mammals include ground squirrels, which must outwit predators like foxes and bobcats.

GILA MONSTER

BOBCAT

Day and night in the desert

Some creatures have ways of coping with searing daytime desert heat, while a host of others are only active when the temperature drops at night.

Daytime action

Although the heat of the day can be very intense, desert animals and birds are well adapted to cope with it. Many species of reptile rely on the morning sun to raise their body temperature to the required level for them to become active. They then hide in crevices and under stones when they become too hot. Most birds and larger mammals often start looking for food before dawn. They then seek shade and rest when the heat becomes excessive, only emerging again to forage toward the end of the day.

POLLINATING AROUND THE CLOCK

Desert plants rely on a variety of pollinating agents, including bees, butterflies, moths, birds, and even small mammals and reptiles. Drawn to the plants' nectar, they unwittingly transfer the pollen to their next destination. Some plants only bloom when certain specialized pollinators are visiting the desert.

DURING THE DAY
Hummingbirds move through deserts, such as the Sonoran Desert, on migration and can visit up to several hundred flowers in a day.

AT NIGHT
Bats are important pollinators of cacti and other desert plants, some of which bloom specifically at night for this reason.

THE DESERT BY DAY
Daytime temperatures can soar up to 120 °F (50 °C). Animals such as meerkats seek shelter in the shade.

EARLY IN THE MORNING
Tortoises and other reptiles emerge and warm up in the sun, before starting to look for food.

BOILING AT NOON
With ground temperatures soaring, shovel-snouted lizards lift their limbs off the hot sand to keep cool.

COOLER AFTERNOON
As the heat eases, birds of prey like this lanner falcon become more active and start scouting for small mammals and reptiles.

TOWARD EVENING
The hour before dusk is a good time to watch herbivores, such as gazelles, gathering to drink.

As darkness falls...

Night falls swiftly in the desert and the temperature can drop dramatically. As the last rays of the sun sink below the horizon there is a changing of the guard for wildlife. Almost all desert birds roost as high up as they can, while most large mammals, such as oryx, also settle down for the night. They are replaced by an army of small rodents that emerge from their burrows to forage for seeds, fruit, and invertebrates. Creatures such as scorpions come out from rock crevices and under stones, and the hours of darkness also provide perfect cover for predators, such as sand cats and foxes.

NIGHT VISION

Watching wildlife at night is not always easy—you should always take great care and, where possible, use a professional guide. A night vision device lets you see wildlife in the dark, but even if you explore just by the light of the moon, you will be amazed at how much there is to see. Look out for signs of movement, walk slowly, and keep your attention on the ground. Also remember to look up in trees and tall cacti, which is where birds, such as owls, sit and scan for prey.

NIGHT VISION DEVICE

ULTRAVIOLET LIGHT
Special optics, such as ultraviolet light, make it easier to see some nocturnal creatures.

DESERT NIGHT
Many desert animals take advantage of the cooler temperatures, and become active at nightfall.

Look for birds, gathering at dusk to roost on cacti.

see a prowling fox hunting at dusk.

NIGHT BLOOMER
The queen of the night cactus unfolds its petals at dusk, but they are closed again by mid-morning the next day.

THE COVER OF DARKNESS
Desert hedgehogs are night foragers that use their sharp sense of smell to hunt insects and small reptiles.

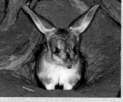

KEEPING WATCH
Some nocturnal rodents, like this greater bilby, have large ears to help detect danger in the dark.

NIGHT CRAWLERS
Tarantulas hunt largely at night and spend the day in burrows lined with their own silk.

Tarantulas eat insects and small lizards.

245

Living in the desert

Deserts are one of the harshest environments on the planet; yet a surprising diversity of plants and animals live here, all specially equipped for the difficult conditions.

Coping with extremes

Epic temperatures and a scarcity of water are the two main factors affecting wildlife in the desert—they also make it a hostile place to explore. A key requirement is the ability to obtain and retain moisture, as well as reduce the impact of the sun and other dehydrating factors, such as wind. Desert animals and birds do this in a variety of ways, including deriving almost all their moisture from their food, thereby reducing the need to drink. Low metabolic rates help them conserve energy, while pale-colored coats and plumage reflect the sun and heat.

WATER STORERS
Water-holding frogs and toads survive the heat by burying themselves temporarily.

UNDER THREAT

Most desert environments are highly vulnerable to human activity. The "greening" of the desert, when irrigation is used to convert arid areas to farmland, can ruin habitats. Equally destructive are activities such as mining and road building, while overgrazing by domestic livestock can cause environmental damage.

DUNE BASHING
Pleasure-seekers driving off-road vehicles over sand dunes can cause lasting damage and disturbance to wildlife.

RODENTS
Small mammals, such as hopping mice, usually emerge from their burrows at dusk to escape the daytime heat.

SNAKES AND LIZARDS
Desert reptiles include Australia's thorny devil, which drinks dew collected on its back from grooves leading to its mouth.

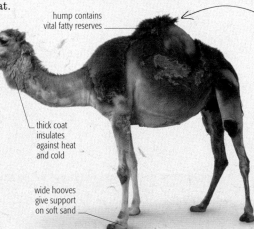

nostrils can close against blowing sand

hump contains vital fatty reserves

A camel's hump shrinks if it doesn't eat.

thick coat insulates against heat and cold

wide hooves give support on soft sand

SHIP OF THE DESERT
Widely domesticated across North Africa and the Middle East, camels were introduced to Australia in the 1800s and now live wild in the outback.

RATTLESNAKES IN RESIDENCE
During cooler winter weather, reptiles such as rattlesnakes and gila monsters move to communal shelters (hibernacula), usually on south-facing slopes, to hibernate.

gila monster

rattlesnake

The desert winter

All deserts are dry, but not all are necessarily hot. In some deserts temperatures can drop well below freezing in winter, especially at high altitudes, and they can remain low for months. Biting winds intensify the cold, making winter deserts very inhospitable. During such periods, wildlife is forced to hunker down and wait for better conditions in spring. Some species survive by becoming dormant or hibernating, while others migrate and only return when the weather warms up.

A COLD BLAST
Even in hot deserts, such as the Sonoran Desert in Mexico and southwestern USA, snow can fall in midwinter, but frost is usually more damaging to plants.

Drought busters

Desert plants have evolved various strategies to cope with the lack of moisture. Many become dormant during very dry spells, springing back into life when rain falls. Their life cycle is often very short, enabling them to take advantage of short-lived times of plenty. Desert plant leaves usually have a small surface area, which helps reduce evaporation rates. In the case of cacti, the leaves are reduced to spines.

TOUGH SHRUB
The creosote bush has waxy, resinous leaves to reduce water loss, and long roots that penetrate deep into the soil.

MOISTURE FROM THIN AIR
African welwitschias extract moisture from mist and dew via special pores (stomata) in their leaves. They can live for more than 2,000 years.

waxy skin with spines growing from it

water storage tissue

water-conducting tissue

DESERT SCULPTURES
The American saguaro cactus can grow up to 50 ft (15¼ m) tall. The main trunk expands and contracts according to how much water is retained.

INSIDE VIEW
Cacti store water within a spiny body that protects against the effects of the sun and browsing animals.

shallow roots soak up water from rainfall

Spotting desert dwellers

Though deserts may seem barren, you can find signs of life everywhere—if you know where to look. Remember to take care to stay safe in this challenging environment.

Social water holes and saltpans

Water is a scarce resource in the desert. Although most desert animals can cope for long periods without drinking, very few species will turn down an opportunity to do so when water is available. Dawn and dusk are the best times to observe water holes—if you do so, it is important to select a safe location where you can sit quietly and out of sight. Some animals will visit for just a few minutes, while others may live there all the time. Saltpans attract a less diverse range of wildlife, but are important for birds such as flamingoes, which often breed in these habitats.

SANDGROUSE ARRIVING AT A WATER HOLE
The breast feathers of a male sandgrouse are specially adapted to absorb water, which he then carries back to young birds in the nest.

WHEN IT RAINS...

Rainfall in the desert is a dramatic event. Often an entire year's precipitation falls in seconds and flash floods are common. Some animals, including certain types of shrimps, take advantage of temporary rainwater pools in which to hatch and reproduce before the water dries up.

RARE BLOOMS
The seeds of many desert plants lay dormant in the soil and burst into life as soon as rain falls. An accelerated life cycle enables them to germinate, flower, and set seed quickly.

Desert homes

All animals need a place in which to shelter, feed, and reproduce. Identifying their homes and knowing what animal lives where is an essential skill for watching desert wildlife. Crevices and holes in rocks are often used by reptiles and small mammals, and as nesting sites by birds like wheatears. Cacti and other plants are excellent places to search for invertebrates, which can also be found under rocks and dead vegetation.

EYED SKINK

Look out for crescent-shaped skink burrow entrances.

SUBSTITUTE TREES
Birds such as cactus wrens use tall cacti as prominent songposts, while desert-dwelling woodpeckers excavate nestholes in the trunks.

GOING UNDERGROUND
Skinks make a distinctive burrow that offers respite from the heat and security from potential predators.

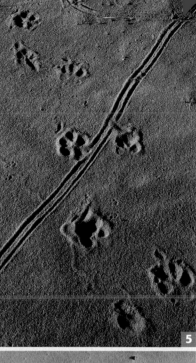

Desert tracks

One of the best ways of finding out what wildlife inhabits a desert is through their tracks in loose sand. Early morning is the best time for this, before wind and other factors have disturbed the evidence. Each animal has a very distinctive trail, so it is worth learning about the different types of track they leave.

1 Grasshoppers and crickets (pictured) usually leave neat lines of footprints in two distinct lines. These can become random if the insect jumps.

2 Scorpions leave a tightly grouped trail with four footprints on each side that may appear fused. The forward pincers are carried up off the ground.

3 The tracks of large antelopes, such as oryx, are unmistakable, with large cloven hoof prints that are usually sunk quite deep into loose or wet sand.

4 Chameleons sometimes walk across open terrain between areas of vegetation They leave distinctive, angled footprints that often have a tail trail in between.

5 Cats leave characteristic round paw prints with no claws showing. By contrast, fox prints are more narrow and the claws are always visible.

6 Beetle tracks are highly variable, depending on the species. Scarab beetles leave a distinctive, but confusing, trail as they hunt for food.

7 Darkling beetles make a very recognizable, tirelike tracks that may run for considerable distances across open dunes.

8 Sidewinding snakes leave J-shaped marks—if the tracks stop suddenly the snake may have buried itself in the sand to escape the heat.

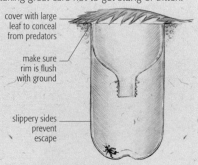

MAKE A PITFALL TRAP

Pitfall traps are a great way to catch insects or other small animals in any habitat. Take a clean plastic soda bottle and cut it about two-thirds from the base. Invert the top into the base and sink it into the sand or soil. Check the trap daily and release your catch, taking great care not to get stung or bitten.

cover with large leaf to conceal from predators

make sure rim is flush with ground

slippery sides prevent escape

Glossary

Abdomen
In mammals, the part of the body between the thorax (chest) and pelvis; in insects, the hind section of the body behind the thorax.

Adaptation
The evolution of features within a species or population, improving fitness for life in a particular habitat.

Agro-forestry
Cultivation of trees as a crop, for lumber, pulp, or other products, such as palm oil.

Algae
Simple organisms, the most complex being seaweeds, lacking structures of plants such as roots and leaves.

Arctic
The region around the North Pole, north of the Arctic Circle at 66° 33'N.

Biodiversity
The total variety of living things, including species and subspecies.

Biome
An ecosystem, or community of plants and animals, living in particular geographical and climatic conditions.

Botany
A branch of biology specializing in the study of plants.

Cambium
A layer of cells within stems and roots of plants whose growth gives an increase in girth.

Chlorophyll
Green pigment in plants, vital in extracting energy from sunlight.

Chrysalis
Pupa, a life stage in insects and moths between larva and adult.

Climate change
A gradual change of global climatic balance, natural or artificially induced.

Cocoon
A silky protective casing produced by some caterpillars.

Colony
A grouping of breeding animals in a specific site, for social stimulation or protection.

Commensal
A life style relationship between two organisms, to the benefit of one with no harm to the other.

Compound leaf
Leaf split into several leaflets.

Contour
Line on map (or, imaginary, on ground) joining points of the same altitude.

Cyclone
An area of winds rotating inward to "fill" a central area of low pressure; also a name for tropical storms in the Pacific and Indian oceans.

Dabbling
The taking of water, debris, seeds, and tiny organisms into its bill by a surface-feeding duck; water is expelled with its tongue, and food is retained.

Debris
Assorted mixture of material washed or fallen from above: from hillside rocks to fine soil and plant material in tree bark cavities.

Deposition
The laying down of suspended items washed along in a current.

Dorsal
On the upper part of the body; view from above.

Ecosystem
Complete assemblage of living things, from soil organisms to higher plants and animals, living in particular conditions and geographical area.

Enzyme
Protein produced by living organism, helping speed up chemical reactions.

Epidermis
Outer layers of the skin.

Epiphyte
A plant growing on another plant without parasitizing it.

Evergreen
Having leaves all year, which are shed and replaced more or less continually, not seasonally.

Fern
A plant with vascular system, roots, leaves, and stems, but reproducing by spores instead of flowers.

Filter-feeder
An animal that takes a mouthful of water containing minute food and expels it through a filter, retaining the food, for example whales with "whalebone" or baleen plates instead of teeth.

Fragmentation
Past extensive distribution of plant or animal, now reduced to small, isolated, or remnant areas, through climate change or human action.

Fresh water
Water from rain, in lakes, rivers, marshes, and aquifers, with low concentration of dissolved salts and minerals (these increase through brackish to salt or seawater).

Friable
Crumbly and easily broken down.

Fungus
Plantlike organism that does not create its own food with chlorophyll, lacking any green pigment, typically feeding on remains of dead plants and animals.

Gall
Growth on plant leaf or twig in response to attack from parasitic insect, mite, fungus, or bacteria; parasite often identifiable by particular shape and color of gall.

Genus
A unit in scientific classification of living things, linking similar species—first of two-word "scientific name," for example *Homo* in *Homo sapiens*.

Germination
Period when seed or seedling emerges from dormant period, such as winter, to begin growth.

Gill
A structure that extracts oxygen from water, in fish or early stages of amphibian; also structure beneath cap of some fungi, containing spores.

Glacier
A mass of ice that becomes so heavy that it gradually "flows" imperceptibly downhill.

Greenhouse gas
Gas, such as carbon dioxide, that allows heat from the Sun to reach the Earth, but prevents it from radiating outward, hence increasing global temperature.

Gyre
A large-scale circulation of ocean surface currents.

Habitat
The amalgamation of features, such as soil, plants, animals, and local climate, in which a particular organism lives.

Harem
A group of females assembled and defended for reproductive purposes by one male.

Heliotropism
Movement of plant during the day, "following" the movement of the Sun.

Herbaceous
Plant that dies back to soil level in autumn and winter.

Hibernaculum
A structure made to give a safe site for hibernating reptiles and amphibians in winter.

Humidity
The amount of water vapor in the air.

Humus
Decaying vegetable matter in the upper layer of soil, giving it a dark brown or black color.

Hyphae
Long filaments of fungi, on or below ground, that form the mycelium; extracts and transports nutrients.

Lateral line
A line of sensitive cells along the side of a fish, able to detect sound and movement.

Leaflet
Division of a compound leaf, such as an ash leaf.

Lek
Communal display of males of some birds, such as black grouse and ruff, to attract and impress females; also the name for the traditional site used for such displays.

Lichen
Organism formed by close liaison of a fungus and a green plant that takes energy from sunlight, such as a green alga.

Litter
Fallen leaves collecting beneath trees and shrubs, decomposing over several months.

Mantle
On a bird, feathers cloaking the upper part of the body; a bird of prey also protects its catch by "mantling," opening its wings over its food.

Meander
Wide, S-shaped bend or loop in a river; fast flow undercuts the outer edge of a bend while slower flow deposits gravel on the inner edge, gradually shifting a meander downstream.

Melanin
Dark pigment, for example in fur and feathers, giving darker, richer colors and black, and also adding strength to color.

Metabolism
The sum of all physical processes that take place in the body.

Metamorphosis
Marked and rapid change between life forms of certain groups of animals, for example from caterpillar to chrysalis to butterfly.

Microbe
Microscopic organism, or microorganism, almost invisible to the naked eye.

Midrib
Central stiff support of flat leaf.

Migration
A regular, often annual, large-scale movement of animals of a particular species, such as wildebeest and swallows, often in connection with seasonal changes in climate and food, or for breeding purposes.

Monsoon
Seasonal wind and associated rainfall, producing majority of annual rain in one short season: West African and Asian–Australian monsoon systems are the biggest.

Mycelium
Network of fibrous filaments, or hyphae, beneath a fungus, which collects nutrients.

Mycorrhiza
A close association between a fungus and roots of a plant, to the benefit of both.

Native
An organism in its natural geographical range, i.e. not introduced, either deliberately or accidentally, by human action.

Nymph
Stage in the life of some insects, looks much more like the final adult form than a typical larva.

Opposite
Describes leaves or leaflets arranged in opposing pairs on a stem.

Outer skeleton
A shell-like, structural outer layer of certain invertebrates.

Oxygen
Abundant, tasteless, colorless gas in the atmosphere, essential to life; also in water and other natural substances.

Palmate
Having a web-shaped form between "fingers," for example the feet of a palmate newt, or the shape of a sycamore leaf.

Permafrost
Permanently frozen soil, often causing waterlogged ground when higher layers thaw out in summer.

Pheromones
A chemical signal between insects, for example laying a "food trail" or attracting a potential mate, often over remarkably long distances.

Photosynthesis
Extraction of energy from sunlight by chlorophyll in plants, and conversion to sugars and carbohydrates.

Pigment
A chemical material that influences the color of reflected light by absorbing various wavelengths.

Plankton
Assorted minute plants, animals, and bacteria living and drifting freely in upper layers of water.

Polar
An area close to the pole: an imprecise definition, but closer to the pole than "Arctic" or "Antarctic."

Pollination
Fertilization of plants as male pollen grains are transferred (by wind, insect, or bird) to female reproductive structures.

Precipitation
Water vapor coagulating in the atmosphere as its capacity to absorb water is reduced through changing pressure or temperature, to form rain, sleet, hail, or snow.

Prehensile
Mobile or capable of grasping, for example a prehensile tail that can be curled to grasp a branch.

Proboscis
Elongated structure from an animal's head, especially a tubular probe from an insect.

Pupation
Period in metamorphosis of some insects in which larval structures break down and adult features develop.

Rut
Period when males, for example of deer, gather females into groups for reproduction, and to defend them against other males.

Saliva
A secretion from the mouth, serving as lubrication for swallowing food and also as "glue" to help create external structures, such as nests.

Scale
A small, rigid platelike structure growing from the skin, for protection and color, for example on fish or butterfly.

Sciophyte
A plant that can thrive in shaded areas.

Schooling
Fish living in groups, with a degree of collective action.

Sediment
Particles initially suspended in water, deposited as water velocity reduces or particles coagulate into heavier items.

Species
A basic unit in the classification of living things that groups together genetically similar individuals: members of a species interbreed and produce fertile offspring recognizably of the same species.

Spinneret
Organ of a spider that spins its silk fiber or web.

Stipe
The stem of a typically toadstool shaped fungus.

Substrate
Underlying rock or subsoil beneath the soil.

Symbiosis
Arrangement in which two or more organisms live inextricably and closely linked.

Temperate
A broad area between more extreme tropical and Arctic climates, without marked extremes of temperature or rainfall.

Thermals
"Bubbles" of rising air, produced as areas of bare or light-colored ground warm the air above them in strong sunshine; never produced over water.

Thorax
The part of the body between the head and the abdomen.

Topsoil
Uppermost layer of soil in which decaying leaves decompose and from which roots of plants and fungi extract nutrients.

Transpiration
The loss of water vapor from leaves of plants.

Tropical
Area between the Tropic of Cancer and Tropic of Capricorn, extending across the equator, typified by high temperatures, lack of marked seasonality, and little change in length of days.

Understory
Shrub and sapling layer in forest or woodland that is below mature trees, but above the herbaceous layer.

Veil (of fungi)
Partial or universal veil encloses growing cap and stem; splits to leave remnant ring on stipe.

Volva
A bag or cup-shaped structure at the base of the stem of a fungus, a remnant of the veil.

Index

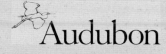

Audubon

This book has been produced in collaboration with Audubon, whose mission is to conserve and restore natural ecosystems, focusing on birds, other wildlife, and their habitats. Through its education, science, and public policy initiatives, Audubon engages people throughout the US and Latin America in conservation. Audubon's Centers, and its sanctuaries and education programs, are developing the next generation of conservation leaders by providing opportunities for people to learn about and enjoy the natural world. Working with a network of state offices, chapters, and volunteers, Audubon works to protect and restore our natural heritage.

To learn how you can support Audubon, contact:

Audubon
225 Varick Street
7th Floor
New York, NY 10014

1-800-274-4201
www.audubon.org

To find out more about
The Great Backyard Bird Count,
visit http://www.birdcount.org

To participate in ebird, visit:
www.ebird.org

Also available from
DK and Audubon:

Bird

Audubon Backyard Birdwatch

**Audubon North American
Birdfeeder Guide**

Acknowledgments

Dorling Kindersley would like to thank the following for their help in the preparation of this book: George McGavin for consultancy, Daniel Gilpin and Elizabeth Munsey for editorial assistance, Sunita Gahir for design assistance, The Cotswold Store and Alana Ecology for supplying equipment, and Peter Anderson and Gary Ombler for additional photography. The publisher would also like to thank the following for their kind permission to reproduce their photographs:

(Key: a-above; b-below/bottom; c-center; f-far; l-left; r-right; t-top)

1 Corbis: Visuals Unlimited (cr). Dorling Kindersley: Frank Greenaway courtesy of Natural History Museum, London (cl). 4 Dorling Kindersley: Frank Greenaway courtesy of Natural History Museum, London (tr). 5 Dorling Kindersley: Frank Greenaway courtesy of Natural History Museum, London (tc); Stephen Oliver (br). 6 Dorling Kindersley: Peter Chadwick, courtesy of the Natural History Museum, London (tr); Neil Fletcher (bc) (fbl); Frank Greenaway courtesy of Natural History Museum, London (tc); Matthew Ward (cl) (tr); Jerry Young (r). 7 Alamy Images: Bob Gibbons (tr). Dorling Kindersley: Frank Greenaway courtesy of Natural History Museum, London (tr) (tc); Derek Hall (bl) (bc) (crb); Tim Ridley (tr); Matthew Ward (br). 8 Corbis: Gisuke Hagiwara / amanaimages. 10 Alamy Images: Paul Glendell (cb). Corbis: Patrik Engquist (br); Frank Krahmer (c); Roger Tidman (tr). 11 Ardea: Francois Gohier (cr/prairie dogs) (cra) (tr). Corbis: W. Cody (ca); Simon Weller (bl). Dorling Kindersley: NASA / Finley Holiday Films (br). Getty Images: Robert Postma (cla). Photolibrary: Shattil and Rozinski (cr/ferret). 12 Corbis: Hans Reinhard (c). Dorling Kindersley: Thomas Marent (cla). Getty Images: Colin Milkins / Photolibrary (ca). 12-13 Alamy Images: WILDLIFE GmbH. 13 Alamy Images: Rolf Nussbaumer (cb). Corbis: amanaimages (c); Scott Stulberg (cb); Herbert Zettl (bc). Dorling Kindersley: Harry Taylor, courtesy of Natural History Museum, London (tl). Getty Images: De Agostini (cl); Dr Sauer (ca). 14 Alamy Images: All Canada Photos (ca). 14-15 naturepl.com: Jane Burton. 15 Getty Images: Jeff Hunter (cr); Joel Sartore / National Geographic (tr). 16 Corbis: E & P Bauer (br). Dorling Kindersley: Frank Greenaway courtesy of Natural History Museum, London (clb). Getty Images: Christopher Furlong (cl). 16-17 Alamy Images: Peter Arnold, Inc. 18 Corbis: Visuals Unlimited. 20 Corbis: Paul Souders (br); Hubert Stadler (bl). Getty Images: Astromujoff (bl). 21 Corbis: Theo Allofs (bl). Getty Images: Philip and Karen Smith (tr). 22 Corbis: Mike Theiss / Ultimate Chase (tr). 23 Alamy Images: Arctic Images (bc); blickwinkel (tc); Ashley Cooper (ca); Eddie Gerald (clb); NaturePics (cr); Ken Walsh (bl). Corbis: Johnathan Smith; Cordaiy Photo Library Johnathan Smith; Cordaiy Photo Library Ltd (cb); Craig Lovell (cla). Dreamstime.com: (cra). Getty Images: Jamey Stillings (br). 25 Alamy Images: Ashley Cooper (cb); imagebroker (cl); Oleksiy Maksymenko (fcl). Corbis: Glowimages (c); Richard T. Nowitz (br). Getty Images: Arctic Images (cla); Jeff Foott (cl). Science Photo Library: Kenneth Libbrecht (tr) (cra) (tra). 26 Alamy Images: Hemis (c). 26-27 Corbis: Peter Wilson. 27 Corbis: Gene Blevins (bc). Getty Images: Alan R Moller (tr); Priit Vesilind / National Geographic (br). Science Photo Library: J. G. Golden (ca). 28 Alamy Images: WildPictures (cl). Dreamstime.com: (br). Getty Images: Brian Stablyk (cb); Kim Steele (tl). iStockphoto.com: (br). NOAA: Carol Baldwin (bc). Image courtesy of Oregon Scientific (UK) Limited: (cr) (tc/bottom) (tc/middle). 29 Alamy Images: Nepal Images (tc/top). Corbis: Jorma Jamsen (br); Tony Hallas / Science Faction (cr). Getty Images: Michael McQueen (cr). Science Photo Library: Garry D. McMichael (tl). 30 Corbis: Larry Dale Gordon (cl). Getty Images: Jeremy Walker (cb). 30-31 Corbis: Mitsushi Okada / amanaimages. 31 Corbis: Laura Sivell / Papilio (bc); Chen Zhanjie / XinHua Press (cla). Getty Images: Johnny Johnson (ca); Visuals Unlimited (cl). 32 Getty Images: Lew Robertson (bl). 32-33 Till Credner & Sven Kohle / allthesky.com. 33 Alamy Images: Peter Arnold, Inc (cr); Galaxy Picture Library (cb). Corbis: Roger Ressmeyer / Science Faction (br). 36 birdmike.co.uk: (cl). Corbis: Roger Ressmeyer / Science Faction. 36 birdmike.co.uk: (cl). Dorling Kindersley: Yuriko Nakao / Reuters (br). Olympus.co.uk: (c). 37 FLPA: Hugh Clark (ca) (cr). rspb-images.com: Malcolm Hunt (tl). 40 Alamy Images: Peter Titmuss (br). 40-41 Alamy Images: Superstudio. 40 Getty Images: Joel Sartore / National Geographic (c). 42 FLPA: Yva Momatiuk & John Eastcott (crb). Getty Images: Gerry Ellis (tr); David Madison (cra); John Miller (c). KATA: Panasonic: Panasonic Industrial Europe Ltd (clb) (cr). Pentax UK Ltd: (br/zoom). Sigma Corporation: (br/wide). Courtesy of Sony United Kingdom Limited: (cla) (c). 42-3 Corbis: Peter Johnson (t). 42-43 Corbis: Gary W. Carter (b). Getty Images: David Maitland (cb). 43 Corbis: Michele Westmorland (cla). FLPA: Robert Canis (bc); David Hosking (cra). Getty Images: Peter Lilja (tl). rspb-images.com: Niall Benvie (bl). Gerald Downey (cb). Getty Images: Marc Romanelli (tr). Marek Walisiewicz: (ca) (bl). 45 Corbis: Bob Krist (cra). Marek Walisiewicz: (c). 48 Alamy Images: blickwinkel (cra). Corbis: Elizabeth Whiting & Associates (tl). Getty Images: Evan Sklar / Botanica (br); Visuals Unlimited (c). 49 Corbis: Toshi Sasaki / amanaimages (tl); Owaki-Kulla (bl). Getty Images: Mitchell Funk (tr). 50 FLPA: Erica Olsen (ca). naturepl.com: John Downer (br); Kim Taylor (cra). Photolibrary: Roger Jackman (c). Science Photo Library: Tom McHugh (c). 51 Getty Images: Tony Bomford / Photolibrary (cb). NHPA / Photoshot: Stephen Dalton (br).

52-53 Alamy Images: Lawrence Stephanowicz. 54 Corbis: George McCarthy (bc). Getty Images: Oxford Scientific / Photolibrary (c). naturepl.com: Laurent Geslin (tl). 55 Corbis: O. Alamany & E. Vicens. FLPA: Malcolm Schuyl (bl). Getty Images: Raymond Blythe / Photolibrary (ca). naturepl.com: Laurent Geslin (br). 56 Corbis: John Hawkins; FLPA (tr). Getty Images: Michael Crowley (bl). 57 Corbis: Gary Carter (crb). FLPA: Toomas Iii (cla); Sven Zacek / Photolibrary (cra); Paul E Tessier (ca). 58 Audubon / wingscapes.com: (tr). FLPA: Roger Wilmshurst (cr). rspb-images.com: (bc). 59 Corbis: Gary W. Carter (c). FLPA: Gianpiero Ferrari (bc); S & D & K Maslowski (bl). Getty Images: Visuals Unlimited (tr). 60 Getty Images: Visuals Unlimited (crb). 61 FLPA: Robert Canis (clb); Mike Lane (tr); Derek Middleton (cr). 62 Corbis: D. Robert & Lorri Franz (bl); Paul Taylor (cla). FLPA: David Hosking (br). 63 Alamy Images: John Glover (cl). Getty Images: Tier Und Naturfotographie J & C Sohns (cla). Cara Tyler: (bc). 64-65 Alamy Images: Stan Kujawa. 65 Getty Images: Yann Layma (bc); George Grall / National Geographic (br). image100 (c) Corbis: (cl). 69 Dorling Kindersley: Kim Taylor (c); Rollin Verlinde (cl). 70 Alamy Images: Nigel Cattlin (c). Corbis: Michael Rose; FLPA (bl); Joe McDonald (c); Roger Tidman (clb). Getty Images: Wendy Shattil & Bob Rozinkski / Photolibrary (tr); David Zimmerman (c). iStockphoto.com: (cr). 71 Alamy Images: Don Geyer (bl); imagebroker (br). Photostock-Israel (cl). Corbis: Roger Wood (cr). Getty Images: Mad MaT (cra); Visuals Unlimited (clb). 72 naturepl.com: Bruno D'Amicis (cra). 72-73 José Luis Gómez de Francisco. 74 Alamy Images: Neil Hardwick (ca). Getty Images: Brian Hagiwara (c); GK Hart / Vikki Hart (cr); Oxford Scientific / Photolibrary (cra); Paul Taylor (cl). Science Photo Library: Bjorn Svensson (c). 74-75 Alamy Images: flabCC. 75 Getty Images: Anthony Bannister (tr). 76 Corbis: Tom Bean (cra); Joe McDonald (cla). FLPA: Nigel Cattlin (c). Getty Images: Michael Leach / Photolibrary (c). Science Photo Library: Martyn F. Chillmaid (br); Terry Mead (cla). 76-77 naturepl.com: Gary K. Smith. 77 Alamy Images: Nigel Cattlin (crb/springtail); Tom Joslyn (crb/dung fly). Corbis: PULSE (br). Getty Images: Andrew Howe (c); Jason Edwards / National Geographic (cr); Rodger Jackman / Photolibrary (bl); Ann & Steve Toon (br). 78-79 Alamy Images: flabCC. 82 Alamy Images: JTB Photo Communications, Inc (br). Dorling Kindersley: Frank Greenaway courtesy of Natural History Museum, London (c); Sean Hunter (tr). Getty Images: David Tipling (tl). 83 Alamy Images: David Noble Photography (tl). Corbis: Gavriel Jecan (br); Larry Lee Photography (t). Dorling Kindersley: Geoff Brightling (br). 84 Alamy Images: blickwinkel (ca). 85 Alamy Images: imagebroker (tl); Stefan Sollfors (cra). 86 Dorling Kindersley: Frank Greenaway courtesy of Natural History Museum, London (tl). Getty Images: Photolink (c); Visuals Unlimited (cr). 88 Getty Images: Jozsef Szentpeteri / National Geographic (ca). 89 Corbis: Karl Kinne (cla). Rob Herr: (tr). 90 Alamy Images: Simon Colmer and Abby Rex (tr). Dorling Kindersley: Rollin Verlinde (cra). Getty Images: Paul Oomen (cl). 91 Alamy Images: David Crausby (cb). Getty Images: Travel Ink (tr). 94 Alamy Images: Peter Arnold, Inc (c); Mark Breturton (bl); John Glover (br); Krystyna Szulecka Photography (bc). Corbis: Roger Tidman (tc); Visuals Unlimited (ca). Dorling Kindersley: Frank Greenaway courtesy of Natural History Museum, London (c). 94-95 Corbis: Ashley Cooper. 95 Alamy Images: blickwinkel (c); WILDLIFE GmbH (br). 96 Alamy Images: blickwinkel (c); INTERFOTO (tr). naturepl.com: Staffan Widstrand (bl). 97 Alamy Images: blickwinkel (c); David Chapman (ca). 98 Alamy Images: William Leaman (c). 99 Dorling Kindersley: Peter Chadwick, courtesy of the Natural History Museum, London (tr) (ca). Sue Robinson: (c). Colin Varndell: (c). 102 Alamy Images: Michael Griffin (bc). Corbis: Lothar Lenz (tr); Manfred Mehlia (cra). Getty Images: Stephen Studd (c). naturepl.com: Philippe Clement (bl). 103 Corbis: David Chapman Natural Selection (c); Fridmar Damm (cr); D. Robert & Lorri Franz (cra). Getty Images: Visuals Unlimited (clb). 104 Alamy Images: Horizon International Images Limited (br); David Hosking (tr). Corbis: Niall Benvie (bl). 104-105 Getty Images: Joel Sartore / National Geographic. 105 Alamy Images: Peter Arnold, Inc (tl); Papilio (bl). naturepl.com: Paul Johnson (tc); Colin Seddon (br). 106 Corbis: Frans Lanting (br). Getty Images: Charcrit Boonsoom (tcl). 107 Alamy Images: Pictorial Scotland (tr). Corbis: W. Perry Conway (tc); Steve Austin; Papilio (ca); Ed Darack / Science Faction. 108-109 Alamy Images: Louise A Heusinkveld. 110 Alamy Images: Gay Bumgarner (br); Danita Delimont (cr); Rolf Nussbaumer (tr). 110-111 National Geographic Stock: Michael Nichols. 111 Alamy Images: Mary Liz Austin (cr). Getty Images: Philippe Bourseiller (tl); Michael Orton (c); Greg Vaughn (tr). 112 Alamy Images: A. P. (tr); Neil Hardwick (c). 116 Getty Images: Peter Lilja (c). 116-117 Alamy Images: First Light. 117 Alamy Images: Arco Images GmbH (tr); Juniors Bildarchiv (cr). Getty Images: Bob Stefko (cra). 118-119 Getty Images: Raymond K. Gehman (c). 119 Corbis: D. Robert & Corri Franz (cra); Steven Kazlowski / Science Faction (br). Getty Images: Riccardo Savi (c); Ronald Wittek (br). 120 Corbis: Galen Rowell (br). 120-121 National Geographic Stock: Michael Nichols. 122 Corbis: Wolfgang Kaehler (c); Michael & Patricia Fogden (bl). Getty Images: Michael Dunning (tr). 123 Alamy Images: Hornbill Images (l) (br). Getty Images: Martin Harvey (c). 124 Corbis: epa (c); Bob Krist (br). Getty Images: Ian Cumming / Axiom (cra); Paul Chesley (cl). 124-125 NHPA / Photoshot: Woodfall. 125 Corbis: Jack Fields (br). Dorling Kindersley: Colin Keates, courtesy of Natural History Museum, London (bc). 126 Corbis: Kevin Schafer (ca). 126-127 Corbis: Michael & Patricia Fogden. 127 Corbis: Rainbow (tc). Getty Images:

Tim Laman / National Geographic (crb); David Tipling (cra). 128 Corbis: Atlantide Phototravel (crb); Jason Edwards / National Geographic (cra). Getty Images: Joel Sartore / National Geographic (cra). 129 Corbis: Theo Allofs (bc); Anthony Bannister (cl). Getty Images: De Agostini (bl); Gerry Ellis (tl); Martyn Colbeck / Photolibrary (c). 130 Dorling Kindersley: Frank Greenaway courtesy of Natural History Museum, London. 132 Corbis: Julie Meech; Ecoscene (tl); Pam Gardner; FLPA (tr). Getty Images: Adam Burton (br). 133 Alamy Images: David Boag (tr). Corbis: Nigel J. Dennis; Gallo (crb). FLPA: Gerry Ellis / Minden Pictures (cla). Getty Images: Panoramic Images (br); Louis-Marie Preau (cla). 134-135 Alamy Images: David Boag. 135 Corbis. 136 Getty Images: Wolfgang Bayer (tr); David McNew (cl); Paul Chesley / National Geographic (cla); Photolink (bc); Visuals Unlimited (cra). 137 Corbis: Peter Reynolds; FLPA (tc). Getty Images: David McNew (cla) (tr). Still Pictures: David McNew (br). 138 Getty Images: Marcus Gosling (cla). Dorling Kindersley: Frank Greenaway courtesy of Natural History Museum, London (bb); Colin Keates, courtesy of Natural History Museum, London (c). FLPA: Frans Lanting (tr); Mark Winwood / Photolibrary (br). Getty Images: Manfred Pfefferle / Photolibrary (c). 139 Alamy Images: blickwinkel. 140-141 Alamy Images: Hoberman Collection UK. 141 Dorling Kindersley: Frank Greenaway courtesy of Natural History Museum, London (cla) (tl). Still Pictures: WILDLIFE / N Benvie (crb) (cr). 142 Alamy Images: Nigel Pye (crb). naturepl.com: Jane Burton (br). 142-143 Alamy Images: Hoberman Collection UK. 143 Alamy Images: Arco Images GmbH (bc); Juniors Bildarchiv (br); Paulo De Oliveira / Photolibrary (cb). 146 Corbis: Frank Blackburn; Ecoscene (tc); Macduff Everton (br). Dorling Kindersley: Frank Greenaway courtesy of Natural History Museum, London (br); Sean Hunter (th). 147 Alamy Images: Peter Arnold, Inc (cr); Visions of America, LLC (tl); WILDLIFE GmbH (clb). Corbis: Eric and David Hosking (bc). 148 Corbis: George McCarthy (bc). Getty Images: DEA / V. Giannella (bc). 148-149 naturepl.com: William Osborn. 149 Alamy Images: Redmond Durrell (cr). Corbis: Roger Wilmshurst; FLPA. 150 Corbis: Hans Pflleschinger / Science Faction (cb). Dorling Kindersley: Jerry Young (ca). Getty Images: Raymond Blythe / Photolibrary (cb). naturepl.com: Meul / ARCO (cra). 150-151 naturepl.com: Kim Taylor. 151 Getty Images: John W Banagan (tl). 152 Getty Images: Jody Dole (cl). 154 Corbis: Tom Bean (cr); Tom Brakefield (cra). Dorling Kindersley: Jerry Young (tr). Getty Images: Russell Illia (c); Michael Poliza (cl); Federico Veronesi (br) (tc). 155 Corbis: W. Perry Conway. 158 Alamy Images: blickwinkel (bc). Corbis: Andrew Brown; Ecoscene (tl); Pablo Corral Vega (bl); Tim Zurowski (ca). 159 Alamy Images: Robin Chittenden (bc); Chris Mattison (br). Corbis: Martin Harvey (c); George Steinmetz (bl). Getty Images: Michael Doolittle (cb). Corbis: Roy Hsu (tr). Getty Images: Konrad Wothe (cr). 160-161 Alamy Images: Art Kowalsky. 161 Alamy Images: Andrew Darrington (cr). Corbis: George D. Lepp (tl). Getty Images: (bl/cycling); DEA / A. Calegari (br); David Epperson (bl); George F. Mobley / National Geographic (tr). 162 Corbis: David Muench (cr). Getty Images: Phil Schermeister / National Geographic (tl); Visuals Unlimited (c). naturepl.com: Kirkendall-Spring (br). 163 Alamy Images: Cubolmages srl (br). Getty Images: altrendo nature (fbl). 164-165 Getty Images: Soren Herbst / Flickr. 166-167 Photolibrary: John Cancalosi. 167 Corbis: Galen Rowell (sl/houette). Roger Tidman (cr). Getty Images: Jonathan Gale (tr); Stan Osolinski / Photolibrary (tr/portrait); Joseph Van Os (tr). 168 Getty Images: Visuals Unlimited (cr). 168-169 Alamy Images: Bob Gibbons. 170 Dorling Kindersley: Frank Greenaway courtesy of Natural History Museum, London (bc); Rollin Verlinde (tr). Getty Images: DEA / A. Calegari (ca); David Littschwager / National Geographic (bl) (tr). 170-171 Photolibrary: Luis Javier Sandoval. 171 Getty Images: Stephen Alvarez / National Geographic. 174 Corbis: Adam Woolfitt (br). Dorling Kindersley: Frank Greenaway courtesy of Natural History Museum, London (br); Rollin Verlinde. Getty Images: Paul McCormick (tr). 175 Dorling Kindersley: Jerry Young (br). Getty Images: Matt Cardy (tl); stockbyte (tr). 176-177 Getty Images: Tyler Gray. 178 Corbis: Niall Benvie (c). 179 Alamy Images: Peter Bowater. 179 Dorling Kindersley: Kim Taylor (cla); Daniel Cox / Photolibrary (bc). Getty Images: Manfred Pfefferle / Photolibrary (cra). 180 Ardea: Tom & Pat Leeson (cr). Corbis: Kennan Ward (clb). Getty Images: Hauke Dressler (c); Visuals Unlimited (crb); Dominic Harcourt Webster (tl). 180-181 naturepl.com: John Cancalosi. 181 Dorling Kindersley: Cyril Laubscher (cr); Jan Van Der Voort (cra). Getty Images: Elliott Neep (tr); David Boag / Photolibrary (br). 182 Michel Roggo: (cl) (br). 182-183 Alamy Images: Wolfgang Polzer. 184 Corbis: Frans Lanting (c); Roger Tidman (br). Getty Images: Catherine Cedner (tl); John Downer (bl); Frank Krahmer (cra); Sven Zacek / Photolibrary (cra); Paul E Tessier (tr). 185 Corbis: Frank Krahmer (c); Oxford Scientific / Photolibrary (br); Gerhard Schulz (cb); Judy Wantulok (bh). 186 Alamy Images: blickwinkel (cr). Getty Images: Spike Walker (c). 186-187 Alamy Images: Papilio. 187 Alamy Images: Daniel Borzynski (br); Premaphotos (br). Getty Images: Oxford Scientific / Photolibrary (bc). 188 Alamy Images: Brian Bevan (tr). Corbis: Colin Milkins / Photolibrary (cr) (cb); Visuals Unlimited (tl). 189 Getty Images: Bianca Lavies / National Geographic (br). 190 Alamy Images: blickwinkel (cra). Corbis: W. Cody (tr); Roger Wilmshurst; FLPA (cl). Getty Images: AFP (br). naturepl.com: Tom Vezo (bl). 191 Corbis: George McCarthy (ca). Getty Images: Theo Allofs (cb); Jan Tove Johansson (br); Harold Taylor / Photolibrary (cla); Niall Benvie / Photolibrary (clb); Tohoku

Colour Agency (tl); Visuals Unlimited (cb) (bc). 192 Alamy Images: Richard Murphy. 194 Corbis: Arthur Morris (cra). Getty Images: Image Source (br); Jupiter Images (tl). 195 Alamy Images: Florapix (cra). Corbis: Frans Lanting (tc); Michele Westmorland (ca). Chris Gibson: (bl). 196-197 Corbis: Andrew Brown; Ecoscene. 198 Alamy Images: John Taylor (cra). Getty Images: Darylyne A. Murawski / National Geographic (bc); Visuals Unlimited (br). 198-199 Corbis: Bertrand Riegel / Hemis. 199 Alamy Images: doughoughton (br); JS Callahan / tropicalpix (cra). Corbis: Eberhard Streichan (cl); Anthony West (tc); Adam Woolfit (cla). Getty Images: Laurance B. Aiuppy (br). 200 Getty Images: Leslie Garland Picture Library (tr). Getty Images: De Agostini (c). 201 Alamy Images: Skyscan Photolibrary (cr). Getty Images: Thierry Grun (br); Camille Moirenc (bl). 202 Alamy Images: Lightworks Media (tl); Peter Titmuss (tr). Getty Images: Bob Pool (br). 203 Dorling Kindersley: Frank Greenaway courtesy of Natural History Museum, London (tr). 204 Alamy Images: Robin Chittenden (tr); Nick Greaves (bc). 205 Getty Images: Rosemary Calvert (tc). 206 Alamy Images: Nigel Housden (bl). Corbis: Ronald Wittek / dpa (bc). 206-207 Corbis: Paul Darrow / Reuters. 208 Alamy Images: David Chapman (br); photow.com (cra). 208-209 Dorling Kindersley: Stephen Oliver (t). 210 Alamy Images: Rami Aapasua (bc). Getty Images: AFP (tl). 210 naturepl.com: Juan Manuel Borrero (tr). 211 Corbis: DK Limited (b). Getty Images: Frank Cezus (cra); Barrie Watts / Photolibrary (bc); Time & Life Pictures (cr). 212 Alamy Images: David Fleetham (bl). Waterframe (cr). Corbis: Brandon D. Cole (bc); Jeffrey L. Rotman (cl). Dorling Kindersley: Colin Keates, courtesy of Natural History Museum, London (cr). Getty Images: Stephen Frink (c). 213 Corbis: Stephen Frink / Science Faction (l); Stuart Westmorland (cr). Getty Images: Georgette Douwma (crb); Mark Webster / Photolibrary (tr); Jeff Rotman (cra). 214 Corbis: Guenter Rossenbach (c); Chinch Gryznziewicz; Ecoscene (tl) (tr); Adam Woolfitt (bl). 215 Corbis: Ashley Cooper (tr); Destinations (ca); Robert Pickett (bl). Dorling Kindersley: Colin Keates, courtesy of Natural History Museum, London (br). 218 Alamy Images: Stefan Huwiler (bl). charliephillips.co.uk: (cr). Corbis: Joe McDonald (bl). Getty Images: Ghislain & Marie David de Lossy (cla). 218-219 Alamy Images: Christina Bollen (r). 219 Corbis: Craig Lovell (br); Winfried Wisniewski (bc). Getty Images: Siqui Sanchez (bl). naturepl.com: Chris Gomersall (tr). 222 Alamy Images: Michael Howell (bl). Corbis: Yann Arthus-Bertrand (cr); Roger Wilmshurst; FLPA (bc). 223 Alamy Images: Loetscher Chlaus (tr). Corbis: Demetrio Carrasco (bl); Tony Hamblin; FLPA (cla). Getty Images: David B. Fleetham / Photolibrary (br). 224 Alamy Images: RWP (cl). Corbis: Chris Collins (tl). Getty Images: Sabine Adamson (tr). iStockphoto.com: (cr). Science Photo Library: Nigel Cattlin (br). 224-225 Chris Gibson. 225 Alamy Images: Mark Boulton (cr). Corbis: Chinch Gryznziewicz; Ecoscene (bc); Roger Tidman (br). Chris Gibson: (tr). Neil Hardwick: (crb). 226 Alamy Images: blickwinkel (cra). Corbis: Frank Blackburn; Ecoscene (cl); Raymond Gehman (br); Eric and David Hosking (br); Robert Marien (cr). Getty Images: Ron Erwin (cla); Christopher Furlong (cr). 227 Alamy Images: Robography (cra). Corbis: Brandon D. Cole (cl); Roger Tidman (bl). Dorling Kindersley: Frank Greenaway courtesy of Natural History Museum, London (cr); Colin Keates, courtesy of Natural History Museum, London (br). Getty Images: China Foto Press (tl). Chris Gibson: (tl). Science Photo Library: Kjell B. Sandved (fcr); Dr Keith Wheeler (c). Steve Trewhella: (c). 228 Getty Images: Jeff Rotman (tl). 228-229 naturepl.com: Jurgen Freund. 230 Corbis: Paul A. Souders (c); Specialist Stock (c). 230-231 Getty Images: Johnny Johnson. 231 Alamy Images: Thomas Hanahoe (tr); Michael Patrick O'Neill (cr); Rosanne Tackaberry (bc). Corbis: Frans Lanting (cr); Karen Kasmauski / Science Faction (cra). 234 Corbis: Galen Rowell (cra). Altrendo Images (bc); Paul Nicklen / National Geographic (cla). 234-235 Corbis: Galen Rowell. 235 Alamy Images: Arcticphoto (c); Karen & Ian Stewart (tr). Dorling Kindersley: Frank Greenaway courtesy of Natural History Museum, London (cr). Getty Images: Geoff du Feu (tl). 236 Corbis: Steve Kaufman (br); Kennan Ward (bl). 236-237 Anna Henly Photography. 238 Getty Images: Louise Murray (bl); WILDLIFE GmbH (br). FLPA: Frans Lanting (c). Getty Images: Sue Flood (cl); Chris Jackson (br). 238-239 Corbis: Bob Krist. 239 Corbis: Momatiuk-Eastcott (br); Paul Souders (cla). Getty Images: David Hallett (c). 240 Dorling Kindersley: Dave King (c). 242 Alamy Images: WoodyStock (cra). Corbis: Lucas Lenci (tl). Getty Images: John W Banagan (tr); Jane Sweeney (bl). 243 Alamy Images: AfriPics.com (cr). Corbis: Gavriel Jecan (br); Joson (ca). Getty Images: Steve Allen (c). 244 Corbis: Steve Kaufman (br); Michael Fogden / Photolibrary (bc). Getty Images: David MacDonald / Photolibrary (c); Visuals Unlimited (cra); Tim Zurowski (cr). 245 Alamy Images: Rolf Nussbaumer (fbl). Corbis: Tim Davis (fbr); Martin Harvey (br). FLPA: Konrad Wothe (bl). Getty Images: Joel Sartore / National Geographic (c); Oxford Scientific / Photolibrary (cra). Green-Witch.com: Deben (c). 246 Corbis: Steve Bowman (fcl); James Randklev (br). Getty Images: Jason Edwards / National Geographic (cb); Pankaj & Insy Shah (cra); Art Wolfe (cl). 247 Corbis: George H. H. Huey (c). Getty Images: Karl Lehmann / Lonely Planet (c). naturepl.com: Jack Dykinga (cra). 248 Corbis: Peter Johnson (tr). Getty Images: Mark Turner / Botanica (c); Jeff Foott (cl); Jason Edwards / National Geographic (br); Visuals Unlimited (bl). 249 Corbis: Franck Guiziou / Hemis (c); Frans Lanting (cl); Frans Lemmens (cla); Paul Souders (tl); Martin Harvey / Gallo (br). Getty Images: Rod Patterson / Gallo (bl). naturepl.com: Richard du Toit (tr); Neil Lucas (bc)

All other images © Dorling Kindersley
For further information see: www.dkimages.com